WASHED
AWAY

WASHED AWAY

How the Great Flood of 1913,
America's Most Widespread Natural
Disaster, Terrorized a Nation
and Changed It Forever

WITHDRAWN

GEOFF WILLIAMS

PEGASUS BOOKS
NEW YORK LONDON

To the men, women and especially the children
whose lives were cut short in the Great Flood of 1913.

WASHED AWAY

Pegasus Books LLC
80 Broad Street, 5th Floor
New York, NY 10004

Copyright © 2013 by Geoff Williams

First Pegasus Books cloth edition 2013

Interior design by Maria Fernandez

Library of Congress Cataloging-in-Publication Data is available.

ISBN: 978-1-60598-404-9

10 9 8 7 6 5 4 3 2 1

Printed in the United States of America
Distributed by W. W. Norton & Company, Inc.

Contents

Author's Note

On March 23, 1913, the United States of America was reminded that when it comes to nature, we're not really in charge. It was an Easter Sunday, but the thunderstorm that almost crushed the Midwest into oblivion could have been straight out of the Biblical story of Noah's Ark—only it didn't rain for forty days, but, depending where you lived, more like four or five. The rain, in any case, was long enough to create the most widespread natural disaster in the history of the United States. Millions upon millions of 1913 dollars of damage. Hundreds of thousands of families and individuals were driven from their homes. There were at least several hundred, and probably more like a thousand, deaths. It was a flood of such epic proportions that it forever changed how the United States manages its waterways.

My first memory of hearing about the flood is about as innocuous and ordinary a memory as you can get, so boring that I'm almost embarrassed to bring it up. I was standing with an uncle of mine, Pat Scorti, in Middletown, Ohio, at a gas station. I think I was eight years old, which would place us in 1978. He was pumping unleaded into a beat-up car that he had probably purchased a decade earlier. What exactly he was talking about as he pumped, I have no idea, but suddenly his monologue landed on the 1913 flood. He mentioned how there was water for miles, and that Dayton, a city just north of us, really was hammered by it, and that about a dozen people died in Middletown alone. It was very serious, he said, his voice full of awe, as if he had been there, but he hadn't. He was born over thirty years after the flood.

That's about all I remember. It was a brief, inconsequential moment in time, which somehow stuck with me, but I think the conversation explains a lot about why this flood has now been forgotten. This was a disaster that felt local and wasn't necessarily viewed by individual communities as a national calamity. But during and after the time the water receded, the Great Flood of 1913—Arthur Ernest Morgan once called it that; he was a famed engineer whose flood control techniques became widely known and disseminated after the disaster—was often compared to the 1906 San Francisco earthquake and fire and the sinking of the *Titanic* just a year before. And for good reason. The Great Flood of 1913 affected far more Americans than both of those previous disasters combined.

Yet the sinking of the *Titanic* and the San Francisco earthquake were disasters that were contained and created an easy-to-grasp story. The rest of the country could read about the thrilling adventures (the papers back then described every near-death escape as "thrilling") and wonder what they would have done if they had been there; and of course, movies, like *San Francisco* in 1936 with Clark Gable walking around in a daze, and the *Titanic* films, not to mention shelves of books, all helped to fuel our collective imaginations of the heroes, villains, and victims within each story. Conversely, the Great Flood of 1913 affected so many people that, arguably, people didn't want to wonder what they would have done if they had been there. They *were* there. Or they had friends and family who were there. After a while, nobody wanted to talk about it. It was too close for too many. If anything, people wanted to forget about this disaster.

The flood disaster also, as noted, became very localized. Water-logged cities adopted the flood as part of their local history, and so instead of becoming known as the Great Flood of 1913, folks around Dayton, Ohio, would talk of the Great Dayton Flood. Residents in Columbus, Ohio, would speak of the Great Columbus Flood. People in Indianapolis thought of it as an Indianapolis flood. My uncle seemed to think of it as a flood that affected only Middletown and Dayton. While

it was a national tragedy, or at least a semi-national apocalyptic catastrophe, hitting over a dozen states and terrifying friends and family
across the nation, the flood tended to be thought of as a neighborhood
event instead of as part of a national narrative.

It may also have been forgotten because the exact death toll of
the flood isn't known and may never be known, so it's easy to forget
how deadly and damaging it was. Historian Trudy E. Bell, who
wrote *The Great Dayton Flood of 1913* (Arcadia Publishing) and has
written extensively on the topic, has placed the death toll at over
1,000, which sounds right to this author, but the numbers bandied
about throughout the 20th century often focused on only the deaths
in Ohio and Indiana, when a considerable number of people in other
states lost their lives.

Four hundred and sixty-seven deaths is the most quoted number
for Ohio, devised by J. Warren Smith, who in 1913 was a professor of
agricultural meteorology at the U.S. Department of Agriculture, and
the number of deaths for Indiana quoted is usually 200. A June 5,
1921 *New York Times* article placed the figure of the deaths in Ohio
and Indiana as 730, which may or may not have included victims from
other states like Illinois, Kentucky, Missouri, West Virginia, Pennsylvania, and the hundreds of others who died in the tornadoes that
came with the storm that initially brought the flood. In other words,
this wasn't a tidy disaster like the RMS *Titanic* had been with her loss
of over 1,500 souls.*

The flood has also been somewhat forgotten because there have
always been floods, and there always will be. It's hard for the history
books to remember the flood of 1913 when it's also competing with
the Mississippi Flood of 1912, the Great Mississippi Flood of 1927, the
Great Flood of 1937, and—well, you get the idea.

After my uncle brought up the flood, I didn't think about it for most
of my life. Sure, I would occasionally hear about it in the local news
when a flood anniversary came up and think, "Wow, sounds pretty
bad," but it never captured my imagination; although in recent years,
I started to develop a healthy fear and respect for rivers. My young
daughters enjoy wading in a creek that feeds into the Little Miami

---

*   Depending on the source, it was either 1,514 deaths or 1,517.

River, searching for tadpoles, minnows, and the occasional toad or turtle. It's a few feet deep at the most and home to a lot of tadpoles, guppies, and the occasional turtle and water snake, but in 1913, this meandering waterway was around 50 feet deep for several days. But looking at the docile, picturesque creek now, you'd never believe it. In fact, the creek and the Little Miami River swamped downtown Loveland, Ohio (population in 1913: 1,476), a community I live near and visit often, putting its downtown five to ten feet under water and submerging twenty-five percent of the homes in the area. But what really got me was a death near Loveland, a little over ten years ago. A sixteen-year-old girl was in a SUV with three teenage friends, and the vehicle suddenly found itself floating on a road after a flash flood. Three of the teenagers were able to get themselves to safety, simply by choosing to climb out of the left side of the car; the sixteen-year-old escaped out of the right passenger window and made her way toward a retaining wall that she didn't see, and she fell over it and into Sycamore Creek. A day or two later, her body was found floating in a lake that my kids and I occasionally visit. It horrified me as a human being and parent, in part because I travel on this road frequently; and I think, for the first time, I started to understand the terrifying, ugly power of a flood.

Still, I only considered writing about the flood a couple of years ago when I was trying to come up with an idea for a book. My agent, Laurie Abkemeier, asked if there were any local events that would have national interest. For a long time, I couldn't come up with anything; and even when the 1913 flood popped into my head, I quickly pushed it right out.

A flood doesn't sound all that exciting. Water comes into a town, it gets high, it leaves. I had no clue.

Now I wish I had started researching the 1913 flood immediately after my uncle first told me about it. In communities throughout the Midwest and parts of the South and Northeast, there are so many stories worth telling that one could make researching this flood their life's work and still feel that they hadn't learned everything there is to know about it. This is my way of saying that if you lived in a community that was walloped by the flood, and it's not mentioned in this book, my apologies. There were just so many towns hit by the flood that I couldn't possibly dig into all of them and still tell the wider story of this flood and what it meant to history.

This was a gravely serious flood, the United States' second-deadliest in history, following the infamous one in Johnstown, Pennsylvania in 1889, in which 2,209 people died after a dam failure. In the spring of 1913, men, women, and children perished in communities across Ohio, Indiana, Illinois, Wisconsin, Pennsylvania, Maryland, Michigan, New York, West Virginia, Kentucky, Arkansas, Missouri, and Louisiana. Even states as far away as Vermont, Connecticut, and New Jersey were affected by the flooding.

What follows are some of the many stories of the thousands of people who lived through this flooding. These are tales of bravery, selflessness, tragedy, and even cowardice and greed, although this is mostly a story about Americans at their best when Mother Nature was at her worst.

SUNDAY,
MARCH 23, 1913

Chapter One

Heading for the Cellar

March 23, Rock, Wisconsin, 5 P.M.–5:12 P.M.

Edward Suchomil deserved a lot more in life than to be struck down by lightning.

At least, the faint remaining paper trail that represents his life suggests that he didn't have this coming. The 24-year-old had made many good friends ever since moving two years earlier to the tiny town of Rock from his home base of Jefferson, just twenty-seven miles north. Suchomil remained close to his parents, visiting them often.

Unfortunately, he had the misfortune to step into the middle of an elaborate weather pattern that began two days earlier when a high-pressure system from the Arctic Circle invaded Canada. From there, the system brought in severe winds from the west and stormed most of the Midwest and much of the East and Northeast of the United States. Hundreds of telephone and telegraph poles were uprooted in half a dozen states. Sleet followed, and many of the telephone and telegraph wires that were still standing were felled by the ice weighing down the wires.

Had those telephone and telegraph poles and wires remained standing, historian Trudy E. Bell has suggested, the U.S. Weather Bureau might have been better able to collect information or send warnings to

3

neighboring communities and come to a quicker understanding of what was befalling the country. The flood still would have occurred, of course, but more lives might have been saved with advance warning.

Suchomil was probably a goner nonetheless. Even if he had known that he was walking into an evening storm affecting not just his own state but Oklahoma, Kansas, Nebraska, Wisconsin, Iowa, Missouri, Illinois, Indiana, Michigan, Ohio, Kentucky, Pennsylvania, West Virginia, Vermont, and New York, he probably would have assumed he could beat the weather. There was the whole invincibility of youth mentality to contend with, after all, and don't we all think we can beat a little old lightning?

Suchomil left a neighboring farm to go back to the farm of Edward Ellion, where he undoubtedly planned to partake in a fine Easter dinner. Suchomil noticed the clouds—how could he not?—but it was a short walk through the wet, melting snow, especially if he made his way through the cornfield. He must have figured he could reach Ellion's home.

He almost did.

Suchomil's right palm was in his pocket when he was struck, a pose that suggests that he may have been in mid-stroll, hands stuffed in pockets and fairly unconcerned about the clouds.* The buttons ripped off his rubber boots, which were otherwise unharmed. His cap blew into smithereens and flew off his head. His pocket watch stopped. His hair was singed, and as the clothes on his body burned, Suchomil fell face forward into the snow, which extinguished the flames. The coming rain also cooled him off.

Ellion and the dinner guests worried about Suchomil, but, given the night and the nature of the storm, they didn't venture out until the next day where they discovered him, forty rows deep in the middle of a cornfield.

March 23, 1913, Omaha, Nebraska, approximately 5–6 P.M.

Thomas Reynolds Porter mentally wrote down everything he saw. The 43-year-old had almost the perfect name for his profession. He went

---

* One might potentially theorize that he was reaching in his pocket for a key, but this was an age when few people locked their doors, and he was going to a house that had people in it, which means he wouldn't have been worried about not being able to get inside.

by the name T. R. Porter, and if one ignored his first initial, you could almost read his middle initial and his last name—R. Porter—as in "reporter." He was a freelance writer, actually, reporting and writing for both newspapers and magazines.

Porter thought the skies looked ominous. The weather had been questionable all day, warm and muggy, with rain here and there, plus the requisite thunder and lightning. At the noon hour, however, the sun came out warm and bright. Churchgoers flooded the streets in their Easter Sunday best and strolled to their homes, or friends and family. The clouds quietly returned, but that didn't trigger any suspicions among most of the city's residents.

But Porter wasn't most city residents. He was trained to watch the world from the moment he was knee-high. After his father died when he was three, Porter's mother, Elizabeth, had taken over his father's job of deputy postmaster and was at the center of the action in Russellville, Kentucky. Then Thomas Porter followed his older brother, Garnett, to Omaha and landed an assistant manager's job with the city court, where he continued his training, studying and learning about the human condition. But it was when Thomas followed in his older brother's footsteps and became a newspaper man that observing the world was actually part of his job description. And for the last sixty minutes, instead of relaxing on the porch and reading or tending to his garden and clipping the pergola or watering his climbing roses or clematis, Porter was studying the weather.

There was good reason to be concerned. It had already been a month with frightening weather. March 15 brought blizzards to the Midwest. A hurricane hit Georgia and Alabama, the day after. March 17, a cold wave hit in Tampa, Florida, of all places. On March 21, the first day of spring, a blizzard hammered twenty states, from as far north as Montana and south as Arizona, and ended twenty-one lives. On March 23, in an article written before Omaha's destruction, *The Washington Post* published a lengthy essay about tornadoes that began: "Not since 1884 has there been such an outburst of tornadic storms as that which occurred in the west and south last week."

The article was referring to a pair of tempests that, two days earlier, had left behind dozens of people dead across several states, including twenty-eight bodies in Mobile, Alabama, and five more in Michigan, where two young boys skating on a river were blown off course and right into the grip of the Straits of Mackinac's icy waters.

Porter couldn't be sure if a tornado was coming. Nobody alive had actually seen a tornado in Omaha, according to a newspaper account of the time, which made the observation that an old Indiana prophecy that had been handed down for centuries stated that Omaha was immune. That wasn't quite true. The newspaper reporter apparently had forgotten that there was a tornado in September 1881 that had leveled a few blocks in the city, although the loss of life, according to an issue of *The American Architect and Building News* that came out that month, was "trifling." Still, Omaha didn't have an intimate relationship with tornadoes, and its residents felt no danger or fear toward tornadoes.

That was about to change.

Porter called for his nineteen-year-old niece, Clem. Porter had doted on her ever since his older sister, Fannie, a poet from Glasgow, Kentucky, had come to Omaha in 1905. Fannie, forty-seven years old and a widow since the turn of the century, had been sick for the last two years, traveling the West and hoping the warmer climates would improve her health. Whether she came to say good-bye, or if it was unexpected, she died close to her family members. Clem, named for her father, Clement, an attorney, was thirteen years old and all alone. Porter, unmarried, was too. That is, until he met Mabel Higgins a short time later. She was a 28-year-old clerk at a law firm. Both late bloomers for a married couple in 1913, three years after saying "I do," they still weren't parents yet. Clem was all they had.

Her uncle showed Clem the skies and explained why he believed a tornado was coming.

Exactly what Clem said next is left to the imagination, but one has to conclude that they probably discussed Mabel and whether they should alert her. Mabel was with her parents, 63-year-old William, a business owner, and Ella, 61 and in poor health, and possibly both of her siblings, her older sister, Bertha, and her younger brother, Leslie. It's possible that Clem or Porter or both ran the five blocks and reported their concern about the tornado, but they knew Mabel and her family were aware of the weather and probably didn't want to worry anyone on just a hunch.

At about 5:30 in the afternoon, the clouds became considerably darker—almost green—and then the clouds formed one massive, dense, black wall.

Porter wasn't the only one who noticed the skies. F. G. Elmendorf, a traveling salesman from Indianapolis who had just arrived from Chicago, discussed with some fellow salesmen the ominous-looking dark clouds that had shown up after a little rain, and they were nervous. Still, Elmendorf went about his business and picked up something to read, killing time in his hotel's lobby.

Another visitor to the city, a man who gave reporters the name of F. J. Adams, didn't like how the sky looked. He decided he was going to get out of the city.

It was a smart decision, made a little too late. As Adams walked toward the train station, the temperature plummeted, and the sky turned black. There were a few drops of rain. It was windy. Still, when the funnel cloud barreled toward him, having first touched down fifteen minutes earlier, eighty miles southwest at Kramer, Nebraska, before racing past Lincoln and into Omaha at six in the evening, nobody, not even Adams, could say that they had been expecting it.

Inside Elmendorf's hotel lobby, the traveling salesman was sitting next to a window. Then he noticed that the sun seemed to have disappeared. He could hear a humming sound, "the most fearful and peculiar sound I ever heard," he would say later, and thunder crashed over the city, as did rain. But he wasn't sure exactly what was happening outside his hotel.

Porter and Clem ran downstairs to the basement. But it was for Clem's benefit only. Porter sprinted back upstairs to watch the tornado. If it developed into anything important, he wanted to be able to give his readers a first-hand account of the storm.

Porter stood on his porch, amazed at what he was seeing. There was a tornado, all right, and it was beginning to carve up his city.

F. J. Adams was thrown against a building, and it must have saved his life, for he was able to remain where he was and watch the world collapse around him.

"I saw a man picked off his feet and blown through a plate glass window of the Odd Fellows' Temple," Adams said. "He was killed. A taxi careened around a corner, seemed to be running solidly, and in the next instant, it tilted and rolled and then lifted over a sidewalk wall about six feet high. The chauffeur, I believe, must have been killed, as the machine was smashed to kindling."

Adams watched the entire roof of a small store blow away. Seconds later, a man who decided he was better off outside than in, charged out of the store. The man was lifted into the air, spun around for more than a hundred feet, and body-slammed back into the earth. The man didn't get up.

Similar to Elmendorf's recollection, Porter would write that "a billion bumblebees could not have equaled the giant humming which accompanied the storm."

Of what it looked like, Porter called the tornado a "black storm cloud" that "rode a great white balloon of twisting electric fire."

Houses, according to Porter, collapsed like cards or simply disappeared. Another house, a three-story residence, was split in two, as if a giant sword had sliced it. Porter watched a cottage sail through the air and strike the fifth story of the Sacred Heart convent and smash apart the south wing as if it had been made out of paper.

Then a house was picked up and hurled a quarter of a block and directly into the house of William and Ella Higgins.

Where Mabel was.

Then the tornado was gone. Porter ran for the pile of rubble that used to be his in-laws' house.

There was no warning of the tornado, no explanation from Mother Nature. The storm crossed diagonally through the city, across the western and northern parts of the city, attacking residential areas both wealthy and poor. It chugged along for about six miles through Omaha, leaving a path of destruction about a fourth to a half-mile wide. Instead of acting like some tornadoes, hopping into the air and then landing again, this cyclone's path of destruction was continuous, staying low to the ground during those six devastating miles.

Almost sixty years later, in 1971, Tetsuya Fujita, a meteorology professor at the University of Chicago, and Allen Pearson, head of the National Severe Storms Forecast Center, designed the Fujita-Pearson scale. The Fujita-Pearson scale designated tornadoes F1 to F5, with the lower F1 representing winds from 117 to 180 miles, and the F5 to describe a tornado blowing at 261 to 318 miles per hour. The tornado that hit Omaha in 1913 is believed to have been an F4, which means winds were ranging from 207 to 260 miles an hour, and its path was a hundred miles long, a rarity for a tornado.

But the power and durability of the Omaha tornado can really be told with this factoid: a sign from a store in Omaha was found in Harlan, Iowa—sixty miles away.

One of the first signs indicating how unique and ugly this tornado was going to become was when a body dropped out of the sky.

Charles Allen was walking at the corner of Forty-Fifth and Center Streets just after the tornado seemed to have materialized out of thin air. He was astonished to have a little girl, about four years of age, fall out of the sky into his arms. His shock turned to horror when he realized she was dead. He would live out the rest of his days wondering what her name was.

At that point, the tornado had already crossed Woolworth Avenue, the street where Dorothy and Leslie King lived. It seems to have never come closer than five blocks away from the King home, but had it veered a little to the east, Dorothy King, and her as-of-yet unborn child, Leslie Lynch King, Jr., might have become casualties of the tornado.

Dorothy King would then have never divorced her abusive and alcoholic husband, remarried, and moved to Michigan. Which means her son wouldn't have renamed himself after his stepfather, and the country would never have gotten to know Gerald Ford, the future 38th president of the United States.

If tornadoes could be described as having a personality, this one was a sociopath, and the details are disturbing. Mabel McBride, a 24-year-old elementary school art teacher, convinced her mother and young brother that they were safer huddling in a corner of a room than running outside. She was probably correct, or should have been, but when the roof blew away, the floors above collapsed, and a heavy board fell and struck Mabel on the head. She died instantly, but perhaps her actions saved her brother and mother, who survived.

At the edge of the city and near the edge of the tornado's path, most of the children in the orphanage, the Child Saving Institute, were indeed saved by virtue of being herded into the cellar, but two babies, Thelma and Cynthia, were sucked out of the windows.

Just outside the Idlewild, a pool hall, trolley conductor Ord Hensley spotted the cyclone coming toward his streetcar, which was packed with about a hundred screaming passengers.

"Everybody keep cool and lie in the center of the car," shouted Hensley, grabbing two women who were boarding the streetcar and pushing them to the floor while dropping down with them. Nobody needed to be persuaded otherwise. Charles H. Williams, one of the passengers, managed a curious glance at the storm and a fleeting thought—*It looks like a big, white balloon*—as he watched houses blowing away and trees rocketing into the sky. But like every other passenger, he dropped to his hands and knees and joined the pile of humans that had collected onto the floor of the center of the car.

Then the windows shattered. Trash, not rain, enveloped the car. A heavy wooden beam crashed through one window and poked out the other. Wooden planks, tossed by the wind, landed on top of the streetcar passengers. Then as quickly as it had come, it was over for the passengers, and Hensley, Williams, and the others staggered to their feet, unhurt.

The patrons of the nearby pool hall were having their own problems. Eight African-Americans were playing at one pool table, with the rest of the crowd watching. Then everyone heard what sounded like a freight train roaring toward them, and the roof shot up into the sky and, along with it, the pool table. Seconds later, the pool table, along with the roof, came crashing to earth, killing most of the onlookers. A fire broke out next. The county coroner managed to rescue three of the men from the rubble and was likely haunted for the rest of his life by the sight of another man burning to death. In all, fourteen men died in the pool hall.

Several blocks away, the conductor of the streetcar on Forty-Eighth and Leavenworth wasn't as brave as Ord Hensley had been. This conductor saw the approaching tornado and jumped off, running for his life and leaving his passengers behind. One of them, Leon Stover, a thirty-year-old bookkeeper for a department store, moved behind the controls and tried to drive the streetcar and outrace the tornado. It was a nice try, but the twister swept past the streetcar, raining glass and splinters onto a bloodied Stover, who was suddenly aware of a father's anguished cries. The father's baby had been ripped from his arms and blown into the void.

The Diamond Picture Theatre collapsed, killing thirty people inside. The Sacred Heart Convent was turned into firewood. Then the tornado turned its attention to William O'Connor.

William was eight years old. He had just been sent by his older brother to go to the drugstore across the street from the family's house to buy some stamps. A few moments later, Lawrence O'Connor, eighteen years old, saw the storm and shouted to the rest of his family—his parents and five other siblings—that a cyclone was coming and to run for the shelter.

Lawrence didn't go to the shelter. He chased after William.

His little brother was reaching the pharmacy when Lawrence grabbed him and pulled him back across the street toward the house. Halfway across the street, the tornado caught Lawrence, who was still clinging to William, and flung the two brothers both into the air. All the way up, and then all the way down, Lawrence never let go of his younger brother.

A group of people were huddled in the garage of a brick building at 40th and Farnam Streets when the tornado made direct impact. It—and they—were suddenly blown away.

Inside the house of Rose Fitzgerald, a 33-year-old widow, guests were sitting down for a birthday dinner. The guest of honor, Patrick Hynes, eighty-one and a widower, must have been feeling pretty good about where he stood. He had seen plenty in his life since his birth in Ireland in 1832. He fought in and survived the Civil War. His children, married and with children of their own, seem to have been doing well. His son, William, in particular, had a successful elevator company. Surrounded by friends and family, Patrick Hynes gave a little speech to raised wine glasses, and as they all began sipping to good health, the house came crashing down.

Hynes climbed out of the rubble with a fractured leg but was otherwise uninjured, and most of the guests crawled out, although not everyone. His daughter Margaret had two broken arms and internal injuries. "Oh, if only it had been me instead," Hynes later said.

Another party was going on at the home of Benjamin Edholm, a 62-year-old Swedish-American carpenter, and his wife, Hanna, 61.

Hanna saw the tornado first. She drew the shades but before she could corral everyone in a cellar, an object burst through the window and slid across the table and crashed onto the floor with most of the dishes.

It took a moment to realize what that object was: a human body. Then, to everyone's astonishment, the naked body, a man, sat up, grabbed the tablecloth and wrapped it around his body. The man asked for some trousers, was hastily given a pair of Benjamin Edholm's, and dashed out the door without even introducing himself.

A Mrs. F. Bryant, 92, was lying in bed on the third floor of her son's house when walls and floorboards blew apart around her. Mrs. Bryant plunged to the ground and even farther than that, landing in the basement. She was covered in debris, but she also was still in her bed and alive. Her son and daughter-in-law, also still alive, managed, with a lot of difficulty, to remove enough rubble to help her out.

When Edward Dixon saw the funnel cloud, he stopped what he was doing and spun around in fear. The tornado was smashing his neighbors' houses into oblivion, and, by the looks of it, planning on paying a visit to the Dixon residence in less than a minute. The 39-year-old chemist fled upstairs, shouting for his wife to gather their three children.

He never reached the second floor.

Strong winds, the tornado's advance team, hit the house, sending explosions of glass from the windows and into the living room. As if grabbed by an unseen hand, Edward was plucked off the stairs and pulled into the dining room, where he landed flat on his face. Dazed, his right ear aching from a shard of glass that had been, moments ago, part of one of his windows, Edward was nonetheless still alive. He struggled to his feet to find he was surrounded by his wife Opal and their three terrified children: eighteen-year-old Nina, twelve-year-old Lester, and six-year-old Doris. It was clear that within seconds they were going to all die.

But Edward and Opal shepherded their kids to the cellar anyway. Behind them, they fastened the lock shut.

And behind the door was the tornado. Before the Dixons had a chance to hide and huddle, the ceiling above them disappeared.

When it was all over, once the tornado had left Omaha entirely, people began taking stock of what had just happened. In Elmendorf's hotel, nobody had moved since the tornado began, and once it ended, for a long stretch of time, nobody emerged outside. According to Elmendorf, they confirmed that it was a tornado when either the telephone rang or someone called from the front desk, which seems unlikely since many and possibly all of Omaha's telephone lines were down. Perhaps because it was getting dark, or maybe the staff discouraged the guests from leaving, Elmendorf and his fellow traveling salesmen would wait around and get reports on the tornado damage, not leaving to look around until the morning.

At another hotel—or possibly it was Elmendorf's—Mary Knudsen, a servant for an affluent family, came into the lobby as a disheveled mess. She was hysterical but managed to verify to everyone that a tornado had blown apart the city.

The Dixons were not sucked out of their basement along with their ceiling. Edward, Opal, Nina, Lester, and Doris somehow were left alive and in their cellar, which was the good news. The bad news was that the cellar was on fire. But Edward scrambled out and managed to pull his wife and children out of the hole in the ground before it became a fire pit.

Afterward, the Dixons stared at their neighborhood, or what was left of it: telephone poles at 45-degree angles, upturned Model T Fords and uprooted trees, and wooden planks, brick, and debris strewn about. It looked like running carefree and barefoot on a lawn would never be possible again. Of course, as is almost always the case with a tornado, there were some fortunate houses standing as they had always been, as if nothing was amiss at all. The Dixons could see fires in the distance—there were about twenty infernos throughout Omaha, although none too serious; they were all put out by firefighters and the rain within the next three hours.* In the trees and on telephone wires hung bedsheets and clothes.

If the Dixon family could have reached into the future to summon the image, they would have thought it looked as if Omaha had been blasted by a nuclear bomb.

But at least they were around to see it. "We had lost our all," Edward later told a journalist, possibly Thomas Porter, "but were thankful for our lives."

---

* If there's anything worse than seeing your lives destroyed by a tornado, it's probably seeing your lives destroyed by a tornado and then being rained on.

One girl, Margaret Matthews, would later write to a popular children's magazine and share what the tornado aftermath was like for some of the Omaha residents.

"I'm sure I shall never forget it as long as I live," recalled the thirteen-year-old. "I didn't see the tornado cloud, but I heard the roar, and that was enough. I was not at home at the time, but over at my chum's for the night. We were up-stairs and the folks were down, and all of a sudden we heard a loud roar, and the lights went out, and we ran down-stairs. My chum's mother had seen the cloud, and had called for us to come down, but we had not heard her. It did not hit their house nor ours, and we are very thankful. All that night, people came running in, asking for help, and we did not sleep much.

"Next day, I went around to see the ruins, and I am glad I went once, but I would not go again. One poor old man had lost his house and family. The house was laying on its side, and he couldn't talk—he just cried.

"Now," Margaret continued, "every time the least little cloud comes up, every one rushes out to look, and most rush to their cellars."

Small wonder people were afraid. Taking in the sights was too much to bear. Approximately 1,250 buildings had been demolished into rubble, including eleven churches and eight schools. Featherless chickens bobbed back and forth as if nothing had happened, and the occasional cow could be found impaled on a fence post. A man's body hung in a tree.

The bodies of Cynthia and Thelma, two babies, were located a good distance from the wreckage of the orphanage where they spent their short lives. Elsewhere in the city, a toddler whose mother was killed was found in the street alive, playing with a dead dog.

Clifford Daniels didn't make it. He was a mail carrier who was described by his pastor as a strikingly good-looking fellow who was well liked by all. He and his wife, Luella, and their two daughters, six and four years old, were found in the ruins of their house; the girls were embraced in the arms of their mother, while Cliff was found on top of them, which suggested to everyone that he had tried to shield them with his body.

Eighteen-year-old Clifford Daniels, Jr., escaped the cyclone's wrath, but only because he hadn't been home.

14

The tornado also pulverized the home of Mrs. Mary Rathkey and her two grown sons, Frank and James. Their clothes were ripped off by the wind, and their naked bodies were flung into a field about a half-mile away.

Families and individuals who did survive rightfully marveled at their fortune to be alive. John Wright, a 64-year-old railroad worker, surveyed the rubble of his house and realized he was probably only alive because he had left for work half an hour early, not wanting to be caught in what he thought was going to be rain. Then he marveled at how sixteen years earlier, when he lived in Norfolk, Nebraska, his house had been destroyed by a tornado, and forty-two years earlier, when he lived in Panora, Iowa, he barely escaped with his life during yet another cyclone.

Others probably didn't know whether to laugh or cry at the tragic absurdity of it all. Professor E. W. Hunt had been in his basement and staring up at the ceiling when the rest of the house began falling onto him. When he regained consciousness, he found a summer straw hat on his head, only to realize it had been two stories above him and hanging in a closet a short while before.

And still others immediately rushed to help the wounded. F. J. Adams found a man with a wound and two broken arms. The man was unconscious but alive and taken away to a nearby makeshift hospital. Adams never learned the man's name or his fate.

Townspeople rallied around the cries of Gladys Crook, a fifteen-year-old who was walking outside when the tornado came. She didn't have time to run inside and ultimately didn't need to: instead of taking cover inside a house, a house covered her. It took half an hour, but someone finally chopped a hole big enough in the side of the home so that Gladys, incredibly, was able to climb out, shaken but unhurt.

It took fifteen minutes, but Thomas Porter managed to pry his wife and her family, hiding in the basement, out of the wreckage. Once it was determined that everyone was all right, Porter had to go to work. He wasn't an exclusive reporter for any of the Omaha newspapers. He was a special correspondent—the term today would be freelance journalist—for a variety of newspapers, and Porter needed to take note of what he saw and get it on the telegraph wire as soon as possible. That is, if he could find a telegraph. Clearly, there was a lot of destruction, and it was obvious that communication lines might be down. Simply from his own front porch, Porter would later count forty-nine leveled houses.

Throughout the streets of Omaha were bodies, although occasionally those bodies would turn out to be alive. Lawrence and his younger brother William were taken to the Webster Street telephone exchange, where an impromptu medical center had been set up. William was relatively fine. Lawrence had been badly banged up with several broken bones and would spend the next three weeks laid up in the hospital, but he, too, would live to tell friends and family about the part he played in Omaha's most infamous tornado in which, according to most tallies, 140 lives were lost, 322 people were injured, and 2,179 men, women, and children were made homeless.

Elsie Sweedler, a telephone operator, was found wedged between two fallen trees; and when someone realized that she was breathing, firemen were called to saw the trees apart in order to free her. Shortly after she was revived, Sweedler went to her employer, the Harney Telephone Exchange, and reported for duty. She worked all night. It was a selfless act that helped bring both normalcy and assistance to Omaha.

But not right away. The first news about Omaha's tornado didn't go out by telephone or telegraph, because the lines were all down. Instead, a message was sent to the Associated Press from Omaha to Lincoln, Nebraska, by train.

This was bad, because during a crisis, telephone and telegraph operators were always crucial, life-saving links to the rest of the world, especially after a tornado, earthquake, hurricane, or flood. Omaha needed food, water, and help—although the mayor, full of pride and stoicism, would be slow to ask for those things—and the communities near Omaha also would have benefited from immediately knowing what was coming their way. With communication lines down, there was no way to properly warn their neighbors of what was coming. They were on their own.

What nobody else could know or predict was that this was just the beginning and the start of something else entirely. Weather forecasts were far from useless in 1913; but in this instance, they might as well have been. In Washington, D.C., the United States Weather Bureau issued an alert that "a severe storm is predicted to pass over the East

Tuesday and Wednesday." Storm warnings were issued from Hatteras, North Carolina, to Eastport, Maine, and cold wave warnings for the west lake region, the middle and upper Mississippi Valley were issued. "No decided fall in temperature is predicted for the East until after the passage of the western storm," concluded the bureau. "Showers are predicted to fill in the time until the storm arrives."

No mention anywhere of tornadoes and not a word about flooding.

The tornadoes were the opening act of a natural disaster that would unfold for the next few weeks, and if one considers the cleanup and aftereffects, months and years. But the disaster would be known not for its wind, but its water. It didn't help matters that the country was in the midst of El Niño season, a period when the surface ocean waters in the eastern tropical Pacific become abnormally warm, a phenomenon that tends to give the United States some pretty funky weather, and the night of March 23 was as funky and furious as it gets. The Omaha tornado of 1913 was the opening salvo of the Great Flood of 1913.

MONDAY,
MARCH 24, 1913

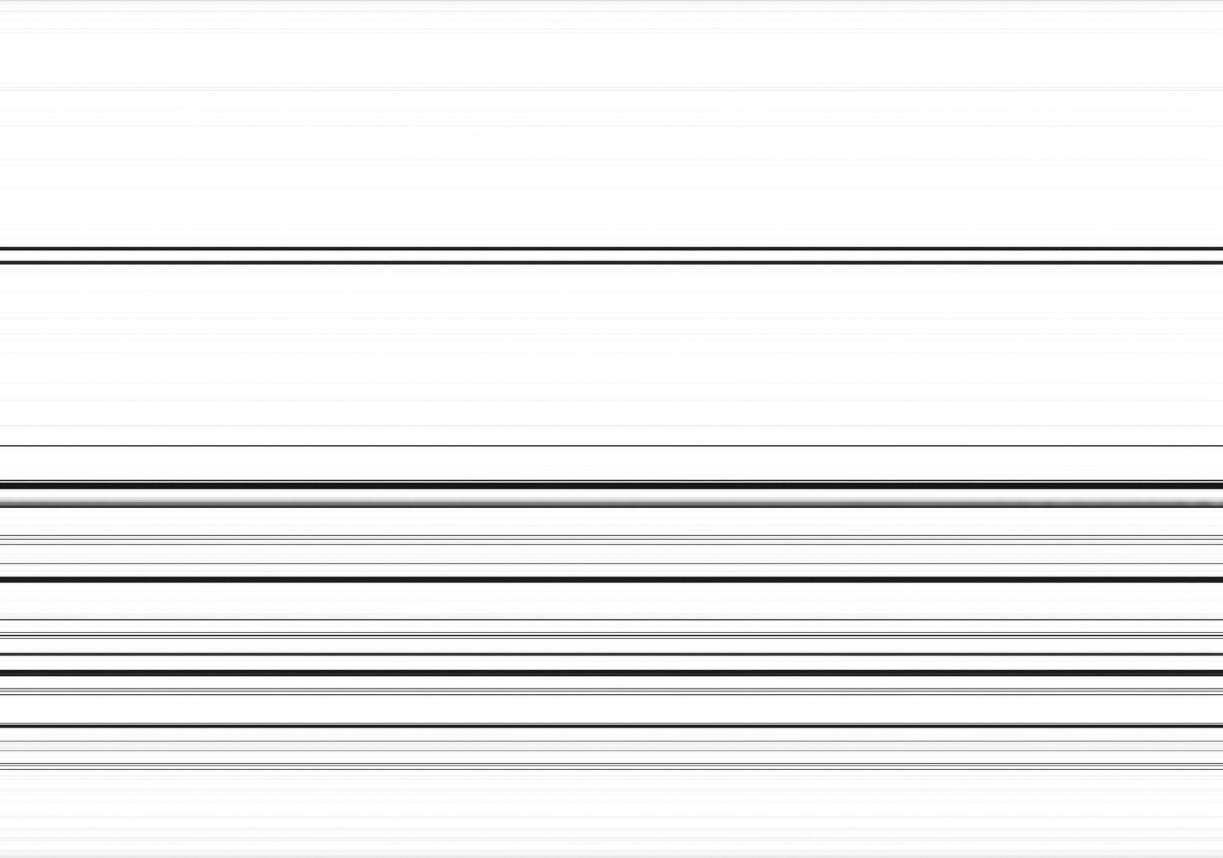

ths

nest P. Bicknell, the
He sent telegrams to
cago, and a St. Louis
to hurry to Omaha
He also telegraphed
ging the Red Cross's
g nurses and doctors,
l towns that had been
could do.
rther reports of the
office, located in the
use, where Woodrow
earlier in the month.
could do more if he

Who's Who of Natural
helping victims in the
estimated casualties,

over 3,000), the 1909 Cherr

during the Mississippi River fl

Traveling to Omaha wasn'

would take roughly twenty-fo

there from Washington, D.C.,

Cross's attention. Bicknell wa

when a crisis wasn't ongoing. N

development of the American

since 1881 when Clara Barton

Cross, brought the concept to

Bicknell's main function see

which invariably called upon

raise money and call attention

called, he pushed all of that a

effort, enjoying the experience

change of pace from the day-to

And while he was gone, the

hands with Mabel Boardman,

actuality a wealthy philanthro

Boardman took herself out of

American Red Cross, believing

a male leader, although Bickne

figurehead. In her current back

much for women's rights, but

Red Cross, devoting her life to

1903 to 1944, just two years be

Bicknell was a man with brow

brown hair that he parted in the

taches were still the norm and mu

be spotted on older gentlemen,

an early adopter of Gillette razo

in 1900. If Bicknell managed to

modern times, other than his sh

early twentieth-century tweed su

Bicknell boarded the train in

believing that he could conduct

Either way, he would be of mo

over 3,000), the 1909 Cherry Mine disaster (casualties, 259), and during the Mississippi River floods of 1912 (estimated casualties, 200).

Traveling to Omaha wasn't a decision made lightly, given that it would take roughly twenty-four hours almost nonstop by train to get there from Washington, D.C., but the destruction demanded the Red Cross's attention. Bicknell was always buried in work, however, even when a crisis wasn't ongoing. Much of his job was spent promoting the development of the American Red Cross, which had been in existence since 1881 when Clara Barton, impressed by the International Red Cross, brought the concept to the United States. Between disasters, Bicknell's main function seemed to be preparing for conferences, which invariably called upon him to write and deliver a speech and raise money and call attention to the organization. But when a disaster called, he pushed all of that aside and devoted himself to the relief effort, enjoying the experience of rolling up his sleeves and having a change of pace from the day-to-day bureaucracy.

And while he was gone, the Red Cross would remain in capable hands with Mabel Boardman, who was technically a volunteer, but in actuality a wealthy philanthropist who ran the entire organization. Boardman took herself out of the running to be at the helm of the American Red Cross, believing the public would more naturally follow a male leader, although Bicknell himself was far from a ceremonial figurehead. In her current back seat, Mabel may have not been doing much for women's rights, but she did a tremendous amount for the Red Cross, devoting her life to it, working for the organization from 1903 to 1944, just two years before her death.

Bicknell was a man with brown eyes that almost matched his sandy brown hair that he parted in the middle. In 1913, when walrus mustaches were still the norm and muttonchop sideburns could occasionally be spotted on older gentlemen, Bicknell was clean-shaven, apparently an early adopter of Gillette razors, which had debuted on the scene in 1900. If Bicknell managed to secure a time machine and travel to modern times, other than his shirt's starch-infested white collar and early twentieth-century tweed suit, he wouldn't seem so out of place.

Bicknell boarded the train in Washington, D.C. that evening, fully believing that he could conduct affairs more efficiently from Omaha. Either way, he would be of more help than half a nation away in

Chapter Two

The First Flood Deaths

March 23, Sunday evening, Washington, D.C.

Once he learned about the Omaha tornado, Ernest P. Bicknell, the Red Cross's national director, did not waste time. He sent telegrams to Eugene T. Lies, a 36-year-old field worker in Chicago, and a St. Louis fellow who went by the name of C. H. Hubbard, to hurry to Omaha and set up a facility to help the tornado victims. He also telegraphed Governor John H. Moorehead of Nebraska, pledging the Red Cross's support and promising that relief trains, carrying nurses and doctors, would soon be in Omaha; and he wired additional towns that had been in the tornado's path to see what the Red Cross could do.

That done, a restless Bicknell waited for further reports of the destruction. He was in the American Red Cross office, located in the State-War-Navy Building next to the White House, where Woodrow Wilson was settling in, having just been sworn in earlier in the month. As the reports trickled in, Bicknell decided he could do more if he personally oversaw the operations in Omaha.

The 51-year-old's resume was like reading a Who's Who of Natural Disasters for the 20th Century. He worked on helping victims in the aftermath of the 1906 San Francisco earthquake (estimated casualties,

MONDAY, MARCH 24, 1913

Washington. If all went as planned, throughout the night his train would pass through several states, mostly Ohio and Indiana, and he could be in Chicago by noon the next day, where he would then board another train for Omaha. But, of course, it didn't all go as planned.

Through the night of March 23 and into the 24th, all across the Midwest

Omaha had the worst of it, but it was one community hit by one tornado. The night of March 23 was packed with tornadoes. Depending on the source you believe, it may have been as few as six or as many as twelve. Omaha, with the tornado cutting through a densely populated downtown, was the most affected, but at least six tornadoes tormented Nebraska, Iowa, Illinois, Missouri, Michigan, and Indiana within the span of about two hours, killing more than two hundred people and destroying thousands of homes. What hit Omaha also attacked Neola, Iowa, where two people lost their lives, and Bartlett, Iowa, where three more people died.

In the Nebraska town of Berlin, which would change its name to Otoe five years later when America fought the Germans during World War I, seven people died. Another twister destroyed half the buildings in the Nebraska town of Yutan, killing sixteen. There were still more tornado-related deaths in Walton and Sterling, Illinois, another in Traverse City, Michigan, and yet another in Perth, Indiana, where most of the buildings were leveled.

Six people were snuffed out by a cyclone in northwest Chicago: two railroad men were killed in the northern suburb of Des Plaines, Illinois, when the chimney from a manufacturing plant was hurled into a caboose of their freight train; another man was crushed in the rubble of his house; yet another was electrocuted by fallen wires; a telegraph lineman was in the wrong place at the wrong time and literally blown off his post into oblivion; a second telegraph lineman was also on a telegraph pole and was electrocuted when the wind came through.

In Terre Haute, Indiana, at 9:45 P.M., a tornado took the lives of twenty-one people; it was theorized later that even more residents, trapped in their homes, would have died from electrical fires, and fires started by lightning, if the rain hadn't started falling. The community was a collage of tragedy, but in the midst of it all, there were a couple of miracles. A baby was lifted out of a bed, carried for a block, and set down, uninjured. Another resident was inside a house that flew a quarter-mile, according to some reports. The woman inside emerged from the wreckage, injury-free. Some people chuckled later, remembering defeathered chickens and how one person's clothing, lain out on a bed, was pulled up into the fireplace and went up the chimney.

Three more people died in the tiny village of Flag Springs, Missouri, which was described at the time as being basically wiped off the map.

All in all, it's believed that 221 people died in tornadoes that night and 761 people were injured.

While the tornadoes were attacking other towns in the Midwest over the next two hours, Omaha swiftly turned its attention to rescuing its citizens. The telephone and telegraph lines were demolished, enough that there was no way to send a message to warn anyone else in time of what was to come. Everyone would be on their own, including those in Omaha, given that there was no quick way to tell the rest of the nation what had happened. T. R. Porter did his best to share the news, however. He made tracks to Fort Omaha, once a United States Army supply depot and now a training center where soldiers learned how to fly in hot-air balloons, which could come in handy during battle, it was believed, and, indeed, during World War I, they were used for observing the enemy below. The fort also taught soldiers radio communication and telegraphy, and as luck would have it, it had a wireless station. The Associated Press may have received word of the tornado first via train, but Porter was apparently the first to get out a lengthy account of what had happened, relaying the news of the tornado one state to the south, to Fort Riley, Kansas, and from there, the soldiers telegraphed the story of the tornado and its destruction to the rest of the country.

Throughout the night with the aid of lantern light, men dug into hills of debris, searching for the living. Doctors tended to the hundreds of wounded. The street railway company had men working, hoping to clear some of the wreckage on the tracks by morning. Families wandered around in a daze. One Omaha resident named John Sullivan sent his daughter to fetch a doctor for his dying mother. After his mother died and his little girl didn't return, Sullivan spent anxious hours wandering the city, shivering and without shoes, looking for her until she eventually turned up. And nobody was particularly excited to see, shortly after midnight, snowflakes falling. It was the beginning of a blizzard.

24

The orphanage, planted on nineteen acres of land, was a three-story brick building with thirty-five rooms that housed sixty-two children from infants to the age of sixteen, but it was capable of caring for as many as seventy-five kids. Not every youth staying there was actually an orphan. Like many such homes across the nation, this one was often used as a place where parents, often overwhelmed single parents, could leave their children—sometimes for only days or weeks at a time, and sometimes forever—when they didn't feel that they could care for them on their own.

The reasons why a parent couldn't take care of their children were as similar as they would be during any age: poverty, alcoholism, death, or perhaps a divorce had broken up the family, so that both parents, or the surviving parent, had to work and the children would wind up here.

Miss Hammond enjoyed spending time with the kids, and she could relate to all of them. She had lost her own father early in life.

Michael Hammond had been a railroad worker, an employee of the Delaware and Hudson Company, first working as a brakeman until he was promoted to freight conductor and extra passenger conductor. On the morning of May 21, 1887, at the station that Hammond was working at, a few cars were in the process of being added, and as the locomotive began to back up, he noticed a woman and a little boy on the track directly in front of the moving train.

Hammond yelled to them to get off the track; but the more he yelled, the more bewildered they looked. Finally, Hammond jumped from the caboose, sprinted along the track, and pushed them off the tracks, but in doing so he staggered backward and was caught by the wheels, thrown under the cars, and instantly killed.

Hammond's death was covered in *The New York Times*, which stated that "Michael Hammond was a popular, industrious and estimable man, about 30 years of age, and well known to railroad men generally."

Theresa was eight months old.

Almost twenty-six years after her father's death, Theresa was employed in one of five orphanages in the county. But the orphanage that Theresa Hammond worked for was the only one in Fort Wayne with the St. Marys River in its back yard. As she and the orphanage's director, Mrs. Ida Overmeyer, would discover, this would become a problem.

Mulberry, Indiana, 9 A.M.

Roy and Roscoe Rothenberger and their friend Elva Myers actually started off in a shallow stream but soon felt confident enough to push themselves off into Wildcat Creek, and for a while they shot ducks. Perhaps they also talked about the brothers' father, David Rothenberger, a carpenter recovering from injuries he sustained falling off a building several weeks ago, or it could be the conversation led to Myers' two younger siblings or how business was going for Myers' dad, a blacksmith. Maybe they talked about the storm that had rolled in the day before, although it seems unlikely that they would have had time to pick up a morning paper and read about the destruction in Omaha, which was dominating the front pages and undoubtedly the discussion in many kitchens and on many street corners across the country.

Whatever they talked about, the Rothenbergers and Myers definitely discussed the river, which was getting deeper and faster by the minute. In fact, the water sped along at about 25 miles an hour, locals later guessed.

The boat was becoming increasingly difficult to manage.

Then when the brothers and Myers hit a whirlpool, the current spun the boat around and toward the river bank, lodging their craft against a willow tree; their situation went from difficult to deadly.

The problem was that the river bank was no longer there, and the tree, which had been rooted in dry earth was now two hundred yards into the waterway. The three men would have done themselves a favor if they had attempted to climb up the tree to wait for help. Instead, they understandably weren't thinking that way and tried to pry the boat off the tree.

The boat overturned.

The men went into the water.

The water was freezing.

Roy was the first to go under, because of his heavy hip boots. The water just poured right into those heavy boots and dragged Roy down to the river floor, where he was trapped, or the current took him for a terrible ride underneath the water and never let him go. Roscoe was perhaps a little luckier, depending on your point of view on how you'd want your life to end in a river on a rampage; he grabbed the edge of his boat and hung on for at least five hundred yards until he went around a bend, just in sight of the Wyandotte Bridge.

But how he died after he went around the bend is anybody's guess. Elva Myers watched his friend float away while dangling from two armfuls of willow tree branches. Myers was able to keep his head above the water, but little else. He started shouting for help.

March 24, noon, Fort Wayne, Indiana

School wasn't in session at the Allen County Orphans Home. The basement had started flooding in the morning, and the adults had decided to do some commonsense planning, in case the river crept a little too close to the building for comfort. But while the basement and the moving of furniture and stoves to the second floor was reason enough to cancel school, when the power and heat went out the teachers must have really thrown up their hands in surrender. Instead, the sixty-two children played on both the first and second stories of the orphanage, and some of the teachers, like Theresa Hammond, went about their usual business, only keeping the youngsters entertained instead of trying to fill their young minds with knowledge. That was what much of the staff had to do, anyway. During the weekdays, the orphanage was a school for the older children and a baby-sitting service for the younger; it was also a home providing social services around the clock. There were many children who were toddlers and at least one baby.

But as the afternoon made its introductions, one can't help wonder if Miss Hammond or any of the children looked outside at St. Marys' muddy waters rushing by and started to second-guess the decision to remain. After all, while everyone expected a fast-flowing river during a heavy rain to be littered with the occasional debris and tree branches, there was something different and creepy about some of the cargo floating in St. Marys this time. There weren't just one or two of these particular items floating down the river, but many, too many for the children to count. At first, nobody knew what they were looking at, but then it became sickeningly clear.

Dead cats.

Mid-morning, somewhere in Ohio or Indiana

Ernest Bicknell's trip was not going as planned. Because the engineer didn't want to find his train rushing into an impromptu river, he kept the speed low and often stopped for interminable lengths of time at stations, mapping out a route. So many bridges were being washed out that crossing Ohio and Indiana was becoming a serious challenge.

As reported in the book *Pennsylvania Lines West of Pittsburgh: A History of the Flood of March 1913*, author Charles Wilbur Garrett wrote: "Trains which were en route on the night of March 24-25 over most of the system were marooned wherever they happened to be when they came to an impassable piece of road—some at stations, some in the open country; some high and dry, some where they were surrounded with water."

Bicknell and the other passengers were continually being told that they would have to be rerouted and would, on occasion, have to wait for other trains to clear the tracks. Bicknell started to recognize that there might be a greater disaster occurring than the Omaha tornado. But for the moment, all he could do was stare out his rain-splattered window.

Mid-morning, Frankfort, Indiana

Elva Myers wasn't the only one engaged in battle with Wildcat Creek. Wallace Garrison, further down the creek, was, about this time, coming to his home in Frankfort from the village of Burlington, seventeen miles away. Unfortunately for Garrison, he didn't realize the bridge ahead was washed out. With his horse and buggy, he kept on the road until it was painfully obvious that there was nothing there.

Around the same time, about eighty miles southeast, John Hagner of New Castle, Indiana, didn't have much of a chance either. The 42-year-old was on a trestle spanning the Blue River, trying to protect the structure that the company he worked for, the Fisher Welch Construction Company, had built.

Trestles, for those who don't have extensive bridge terminology, were bridges constructed for the railroad. They were sturdy, to be sure, since trains passed over them, and usually constructed of timber and iron, but they were built hastily and never meant to be permanent thoroughfares. They were constructed cheaply and fast, as a stop-gap until the railroad could get around to spending money on stone or iron structures.

When his own private tidal wave came rushing toward him, Hagner, married and a father of four, must have recognized the futility of trying to protect the trestle. The wave of water was shockingly high, although not higher than the trestle. As the water thundered into the makeshift bridge, if Hagner hadn't lost his balance, he might have had a shot at getting off it. Instead, he fell and was swallowed up by the river.

During this time, Elva Myers continued to hang on to his willow tree branches, shivering. Among the dirt and debris, the river carried ice chunks in it, and for hours now, Myers had been rained on. His spirits, however, were buoyed by the sight of some farmers who appeared on the river bank shortly after his and his friends' boat overturned. But his euphoria was short-lived; the farmers had no way to reach him.

The men yelled for Myers to hang on, and one of the farmers ran off to fetch a rope. When he eventually arrived with a lengthy coiled one in hand, he threw it out to Myers, but it never quite reached the 21-year-old. Myers was in a bad situation, in any case. His hands and arms were locked in a death grip, and every time the rope landed in the water, it was yanked away by the current. To let go of even one branch and then attempt to simultaneously grab the rope before it was pulled away, especially after being in the water for some time and having little strength, would have taken some dexterity that most humans don't have. He just couldn't do it. Arguably, nobody could.

As the crowd by the riverbank started growing, and people shouted words of encouragement to Myers to just hang on a little longer, the farmers sent someone to get a boat.

Eventually, a 31-year-old man named Dana Hoch, a retail coal merchant, emerged with some sort of boat or raft. Myers somehow was still clutching the willow tree branches. Hoch tied a rope around his waist, giving the other end of the line to some of the spectators, to use in case he capsized and needed to be pulled in. Then he paddled his boat into the raging current. He was able to help Myers into the boat and get the shivering, exhausted youth back to shore.

It was three o'clock, approximately six hours after Myers and his friends had fallen into the river.

Immediately, as Myers was taken home to recuperate, a search party was organized for Roy and Roscoe. Little hope was held out for Roscoe once everyone learned that Myers had seen him go under, but since Roscoe had hung on until he disappeared around the bend in the river, there was still a little hope for his safe return. The search party took whatever optimism they could muster, but they didn't have much. They took with them grappling hooks.

Contrary to whatever anyone might think, there should be no doubt: Roy and Roscoe Rothenberger's deaths were painful and terrifying.

Sure, that sounds like the most obvious statement in the world and worthy of a resounding "duh," but for centuries, drowning has been romanticized in literature as a peaceful and almost pleasant way to check out of life. In Greek mythology, Sirens sang so beautifully, sailors were willing to leap off ships and swim to them, only to then be turned on and drowned. In William Shakespeare's *Hamlet*, Ophelia's drowning scene has her surrounded by garlands of flowers, imagery that would be admired by artists, authors, and poets for centuries to come. Edgar Allan Poe starts off his romantic poem "For Annie" with the words: "And the beauty of Annie, drowned in a bath, of the tresses of Annie."

And just as you're adjusting to the idea that Annie looks beautiful as a drowning victim, Poe continues with: "She tenderly kissed me, she fondly caressed, and then I fell gently to sleep on her breast, deeply to sleep from the heaven of her breast."

In Thomas Hardy's *Tess of the D'Urbervilles*, Retty Priddle attempts to drown herself; and death by water figures significantly in T. S. Eliot's *The Waste Land*. True, authors have only so many ways to kill off characters or provide them with a near-death experience, so you could chalk up some of these examples as coincidence; but there is little doubt that some authors found drowning enigmatic and a romantic way to check out.

Charles Dickens did no favors to any suicidal readers. In his first novel, *The Pickwick Papers*, a character known as the dismal man says to Mr. Pickwick: "Did it ever strike you, on such a morning as this, that drowning would be happiness and peace?"

Mr. Pickwick, to his credit, is horrified at the suggestion, but then the dismal man explains his rationale, and darned if he doesn't make drowning sound like a day at the beach: "I have thought so, often. The calm, cool water seems to me to murmur an invitation to repose and rest. A bound, a splash, a brief struggle; there is an eddy for an instant, it gradually subsides into a gentle ripple; the waters have closed above your head, and the world has closed upon your miseries and misfortunes forever."

And drowning hasn't been limited to writers' imaginations. The twentieth-century poet Hart Crane—who was a fan of Eliot's *The Waste Land*, incidentally—committed suicide by jumping overboard in the Gulf of Mexico. He should have known better than to drown himself: Crane grew up in Garrettsville, Ohio, which had its share of flood in 1913 when he was a fourteen-year-old lad. But the most famous writer to drown on purpose was British author Virginia Woolf, who, on March 28, 1941, wrote a last good-bye to her husband, filled her overcoat's pockets with stones, and walked into the River Ouse.

It's easy to see why drowning might be considered a relatively peaceful way to go. There is no gun, no knife, no being clocked on the head by a tire iron. No gore or gratuitous bloodshed, and often drowning occurs underneath a spectacular vista, as the sunset shimmers over the water or near a grove of trees or a burbling brook or even in a swimming pool where often the sound of children's laughter can be heard.

But, in reality, drowning isn't pleasant at all. It must be one of the most miserable, agonizing, and unpleasant ways to die. You really don't want to know what it's like.

If you were to know, you would discover that your first inclination, even if you were attempting to drown on purpose, would be to automatically hold your breath and buy yourself some time. If you are in danger of drowning, and you are lucky, you aren't panicking, which means you could buy some time that might help your situation. For instance, where are the bubbles you're releasing going? If you're confused and don't know which way is up and which way is down, follow the bubbles.

Unfortunately, if you are drowning, especially in a fast-moving river, you probably are panicking—you're moving fast, maybe 25 miles an hour or faster, and you can't see because mud, sand, and silt are blocking your view, all while the current is tossing you every which way, further hindering your ability to figure out which way is up, so it would be virtually impossible not to panic. If you are in strong physical condition and drowning in a river, you may last a full minute or two holding your breath. If you are unhealthy or elderly, or your lungs aren't very strong, you may only be able to hold your breath for a handful of seconds, which is probably a blessing. Either way, while you're not inhaling and doing what you can not to drown, carbon dioxide is building up in your muscles and organs and being carried through your bloodstream to your lungs.

Your lungs do not like carbon dioxide. Which means, like it or not (and you won't like it), your oxygen-starved brain will send a signal to your mouth, which will then, to your utter horror, open.

You will then swallow water, and, desperately wanting air, you will gasp, and you will panic as water, not air, fills your lungs. As your throat spasms, trying to block the path of the water, your stomach will begin filling up. So will your bloodstream. Not that you'll care to know the definition at this point, but *hyperkalemia* is setting in, which means there's a concentration of the electrolyte potassium in your blood, and it's elevated. The water is breaking down your red blood cells, and potassium is being released throughout your body. This is bad because on top of drowning, you're also dying of potassium poisoning, which means that your muscles and nerves are about to malfunction. The potassium and the lack of oxygen will cause your already wildly beating heart to beat irregularly.

Fortunately, or unfortunately, depending on your point of view, the lack of oxygen will then begin to shut down your brain; and from there, yes, the poets and authors are right: drowning can be described as rather peaceful. You're still alive, and your heart and lungs are still trying to work, but at this point you don't know that.

But during the time when you are conscious, and you know exactly what is happening, drowning is a grisly way to go, and drowning in a river flood, instead of a still pool of water, has even more challenges. Hagner, Garrison, and the Rothenberger brothers were in a stew of destruction. Roy may have found himself stuck in underbrush while he was drowning; Roscoe might have been struck by branches, stones, bricks, electrical wiring, and whatever else was caught in the torrent. Garrison and Hagner may well have died not from drowning but from slamming into a bed of rock or a pile of debris.

Ray and Roscoe Rothenberger, Wallace Garrison, and John Hagner were among the first, and possibly the first, drowning victims of the Great Flood of 1913. There wasn't anything peaceful or romantic about it.

TUESDAY,
MARCH 25, 1913

Chapter Three

Some of the People in the Way

Monday, March 24
Cincinnati, late afternoon

Standing in the rain after school, several boys found themselves on an embankment near a sewer tunnel. They could as easily have been exploring some of the nearby factories or following the nearby railroad and daydreaming about riding the boxcars. But the sewer tunnel was far more interesting, for below them was a pond that hadn't been there a couple of days before. Boys being boys, ten-year-old Ralph Korengel and his friends felt compelled to check it out.

That having been done, the boys started tossing pieces of wood into the pond, watching each piece swiftly sail into the open sewer tunnel and disappear into the darkness. Then Ralph picked up a railroad tie, or, in layman's terms, a wooden plank that the steel part of railroad tracks rest on. Thinking the wooden plank might float nicely, Ralph pushed it over the edge of the dirt cliff. Unfortunately for him, he also went tumbling down the side of the embankment and into the pond.

Even if Ralph could have swum, it wouldn't have mattered: he was sucked right into the sewer tunnel. Screaming for help, the remaining boys raced to the factories, one of them being a rubber factory where Ralph's father worked as a foreman. At least two men, Edward Miller and Mike Cassidy, came running to help.

Quickly surveying the situation, Miller and Cassidy decided that they needed to rush to the other side of the sewer, three blocks away, where Ralph would come out and, with any luck, still be alive.

Inside the tunnel, Ralph was fighting to keep his head above water and losing badly, until he suddenly saw his railroad tie floating past him. He lunged for it and hung on.

Above ground, the boys and men reached the end of the tunnel, where water spilled into Duck Creek. There was no sign of Ralph. The boys or men would later report that another ten minutes would pass. If that's true—it may have just seemed like ten minutes—it makes one wonder what Ralph was doing all that time. Maybe he was able to stop himself from shooting down the tunnel for a while and attempt to crawl back the way he came. In any case, Ralph shot out of the tunnel and into Duck Creek, and, while he didn't look well, he was alive. Before being carried down Duck Creek, Ralph managed to grab a hanging tree branch, which quickly snapped, and he was swept away again. The boys and men gave chase.

Ralph grabbed another branch, but that broke too, and Duck Creek, which wanted him badly, carried him further until he crashed into the side of a tree. Screaming for help, Ralph then sank out of sight. Miller and Cassidy dropped into the creek, the water coming up to their necks, and fished him out. Ralph didn't appear to be breathing.

Miller and Cassidy carried Ralph to a nearby barrel, draping his body over it so that water easily spilled out of his lungs. It took a few minutes, but Ralph eventually came to.

A doctor was called, and just before Ralph was taken home, he weakly offered instructions to everyone. "Don't tell Mother I nearly was drowned," Ralph pleaded. "Just say I got wet."

Ralph Korengel, who would live a good long life and pass away in 1980, lived in a world in which swimming was not yet much of a sport, and as a pastime was only now starting to become mainstream. In 1909, the YMCA—which was still off-limits to anyone without a

Y chromosome—began a campaign to teach every man and boy in the country to swim. But in May of 1913, Syracuse, New York's park commission let it be known that girls were going to be given swimming lessons, and three months later, forty-eight girls in Janesville, Wisconsin, participated in the town's first swimming lessons. Some universities were even making swimming lessons a required part of the curriculum, a trend that really caught on for a while. At its peak, in 1977, forty-two percent of colleges had a swimming requirement. Just five years later, the number of colleges that mandated swimming before handing out a diploma had plummeted to only eight percent. Today, there are just several universities and colleges across the country that enforce swimming. Some high schools require students to swim, but many don't, and as budgets shrink and public swimming pools close, arguably, large swaths of the population aren't learning to swim. There are some understandable arguments for not forcing students to swim—not everyone is physically adept enough to swim well enough to pass a test, some people don't feel comfortable being in a bathing suit in public—and yet, anyone who goes throughout life not knowing how to swim is putting their life at risk. That's underscored every time there is a drowning in the news, of course, but during the summer of 2010, when six teenagers in the Red River drowned in Shreveport, Louisiana, it put a spotlight on how many African-Americans don't know how to swim: seventy percent of black youth, according to many of the reports that came out shortly after the tragedy. Children at a family get-together waded into the Red River, and one of the teenagers stepped off a ledge, falling into water almost twenty-five feet deep. A cousin tried to rescue him but also slipped over the ledge. More teenaged relatives and friends attempted to help the two, but they didn't know how to swim and drowned. The grownups watched, horror-stricken, but none of them knew how to swim either.

It wasn't a tough call for many communities to include the female persuasion in swimming lessons. Women and girls drowned just as easily as men and boys, although it did seem to usually be the latter who did drown. In a culture in which girls were considered nonathletic, dainty, and pure, the boys took more risks. One syndicated article that ran in May 1913, around the country in papers like Frederick, Maryland's *Daily News*, observed: "Every mother of a boy who is near enough a swimming pool is haunted during the summer by the fear that her child will meet his death. . . . Every boy likes to show his prowess by going out farther than the others and oftentimes this venturesome spirit is the cause of drowning."

In fact, since at least the 1880s, the term "drowning season" has been employed to describe the summertime. As *Washington Post* noted in a July 15, 1913 editorial, two days earlier, eight people in Boston had drowned and four more near Philadelphia, "and every large city reported one or more similar accidents on the same day." The editorial pointed out that boys who grew up near the wharves of a big city, "the kind we call street urchins, rarely die from drowning. They learn to swim when they are 7 or 8 years old, and they never forget how to take care of themselves in the water."

The editorial concluded with a chilling suggestion that was clearly influenced by the March and April floods in the country just a few months before: "Both boys and girls should be taught to swim, not only in bathing suits, but with heavy clothes on their bodies."

Nobody could argue that. In fact, the phrase "don't rock the boat" appears to have started because so many people didn't know how to swim, and the last thing you wanted, when you were climbing into a tiny vessel floating in a muddy, fast-moving current, was for the boat to rock.

March 24, Dayton, Ohio

John H. Patterson wasn't preparing for a flood. He was preparing to go to jail.

Several weeks earlier, on February 13, Patterson, the founder of Dayton's famed National Cash Register Company, and his right-hand man, sales manager Thomas J. Watson, who would someday create a little company known as IBM, were found guilty in an anti-trust suit, accused of creating a monopoly.

This was not, at least not for Patterson's competition, simply about trying to get a piece of the pie of the lucrative cash register market in an ethical and legal way. If the charges against Patterson were true, and there is ample evidence that they were, Patterson's salesmen literally threatened their competitors' salesmen. They bribed freight agents to hold up shipments of the other guy's products and then poured sand in their competitors' machines to put them out of order. Patterson's men then opened offices next door to new companies selling cash registers with super cheap prices that would knock them out of business. They hired salesmen at rival companies and paid them to spy on their employer and report back to NCR. Patterson's tactics were ugly but effective. By 1905, when Patterson was sixty-one, it was believed that NCR had about ninety-five percent of the domestic cash register market.

In 1913, there had been a lengthy court case, after which a judge sentenced Patterson to a year in prison. His attorneys were appealing the conviction, but the 69-year-old was facing the very real possibility that on top of a $5,000 fine, negligible for a man like Patterson, he might soon be sitting in a cell at the nearby Miami County Jail in Troy, Ohio for a full year, with common criminals as bunkmates. This was not a luxury hotel for white-collar criminals—the term white-collar criminal wouldn't even be coined until 1939—but a jail with dirt floors. (In October 1913, Wilbur Ballard, a sixteen-year-old in jail for stealing a horse, would tunnel his way out with a spoon.) In the 1920s, one criminal attorney-turned-bootlegger, George Remus, would spend some time in the Miami County jail and call it a "dirty hell hole," and one presumes it wasn't any better and may just have been even worse when Patterson was facing the prospects of living there. But if he was worried, he didn't show it. When he was convicted in court, he was very calm, much more so than the agitated spectators, and after receiving his sentence, Patterson thanked the court for their service, and when the judge asked if he wanted to speak further, he replied, "I have nothing to say, your Honor," and he sat down.

A jail sentence would be the period on what had so far been a spectacularly interesting life. Patterson was born on a family farm near Dayton in 1844, and although he grew up with money, he understood the value of a dollar and what it took to earn it. As a young man, Patterson spent time working as a toll collector on the Miami and Erie Canal, and in 1864, as was common then for many youth who didn't enlist to fight, he spent a hundred days as a Northern soldier in the Civil War, taking on duties away from combat, which allowed more veteran soldiers to stay on the front lines. He was a school teacher around 1870, and then in his mid-thirties he joined his brother to develop coal and iron mines in Jackson County, Ohio.

From there, he went to Coalton, Ohio, to become the general manager for the company store at the Southern Coal and Iron Company. In running the shop, the future business magnate recognized the need for something like a cash register machine. The store was losing money despite doing brisk business, and Patterson read that manufacturers John and James S. Ritty had invented a machine that would tabulate sales as they were made, and that it also had a receptacle for money. Patterson ordered two machines, loved what he saw, and, with his brother, immediately bought stock of the National Manufacturing Company. Two years later, in 1884, they bought enough that they were given control. They weren't thrilled with the plant, however, and decided to build a better factory on better land. They selected a site near the family farm, on land where they had played, worked, and grown up.

Ultimately, their company became one of the world's most successful enterprises, a company still thriving today as a global technology firm that focuses on ATMs and software and other technological marvels that are light-years away from the simple cash register. Patterson would have approved the changes. He was all about following the money.

In 1913, Patterson's business, long since renamed the National Cash Register Company, which everyone referred to by its initials, NCR, employed 5,500 and, aside from the main factory in Dayton, had branches in Toronto and Berlin. But it was Dayton where NCR's success was impossible not to notice. Its headquarters covered thirty-six acres of floor space in fifteen buildings on a manufacturing property occupying 140 acres of ground. Fortunately, for Patterson and everyone in Dayton, the headquarters was on the highest ground of those 140 acres.

Patterson was a tough competitor, but he was a good boss and became better as the years progressed—especially if you compare him to other employers of the age like George Pullman, inventor of the Pullman Sleeper Car, which allowed people to sleep in trains. Pullman's claim to evil-boss fame stems from the company town that he had built just south of Chicago for the employees of his railroad car business. The town really was a town. There were churches, a library, and places to shop; but as landlords go, Pullman was the worst. In 1894, when he cut employees' wages by twenty-five percent, he didn't lower his employees' rent; there was a strike and violence that ended after President Grover Cleveland sent in federal troops to restore order. After Pullman died on October 19, 1897, he was interred in a pit eight feet deep with floors and walls of steel-reinforced concrete. Why? People were afraid his former employees would try to desecrate his corpse. Patterson also acquits himself quite well if you compare him to Max Blanck and Isaac Harris, the owners and operators of the Triangle Shirtwaist Company in New York City, where the men employed immigrant women, paying them next to nothing and keeping them in a building that was locked from the outside; on March 25, 1911, two years to the day before the start of the Great Flood of 1913, there was a fire in the building that killed 146 people, 17 men and 129 women, ranging from forty-eight down to eleven years old.

Around the time Pullman was dealing with his strike, Patterson had a major epiphany after a $50,000 shipment of cash registers was returned from England because the mechanics were faulty; acid had been poured into them, apparently by a disgruntled employee or perhaps several workers.

Patterson went to the floor of the factory to see how it had happened that his employees would turn in such shoddy machinery; and in looking at their work environment, he had to admit that if he were his own employee, he wouldn't care about what he was producing. Patterson raised wages, cleaned the factory, added ventilation, and made dangerous manufacturing equipment safer. He soon went further: dressing rooms and showers, available for employees to use on company time, were introduced, and he opened a factory cafeteria that served subsidized hot lunches. Eventually he went even further: long before corporate retreats became part of the lexicon, NCR employees occasionally went on morale-boosting field trips, like to the 1904 St. Louis World's Fair. The National Cash Register Company started a lending library and started offering free medical care. If those "Best Boss Ever" mugs had been around, Patterson would have had a few hundred in his cabinets.

He was a visionary in other ways as well. It was once estimated that from 1910 until 1930, one-sixth of the business executives in the United States had once worked for Patterson's company. Patterson was a pioneer in sales, giving salespeople scripts and urging his staff to look at the sales cycle as a four-stage process: the initial approach, the proposition, the product demonstration, and closing the deal.

But Patterson wasn't perfect. He could be petty and vindictive, and just plain odd, taking the eccentric-millionaire-boss stereotype to new heights, or depths. When some of his executives weren't around, and Patterson found their desks to be too messy, he'd dump the contents of the drawers into the trash, so they could start work fresh. When he got the idea that everyone should learn to ride a horse properly, which he believed would help his executives master other facets of life, Patterson started making them come to the factory before 6 A.M., for an early morning ride. Company lore has it that Patterson even fired an employee for not being able to ride a horse properly; another employee, he is said to have terminated for not knowing why a flag was flying a certain way.

One of Patterson's righthand men, Charles Palmer, a personal trainer in England before they met, enabled his quirks. Palmer claimed he could read faces, and; so the story goes, Patterson asked Palmer to read the faces of his executives, and then, based on some of those "readings," fired several stunned men.

Patterson, who became something of a health nut later in life, had his employees weighed and measured every six months. Those who were underweight were given free malted milk. Combs and brushes, sterilized every day, were available for grooming, and whenever it rained, company umbrellas were given to female workers going home. Palmer also, with Patterson's blessings, banned bread and butter, tea and coffee and salt and pepper from sales meetings (and replaced them with what?), which didn't go over well with the sales folk. Hugh Chalmers, an NCR vice president who had worked his way up through the company from an office boy, overruled that decision. When Patterson got wind of this, he canned Chalmers and several other top sales coffee-loving executives. Chalmers, who was pulling in $72,000 in salary every year, a fortune at the time, was infuriated and vowed to bring Patterson down.

This was all started over, remember, drinks and condiments.

Five years later, Chalmers, now making automobiles at the Chalmers Motor Company in Detroit, got his chance to exact revenge. When Patterson was taken to court for violating the Sherman Antitrust Act, Chalmers was a convincing key government witness during the fifty-day court case, in which a grand jury took just ten hours to declare

Patterson and his executives corrupt. Patterson and most of the executives on trial were sentenced to a year in jail.

In previous years Patterson had dined with heads of state, but now people across the country were reading the headline INDICTED CASH REGISTER HEAD. Below the awkwardly worded headline was Patterson's photo, showing a somber-looking man with bifocals, a receding hairline, and a neatly trimmed white mustache. The headline, photo, and brief caption explaining his conviction had been syndicated, appearing across the country almost every week. Even as late as March 20, the *Atchison Daily Globe*, in Kansas, had run the news item, which was by now over a month old. Word was gradually getting out. John H. Patterson was a sleazy white-collar crook.

There was a downpour of rain in Dayton on Monday; it had been raining since around midnight, in fact, but most people weren't thinking at all about any serious flooding. But if Patterson had been privy to a flood coming his way, it would have seemed appropriate. He was drowning, all right.

Sometime in the evening, Fort Wayne, Indiana

The St. Marys River finally reached the first floor of the Allen County Orphans Home; once it did, the teachers hurried the children upstairs. It was about this time when two men and a boat arrived, sent by Henry E. Branning, one of the city's trustees whose title was Overseer of the Poor. The boat was small, though, and it could only fit six people, including the two men. Mrs. Ida Overmeyer, the headmistress, did her quick calculations, figuring for sixty-two children and about a dozen adults. Just for the children, assuming the two men were in the boat with four children, fifteen trips would be required. With darkness falling, and the water only grazing the first floor of a sturdy brick building, it didn't seem necessary to go to all that trouble for a little flooding, and it seemed the children would be safer remaining where they were.

It was a tough call, and ultimately the wrong one, but Mrs. Overmeyer understandably decided that they would remain where they were. The children seemed happy, and they had ample food and water for the time being, and coal for the three stoves that had been moved upstairs, although it was in short supply. The flooding couldn't continue much longer, and they could revisit the idea of leaving the orphanage in the morning.

Sometime in the evening, Cincinnati, Ohio

The Queen City hadn't seen much flooding, but there was plenty of wind: witness a 22-year-old male whose name, according to the papers, was Valenti Boeh, son of a cafe store owner. One can only wonder what went through his mind in the last moments of his life as he was blown off the street and into the raging waters of the Ohio and Erie Canal.

7:10 p.m., Makanda, Illinois

Whether technically part of the storm system affecting the Midwest, Northeast, and parts of the South, or just some additional fun that nature wanted to throw into the mix, a storm with 75-mile-an-hour winds ripped through the village. Almost nonstop lightning kept the sky bright, and a funnel cloud emerged, possibly the seventh or thirteenth tornado, depending, again, on what sources one wants to go with. The wind targeted an Illinois Central freight train with forty-one cars, blowing twenty-one of them off the track and obliterating ten of them, such was the power of this tornado.

The contents of the train and much of the village spilled onto the track, fields, and roads but were soon washed away by three inches of rain.

Thirty-nine farmers saw either their house or barn blown to bits, ten people were injured, and three people were killed.

7:30 p.m., Peru, Indiana

The flooding didn't seem all that serious to many people in this town of approximately sixteen thousand, located seventy miles north of Indianapolis and sixty miles southwest of Ft. Wayne. It was probably easy to dismiss something like the weather. The bustling community was on the move, with plenty to distract it. The city had five public schools, several society clubs, a much-admired library, and numerous manufacturing plants. Six rail lines, three electric and three steam, brought goods and passengers into the city. Peru supported three daily newspapers and two weeklies, and in recent years, the community had opened up a city park with electric lights and a bandstand. The fire station had just been modernized in the last year, purchasing two trucks, with pumps that could spray five hundred gallons of water per minute. It was a growing, dynamic city that would soon be covered in muddy river water. The eleven-man police force would be tested as never before.

But on the evening of March 24, Peru residents had no idea what was coming. Nobody could turn to a 24-hour news network to learn that some random people had drowned in communities several hours away and start putting the dots together that this was not an average seasonal flood. There were no radio stations to listen to, although radio technology was making inroads into some levels of society, with the *Titanic* memorably using their radio room almost a year earlier. Information was dribbling in to the local newspapers, which were preparing issues for the next morning. People could look out their window or get the occasional phone call or telegram to learn what was going on away from their own home.

The river ambushed Peru in a surprise attack, with the river storming the city all at once, versus gradually coming into the streets. Officials would conclude that part of the reason the river rushed out of its banks was a railroad bridge that had been built too low. Debris piled up, creating a dam that eventually burst, allowing an obscene amount of water to come into the city at full force.

The water attacked downtown Peru. Clarence Breen, the section foreman for the railroad leading into Peru, was one of the first to see it coming. He didn't stick around to regard it for long, of course, since he and his crew were too busy running for higher ground. Up until then, the 33-year-old and his men had been clearing the railroad of debris. The storm that had come through the day before, part of the tempest that hit Omaha, Nebraska, littered the tracks with ripped-off barn roofs, fragments of horse-drawn buggies, and, mostly, downed tree branches. Breen and his crew had spent much of Sunday night and Monday tending to this task.

But then, after the dam at the bridge broke apart, Breen's job instantly became impossible. From out of nowhere, the water from the 500-mile-plus Wabash River, which passes directly through downtown, covered the tracks of the Lake Erie & Western railroad and then invaded Peru.

Breen and his crew spent the rest of their evening trying to warn the town of what was coming.

Some people didn't need to be told. When the dam broke, the fire whistle blew, alerting residents that trouble was coming; but they were already clued in, since the lights immediately died. Glenn Kessler, a visitor to Peru from northern Indiana staying with a cousin, told the paper later that he had just finished dinner, and that he, along with everyone else, it seemed, went outside after the power went out. It was dark and raining, making it impossible to see and hear what was coming.

Once it did, it swirled around his ankles. Kessler rushed back to his cousin, and by the time he found her in the darkened house, the water was at their waists. Neighbors were crying and screaming. Gunshots punctured the air as a warning to others, and in the din, Kessler and his cousin could hear people shouting "To the courthouse! To the courthouse!" which was seven blocks away from the river, and it was a building plenty sturdy enough to withstand whatever the river had to offer. The courthouse was made of oolitic limestone, mined in Oolitic, Indiana, which twenty years later would provide the limestone for the Empire State Building. More importantly, the courthouse was one of the most modern buildings in the state of Indiana—only two years old—and it was three stories high. It was one of the few places in the city people could be reasonably sure of being safe.

Half running and swimming, Kessler and his cousin floundered their way to the courthouse, the sanctuary for the beleaguered and drenched. It was also the destination for resident Alexander Clevenger, who carried each of his children and then his wife on his back through water waist-deep from their home to the Miami County courthouse. After that, he found a rowboat and rescued a neighbor and her baby.

But then if Clevenger hadn't completely figured out what his town was dealing with, he knew now. A telephone pole came crashing down onto the boat, crushing it into oblivion. When he emerged from under the freezing water, gasping for air, Clevenger saved the mother, who had grabbed some wires to help her stay afloat. But her baby—in the crashing of the telephone pole, the confusion, the cold water—could not be found.

48

Many residents inland had no comprehension of what was happening to their community. The river had overflowed its banks before, coming up as far as five blocks in from the water and hitting Fifth Street. But since it wasn't yet at Fifth Street, everyone from Sixth Street, especially those with second stories to retreat to in an emergency, didn't see much reason to panic.

Oblivious to the idea that they were facing something unprecedented, many families went to bed, unaware that the waters were rising six inches every hour.

There was a reason many Peru residents—and people throughout Indiana, Ohio, and other states—were not terribly concerned about the rain over the past three days. Flooding was terribly common, as it had been throughout the nation's history.

It was common throughout world history, actually. Europe had had ample floods in its past, one of the most famous being in 1236 when the Thames River overflowed into the Palace of Westminster. Palace and rescue workers wound up steering their boats through the halls. On December 14, 1287, a dike broke in a storm in the Netherlands and Germany, and the resulting flood killed ten thousand, and a similar incident happened again in the Netherlands on the night of November 18, 1421. Millions of people around the world since the days of the Ice Age have come to a miserable end due to flooding.

But in the United States, as early as 1726, French residents built a levee made of earth six feet high and a mile long near the opening of the Mississippi River for protection.* Israel Ludlow, the founder of Dayton, Ohio, which bore the worst that the Great Flood of 1913 had to offer, was—according to local legend—warned in 1796 by the few remaining Indians about the floods. But Ludlow ignored their warnings. Consequently, the city of Dayton had its first serious flood—on record—in March 1805. Thawing deep snows and heavy rains were to blame for the flood, which covered most of the town except for a part of the business center. Townspeople considered moving their downtown

---

* For those who are not familiar with dam terminology, a levee is a dam, but a dam is not a levee. A levee is generally an earthen dam, not damming up and stopping the water altogether, but built alongside the riverbank, with a high wall designed to keep the river inside the riverbed. Conversely, a dam like the Hoover dam stops a river altogether at one end.

to higher ground but decided against it. The next big flood came in 1814, where it was deep enough that a horse could swim in the streets. Yet another tempest came on January 8, 1828, when a warehouse was washed away from the front of Wilkinson Street and the southern part of the city was submerged. And another arrived on January 2, 1847, in which the entire town was covered with water, although it wasn't as deep as it had been back in 1805. September 17, 1866, brought a fairly deep flood—it was four inches deep on the floor of the Phillips Hotel, and there was $250,000 in damage, a pretty serious blow considering there were only fifteen thousand residents in the city and that $250,000 in today's dollars would be $3.6 million.

More flooding hit Dayton in 1883 and then in 1896, during the centennial anniversary of the city, historian Mary Davies Steele wrote about the flooding her community had seen. "Some of us can remember how certain aged pioneers used to upbraid the founders of the town for putting it down in a hollow, instead of on the hills to the southeast, and expatiate on the folly which the people were guilty of in voting against the removal, after the terrible freshet of 1805, to high ground," Davies wrote. "'Someday there will be a flood which will sweep Dayton out of existence,' those ancient men and women used to prophesy to their grandchildren."

Steele, in her mid fifties, would not live to see the 1913 flood. She passed away in February 1897, a year of a big flood in Dayton, followed by a worse flood in 1898, which was especially grim. Six more inches, and it would have gone over the levee.

But, of course, it didn't overflow the levee, and that was the problem for the people of 1913. As communities grew and built businesses literally along the riverbank, every generation could look back to floods of the past, and as long as it only affected a minority of the people who lived or worked along the riverbanks, or was a close call, a flood could seem not all that threatening. It might even almost appear amusing and certainly interesting as a work of Mother Nature—especially if you lived far enough from the river.

But for the unlucky soul who didn't take floods seriously, or simply showed up in the wrong place at the wrong time, the power of water was fatally evident, and it certainly wasn't only Dayton that repeatedly found itself threatened by flooding. In 1913, anyone eighty and over who happened to live in Philadelphia would have remembered the serious flood the city had had in 1843. One paper during the time, after telling of bridges being destroyed, brick houses being knocked down, and pigs struggling in the current, reported that two young men, Russell Flounders and Josiah Benting, had been killed in the flood.

"It is supposed that they were crushed by the bridge, as a portion of its materials were seen to roll over onto them as they were engulfed in the flood," reported the *Adams Sentinel*, of Gettysburg, Pennsylvania. "Their bodies were never found."

The paper went on to say that a house had been carried off, and a Mrs. Julia Nowlin and her four children had been drowned.

During the early days of the Civil War, in November 1861, a Union captain from Pennsylvania, and some members of a New York regiment, discovered five bodies floating down the Potomac after some heavy flooding. Two were a husband and wife and a third a private from Massachusetts, named either Bumford or Burford, of Company K, Fifteenth Massachusetts Volunteers, judging from the soggy identification papers. Those weren't the only items Bumford—or Burford—had in his possession. Newspaper editors and reporters, either feeling it was important information or believing readers curious and gossipy, always seemed to go out of their way to report what contents were in the pockets of flood victims. Bumford—or Burford—had in his possession a medallion and $25 in gold.

Mark Twain, who died three years before the Great Flood of 1913, wrote about the flood of 1882 in his book *Life on the Mississippi*, saying about it: "It put all the unprotected low lands under water from Cairo to the mouth; it broke down the levees in a great many places, on both sides of the river; and in some regions south, when the flood was at its highest, the Mississippi was seventy miles wide! A number of lives were lost, and the destruction of property was fearful."

The Johnstown flood of 1889 also highlights how common flooding was, in that at least a couple of its survivors went on to experience the Great Flood of 1913. The *New Castle News* of New Castle, Pennsylvania, reported that a Mildred Abel, who lived in Johnstown at the time of the flood, also was stuck in her surrounded, flooding home in Belle Vernon, Pennsylvania, for two weeks in 1908, and then once again was trapped in her house in New Castle, Pennsylvania, during the 1913 flood. And according to the *Columbus Citizen-Journal*, a Mr. and Mrs. C. M. Sipes* were living in Johnstown, Pennsylvania in 1889 when they lost everything. In Columbus, Ohio in 1913, they would lose everything yet again, becoming some of the more unlucky people in history. On the other hand, considering that they lived to tell the tale of surviving major floods twice, they might also be considered some of the luckiest.

The Flood of 1898 was memorable as well. Richmond, Indiana lost a bridge. Middletown, Ohio saw its nearby Great Miami River, normally about four hundred feet wide, stretch out a mile wide. In nearby Hamilton, Ohio, where every boat in the city was pegged as a rescue boat, seven people died, including a mother and three young daughters. In Columbus, the flood took out the water pumping system, denying people fresh water and flooding homes, some businesses, and the local asylum.

And in Creekside, Pennsylvania, on March 23, 1898, Martin Fisher tried to set an example of what it means to be a good citizen—or, if you'd rather, people who hate the idea of serving on jury duty can point to him as an example that there may be something to their complaints. Fisher, a postmaster and merchant, not to mention a father and husband and provider to his aging mother, was determined to do his duty and get to the courthouse in Indiana, Pennsylvania, despite rain and severe flooding.

There was some water in front of the bridge, but not much, and Fisher, in his horse and buggy, believed—surely like other drivers had before him and many more would later in their cars—that he could traverse a little water without any problems. It must be a quirk of human nature. We as a people become so wrapped up in our day-to-day issues, like trying to get to jury duty or reach a friend's house, that we minimize the danger in front of us. Fisher, like so many people before him and after, surveyed the swollen river and decided he was perfectly capable of crossing it.

Unfortunately, he didn't know that underneath the water there was a ditch waiting for him. His horse and buggy waded in fine, but then

---

* C. M. Sipes was possibly house painter Charles M. Sipes and his wife Stella, who were both born in Pennsylvania, according to 1910 census records.

the wheels got stuck and the buggy pitched forward, throwing Fisher out. Several bystanders attempted to save Fisher, who was able to stay afloat long enough to scream for help. One man ran to grab a boat but couldn't lift it over a fence, and two men unsuccessfully attempted to throw out a rope to Fisher.

There was the will but not a way to save him. Weighted down in his overcoat and shoes, Fisher drowned and was washed away.

The next day, the village authorities found his body stuck in the willows. In Fisher's possession, the *Indiana Weekly Messenger* couldn't help noting, were a watch and a pocketbook containing almost a hundred dollars. Yet his sad story would prove to be repeated again and again and the lesson of not trying to ford the water went unheeded in the years to come.

Chapter Four

The Long Rain

March 25, Tuesday

In the wake of a homicide, a police officer or detective searches for a murderer by trying to discover a motive for taking out a person's life, determining if the killer has an alibi and hunting for clues that prove beyond a reasonable shadow of a doubt who did it. In other words, there are many elements factored into solving a murder mystery.

In the same way, city officials, scientists, and the public at large started looking for causes for the flood right away, especially in its aftermath, and, as it would turn out, rain wasn't the only culprit. Far from it. Mankind shares the blame as well.

Throughout the nineteenth century and into the twentieth, railroads built their tracks near the water without permits or supervision or consideration that perhaps at some point, these tracks will be underwater. Construction crews built their buildings right up to the water's edge, their foundations resting on nothing but silt and sand. Mini-dams and blockades were being created all the time, so that after a heavy downpour or even a light rain, mini-floods were constantly being created.

Arthur E. Morgan, the engineer who would later be brought into Dayton, Ohio, to create a flood-control system for the region, wrote about the flood in his book *The Miami Valley and the 1913 Flood,* published in the year 1917, and laid out a long list of reasons why the river and creeks didn't stay in their beds, most of the reasons for which were man-made. He did account for some factors that had nothing to do with human beings, like "the rolling country with its short, steep slopes leading to innumerable little brooks and gullies, which in turn empty into the larger streams, tends to hurry the rainwater off the land and into the rivers." He added: "The soil, a mixture of clay, sand, and gravel, is sufficiently dense to prevent water from sinking into it rapidly during heavy rains."

But generally, Morgan gently placed the blame on people, citing the following reasons:

1) We were shovel-happy. "The digging of more than two thousand miles of ditches and drains for agricultural drainage and along highways and railroads, within the Miami watershed, has removed innumerable little storage reservoirs over the surface of the land, and by improving the overgrown and obstructed paths of the water, has tended to hurry it much more rapidly to the main streams. . . ."

2) We were chopping down too many trees. ". . . while cutting of the forests, with the removal of the surface layer of leaves and mold, probably results in a similar tendency."

3) We were building too much, too quickly. "The paving of city streets, and the construction of sewers would also hasten the flow of storm water, but the areas affected by city improvements are so small that their effect is negligible."

4) Our dams were sometimes doing more harm than good. "The rivers of the region have formed for themselves natural channels of only sufficient size to carry the usual flow, and as the flow during the great floods is many times as great as that of ordinary spring freshets, the river channels fail entirely to meet extreme conditions," wrote Morgan, who had a tendency to be wordy. "Here and there along the rivers artificial obstructions have been created which to a greater or less extent interfere with stream flow, and the construction of cities in the valley hinders the free passage of overflow water. The levees built along the winding rivers to confine the flood waters, while they serve the purpose admirably until broken or overtopped, thereafter act as submerged dams."

There was a fifth factor in the large death toll surrounding the flood if not the flood itself, and it was yet another manmade one, which Morgan does not mention. Garbage. People across the country were dumping it into rivers and streams. In January 1913, the city council of Lowell received permission from the Massachusetts government that it had the authority to keep their part of the Merrimack River clean and fine anyone who ignored the laws. In years past, residents had been tossing in barrels, tin cats, cotton waste from the textile factories, and even dead cats and dogs. Cities and towns across America eventually came around to Lowell's way of thinking, but it would take time.

But the local laws weren't always much help, which illustrates why the states and federal government eventually had to get involved in the clean water cause. During the same month, the *Daily Courier* in Connellsville, Pennsylvania reported that several businesses had been dumping garbage into the Youghiogheny River all winter, despite a law from the board of health that forbade them to. It was getting to be an eyesore, too. The Connellsville Garbage & Fertilizer Company had recently started dumping their refuse on the edge of the riverbank. "Must dump it somewhere," an unidentified official was quoted as saying.

But while public officials saw blight, Connellsville's impoverished residents saw an opportunity. Mothers and children quickly made a beeline for the river's edge and snatched up the potatoes, grapes, oranges, and other fruits and vegetables that stores hadn't seen fit to sell.

Across the country, mines were dumping waste into rivers, streams, ponds, and lakes, and for decades, even local governments were putting their trash into the waterways. In the 1906 trade magazine *Municipal Journal and Engineer*, it was noted that "many of the inland cities on the great rivers continue to use the primitive method of stream dumping."

The article then cited some figures, which were then "some years" old, but still, it gives an idea of how the nation's water supply was probably faring in 1913. In recent years, according to *Municipal Journal and Engineer*, eight cities were dumping into the Mississippi River 152,675 tons of garbage, manure, and the entrails of meat from butchers' shops, 108,250 tons of human excrement, and 3,765 animal carcasses.

Speaking of which, federal regulation of drinking water quality wouldn't begin until the next year when the U.S. Public Health Service would begin setting standards for the bacteriological quality of drinking water. Unfortunately, those standards were only for drinking water for ships and trains, but we were getting there as a nation in terms of setting some long-overdue water sanitation guidelines.

Still, by the early 1900s, even though it had long been proven that you could catch diseases like cholera from polluted water, cities finally began on their own working on cleaning their water, many of which went with a cloth filtration system; others, a slow sand filtration. Five years earlier, in Jersey City, New Jersey, the water pumping station began putting chlorine in their water. Great strides were being made in offering people what they drank, though it's hard to imagine that anyone today would feel comfortable drinking a nice tall glass of water that came out of a kitchen faucet in 1913*—especially when you consider that most water pipes were made of lead. Most cities by 1913 recognized that drinking water from lead pipes was a good way to get lead poisoning—that had been on health officials' radar since the late nineteenth century. But it would take another ten years, at least, before cities and towns began curtailing the use of lead pipes. It took a while, partly because the Lead Industries Association argued their cause and convinced plenty of water-regulating officials that lead pipes were a perfectly safe manner of transporting drinking water.

So by the dawn of the flood, many of the larger cities were cleaning up their acts, but the smaller communities with less river traffic and weaker budgets were far behind the collective understanding that dumping trash into waterways was a bad idea. If the rivers, creeks, and streams in the states affected by the Great Flood of 1913 had all been clear, yes, the flood would have occurred and would likely have still been grim, but the garbage made matters worse. Just as the debris piled up and eventually broke free, releasing the Wabash River onto Peru, it contributed to the problems in many other overwhelmed communities

---

* The nation was still 35 years away from the Federal Water Pollution Control Amendments of 1948, the federal government's first stab at trying to give the public clean water to drink, bathe, and cook their food in.

in the region. There was one last reason for the flood, and it does not allow for any real historical or scientific analysis: just plain bad timing.

It was the end of the winter. The ground wasn't frozen—which can be problematic when there's flooding—but it was still oversaturated with melted, and melting, snow. The rain that came with the tornadoes couldn't evaporate, or be absorbed, fast enough. Additionally, the melting snow already had rivers at a higher volume than was typical for this time of year.

A week after living through the flood himself, Professor William R. Lazenby, the head of the department of forestry at Ohio State University, explained to a student reporter what had happened: "Conditions in Ohio at the time of the recent flood were unusual. The ground was filled with water, literally watersoaked. Had the same amount of rain fallen in Ohio when the ground was in a dryer condition the flood damage would have been less to a great extent. The intensity of a flood is due to its rapidity. Only when the surface water passes off quickly is the greatest damage done and the danger great."

The Flood of 1913 never would have happened if an identical storm had visited during the end of a dry, hot summer. It also might not have happened if Arthur Ernest Morgan had come along earlier, and the nation had been a little wiser and more sophisticated when it came to flood control. But we weren't there yet in 1913, and in the early wet spring after a long cold wet winter, much of the soil throughout the United States, particularly in Ohio and Indiana, was still frozen. The cracks in the earth, the loose, wind-blown and dry dirt, that would normally capture much of the rainfall, was nowhere to be found. When it began to rain, the water had nowhere to go except the muddy and polluted rivers, streams, and creeks, and they were already dangerously full.

March 25, midnight, Dayton

It was still raining and had been for about twenty-four hours straight now. The police are warned that the Herman Street Levee is weakening. They begin blasting the warning sirens.

Peru, Indiana, around midnight

It was still raining here too. While many families went to bed as usual, many people started waking up when the river smashed open their front doors. Residents were also roused awake by the sounds of lions and tigers roaring and horses neighing furiously.

Gilbert Kessler, with his cousin, heard the sounds from the courthouse, and it slowly dawned on them that the sounds were coming from the Hagenbeck-Wallace Circus, one of approximately thirty traveling circuses that made its way around the country. This one had its headquarters just outside of Peru, an expanse of 1,500 acres, and spent the winters here, preparing and planning out their shows during the warmer months. In fact, they had a big show planned in about two weeks, on April 12, in St. Louis.

The circus owner, Colonel Benjamin E. Wallace, sixty-five years old, lived inside the city limits of Peru, apart from the winter headquarters, which was two miles east of the community. The phone lines leading to the circus headquarters were quickly toppled by the flood, and he couldn't reach his employees to see how the seventy-five men and the animals were faring.

His animals were a major attraction for the circus. Many of them had been caught by Captain Emil Schweyer, an eminent animal trainer from Switzerland and, by all accounts, fearless when it came to animals. One story making the rounds around town was that a few weeks earlier, he had come to Peru for a visit, and Colonel Wallace showed him around, warning Schweyer to be particularly careful with the jaguar.

"Show him to me. I'll eat him alive," Schweyer reportedly said.

If the account is to believed—it could have been a story manufactured for the press and an impressed public—after Wallace showed him the jaguar, Schweyer entered the cage and grabbed the jaguar's jaws. Wallace, thinking the guy was a nut, shouted for the trainers, but Schweyer laughed and put his head in the jaguar's mouth. The jaguar seemed paralyzed until Schweyer left the cage, and then the animal ran for the bars, hoping to nail the animal trainer but instead crashing against the metal. Schweyer laughed again. He sounds like a swell guy.

But Wallace's prized animals were not doing so well now. The lions and a cacophony of other animals, including camels, bears, monkeys, and exotic birds, kept roaring and making terrified sounds that reached the ears of Wallace and other townspeople, reverberating across the flooded streets of Peru as the Wabash and Mississinewa rivers' levels climbed higher and higher. Although, after an hour or two, Gilbert noticed that some of the strange sounds had ended and wondered if it was the water that silenced them.

Somewhere around the midnight hour, some townspeople drove out to a nearby village called Peoria, not to be confused with Peoria, Illinois, or even another Peoria, Indiana, in Franklin County. This Peoria was in Miami County, the same county that Peru resides in. This particular group of Peru residents knew there was one man who would be of big help to their community. His name was Sam, and he was a Miami Indian.

The days of wanting to kill American Indians had been a fading memory for many generations in 1913. Just a little over a month earlier, on a rainy February 22, twenty-nine American Indian chiefs from reservations in the west, marched up a hill at Fort Wadsworth, Staten Island, with President William Howard Taft and members of his family.

After a 21-gun salute, they solemnly broke ground for the National American Indian memorial, a sixty-foot bronze statue of an Indian warrior, which would tower 165 feet above the highest elevation around New York harbor. Hollow Horn Bear, sixty-three, once a Brulé Lakota leader who fought against the United States Army on the Great Plains, was chosen to overturn the earth, not with a shovel, but what he would have used years before: a buffalo thigh bone. Pretty Voice Eagle, sixty-eight years old, of the Sioux, was present. He had fought almost seventy battles with the U.S. Army. Two Moon, once a North Cheyenne warrior who fought against General Custer but was now hovering around seventy years of age and almost blind, had also come for the ceremony. Indian folk songs were played by a band, and so was the Star Spangled Banner. Each Indian leader present was given as a gift the first American nickels to feature the profile of an Indian on one side and a buffalo on the other.

President Taft, in one of his last public appearances, offered a short, eloquent speech, arguably delivered several decades too late. "For two centuries, the North American Indian has had a right to be treated not as a relic of pre-historic man but as an existing force with great and immediate and direct influence upon the settlement and development of this country by the white races."

If you live in New York City or thereabouts and are wondering how in the heck you missed this grand spectacle, you aren't unobservant.

Nobody could get the funding for this memorial, and it was never built. The site chosen is now an abutment for a bridge. Still, the sentiment was nice, although Hollow Horn Bear probably found himself wishing he had skipped the whole thing. He caught pneumonia after being out in the rain and died.

So even if the white man continued to treat Native Americans rather shabbily and keep them quarantined on various reservations throughout the country, the lust for violence and snuffing the Indian out had been replaced with something that seemed close to respect. Samuel Bundy was thirty-one years old, a curiosity but well liked by his white counterparts. Some people—maybe more as a joke than anything—called him Chief Bundy. Most people just called him Sam and knew him to be a good man with a lot of character. They also knew he owned a boat.

It was sixteen feet long and four feet wide with a flat bottom, and Sam Bundy had had some very successful fishing expeditions in his vessel. Perhaps due to the knowledge passed on from his parents and their parents, he truly understood the water.

Bundy wasn't actually a full-blooded Native American. He was a great-great grandson of Frances Slocum, a white pioneer who would become famous for having been kidnapped on November 2, 1778, by the Delaware Indians. She was taken when she was just five years old.

Slocum was renamed Young Bear, raised by the Delaware, and in her late teens married a fellow tribesman. Apparently, he was killed and she married again, because her second husband was a Miami warrior called Deaf Man because he somehow became totally deaf between thirty and forty years of age. After the War of 1812, Young Bear, who had four children with Deaf Man, moved with her family to the Mississinewa River Valley in Indiana. In 1835, Young Bear mentioned her identity to an Indian trader, which eventually led to her being reunited with her brothers, who wanted her to come back to Pennsylvania. She didn't. She couldn't understand English, and as a woman in her early sixties, she was completely assimilated as a Miami Indian. She was, however, allowed to remain in the Mississinewa River Valley, with her immediate family while the rest of her tribe was pushed off to Kansas. Young Bear died in 1847 at the age of seventy-four, over thirty years before Sam Bundy came into the world on August 31, 1881.

Bundy was assimilated among the white men, but he hadn't forgotten his heritage. He lived in Peoria, for starters, which was populated with Miami Indians. And when some of the Peru locals showed up at Bundy's doorstep in Peoria, he understandably wanted no part of plunging into the darkness and rowing his boat through the river. But the more he was told about the flood, and as he came to realize that this was truly unprecedented, he didn't need to be convinced. He said he would be happy to go, which is how at one o'clock in the morning, Sam Bundy came to sliding his boat into a wild river and found himself looking for people to save.

March 25, New Castle, Pennsylvania, midnight

There were ominous signs that some communities in western Pennsylvania might find themselves in the midst of a flood. It had been raining nonstop all day Monday, and the Shenango River and Neshannock Creek were rising. The latter took over Neshannock Avenue, East Street, South Mill Street, and several other roads, but that in itself wasn't alarming. It was an area of the city that always flooded during heavy rains. Still, city officials were warily on watch.

March 25, 1 A.M., Chicago

Ernest Bicknell's train finally pulled into the station, a full thirteen hours late. Exhausted, the Red Cross director had been keeping up with the news of the flood by talking to conductors and grabbing every newspaper he could get his hands on at train stations along the route. He had long since decided that as bad as things were in Omaha, the worst there was over and he was needed more in Indiana and Ohio. He stuck around in Chicago long enough to have a meeting with the officers at the United Charities of Chicago (the forerunner of a nonprofit that's now called Metropolitan Family Services). The officers then started raising money for the flood victims and within a few hours, several thousand dollars, clothing, supplies, and furniture had already been pledged or collected.

Bicknell doesn't say in his biography, but you have to think that he must have looked at his train, heaved a deep sigh, and wondered why airplane travel wasn't fully developed yet. He boarded in any event, so he could once more travel through the flood-stricken lands of Indiana and Ohio.

1:30 A.M., West Liberty, Ohio

The railroads were well aware that flooding might swamp railroad tracks, and rivers had a way of weakening bridges. So that's how and why Phillip Henn, a 47-year-old passenger conductor, found himself, late at night and in the rain, inspecting a bridge for a train that traveled between Indiana and Pennsylvania. Henn was walking on the bridge, looking for trouble, and, boy, did he find it: one of the spans on the trestle collapsed, and he plunged into the Mad River below. If he screamed, nobody was there to hear it.

Shortly after, at 1:30 A.M., the Pennsylvania Railroad passenger train No. 3 came roaring toward the Mad River and onto the bridge that was now mostly no longer there. The engine fell through the rest of the bridge, and gravity brought at least several more passenger cars into the Mad River.

Incredibly, there weren't many deaths in the train crash. The passengers were able to stagger to their feet and climb out of the windows, shaken but alive. The engineer, James Wood, and the fireman, C. E. Tilton, were first into the river, but somehow survived. The brakeman, Elwood Howells, drowned.

Claibourne, Ohio, about 2 A.M.

Pearl Clifton Biddle, a 34-year-old family man and roofer specializing in tin, awakened to hear frantic barking. Biddle's dog slept under the back porch, and so Biddle opened the door, expecting a coyote, a cat, perhaps a burglar—but what he saw was much harder to comprehend.

His dog was in the back yard—swimming.

Biddle didn't let the surreal sight delay him for too long. He ran out into the rain and rescued his dog and waded out to his chicken house to bring his chickens in, probably with the help of his wife, Lillian, and their nine-year-old daughter, Florence. Once that was done, he raced to the pigpen, managing to steer seven piglets and their mother through the water and to his back porch. Then, leaving the animals behind on his porch, he ran through the neighborhood, a modern-day

Paul Revere on foot, warning of an impending danger, pounding on doors and waking up everyone he could find.

Biddle must have missed Alma Donohoe, sixty, for she woke up a few hours later. She discovered water lapping against the shore of her mattress, and terrified, she waded into her living room. She must have been amused—at least later when she thought about it—to see her kitten, floating in the room, alive and well, a passenger in a sewing basket. She and her kitten then hurried to her younger brother Joseph's home.

Miss Donohoe was fortunate, however. She escaped the flood with an amusing story to share with her family, friends, and hopefully Pearl Biddle.

Delaware, Ohio, about 2 A.M.

Approximately twenty miles southeast of Richwood, about the time Biddle was banging on doors, nobody in Delaware needed to be told that a flood was coming. The Olentangy River had taken over eight blocks of the town that resides twenty-seven miles north of Columbus, Ohio. Delaware's 45-year-old mayor, Bertrand V. Leas, who a few short years earlier had been a hardware store owner, first rowed his wife, Marie, and two young children, Florence and Bertrand Jr., to safety and then went back for his neighbor.

Samuel Jones, the patriarch of the family, wasn't there, possibly because he was back at the lumber yard where he was a foreman. Mrs. Sophrona Jones and her fifteen-year-old daughter, Esther, were at the house, however, along with at least two neighbors, Hazel Dunlap, twenty-two years old, and an unknown woman, possibly Hazel's mother. Guided by a lantern and the other lantern light from other rescue boats in the neighborhood, Leas began taking his passengers through the fast-moving current. The rain was dumping on them, and the water and sky were dark, but while they couldn't see what was out there, the sound of rain and rushing water and debris crashing by made it abundantly clear that maybe they were better off not knowing.

And then it happened just twenty feet later: a wave, crashing over the boat and knocking everyone into the water. Somehow, the mayor clung to Mrs. Jones and managed to keep her afloat until rescuers could get to her. But they couldn't get to him. Mayor Leas was swept away.

But not for long. He grabbed on to a rope hanging from the window of a lumber building and climbed up to the roof. Rescuers, however, thought he was a goner, and initial reports went to newspapers across the country that Mayor B. V. Leas had drowned, along with twenty other residents. The numbers were a little off, but they were grim nonetheless—it was probably closer to fourteen who died, and among them were three of the mayor's passengers: Esther Jones, Hazel Dunlap, and the unknown woman.

Deep into the night, still in Delaware, Ohio

Throughout the previous day in the college town of Delaware, Ohio, the flooding at first was subtle: six inches deep in some of the lower streets. But as the day wore on, it was a foot deep. By evening, the Olentangy River had covered the entire lower part of the town, with the second stories and roofs sticking out of the water.

Florence Wyman, a student at Ohio Wesleyan University in Delaware, later said that about two hundred young women in Monnett Hall, their dormitory, walked the floors and cried and prayed. Their university was on the highest hill in the town, but they were only a few blocks away from homes that were deluged. Even if the women closed their windows, they could still hear the water's roar and people, on their roofs, begging and screaming for help. Every once in a while, the young coeds would hear a woman shrieking, which everyone took as the sound of someone seeing a loved relative losing their grip or footing and falling into the water.

There were no boats at the university, and with it being dark, and the town drenched by what was now a cold drizzle, there was nothing anyone could realistically do until morning.

Tiffin, Ohio, middle of the night

It was still raining. People in the northern half of Ohio were recognizing the danger that they were in, and the streets of Tiffin were emptying. But it could be difficult to know what to do when your family wasn't together. Theresa Klingshirn, nine Klingshirn children ranging from a nineteen-year-old to a two-year-old, and her son-in-law, Ray Hostler, and a future daughter-in-law, Regina Ranker, were inside the house. The evening before, when her husband George left for work on the night shift at the lime kiln, when it was apparent that the streets were dangerous but he believed the home was their sanctuary, the father and husband had put on his coat and stressed to the family: "In any event, do not leave the house."

Mrs. Klingshirn listened. Even if he hadn't said those words, the 39-year-old mother might well have wondered where to go in the middle of the night and surely fretted that her husband might come to the house, believe they were still inside, and attempt to rescue them. But hearing that directive and probably something of a plea probably kept coming back to the whole family.

Staying put must have seemed like the wise course of action to remain where they were, even as several neighbors on East Davis Street packed up and fled; but Mrs. Klingshirn, Ray Hostler, Regina Ranker, and the rest of the children would have been far better off if one of the adults had persuaded everything to enact the old chestnut, well worn even in 1913: better be safe than sorry. It was an expression made for moments like these.

Columbus, Ohio, 3 A.M.

The first call for help to the police came in from a house on West Mound Street. The entire area, particularly the Hocking Valley railroad yards, was flooded. The authorities were ready for flooding, they thought. Columbus's weather forecaster had warned the city the evening before of possible flooding, and throughout the night, they had been patrolling the streets in the rain. Not that anyone expected anything all that serious.

Dayton, Ohio, 4 A.M.

Mr. E. T. Herbig, the traffic chief of the Bell phone exchanges, had issued orders to the operators to clue him in if anyone saw anything unusual; and having been wakened throughout the night by calls of water rising, the bleary-eyed telephone man came to the company to start work.

Still, people downtown didn't think a full-fledged flood would reach them. Fred Aring, a telegraph operator, noted in his diary that at about 4 A.M. on this day, "We had received meager reports from operators in north and south of Dayton that the Miami River had been and still was rising rapidly." But there were no levees in South Dayton, noted Aring, and so some flooding "was to be expected. . . . Certainly no general flood is expected."

Dayton, Ohio, 4:30 A.M.

The Platt Iron Works' day engineer was roused awake by a neighbor who informed him that the water was spilling over the levees, and while it wasn't much, it was coming over faster with every passing minute. The day engineer made a few quick adjustments to his home—taking some family photos, valuables, or important papers upstairs—and raced to the plant, where he gave the night engineer and watchman the scoop. They blew the whistle for the next twenty minutes.

Many people heard it, as far as five miles away, but many people had no earthly idea what it meant. People like John P. Foose, a Civil War veteran, didn't know what was happening, but he looked outside at the torrential downpour, and, as he mentioned in a letter to his brother, he saw a troubling sight that gave him an idea of what was coming: "Across the street, the people were up and moving their things upstairs."

About twenty minutes later, as the Platt Iron Works whistle sputtered to a stop, Foose's two daughters ran to the river to see what was happening. They came back to report that the water was as high as the levee. Foose and the family wolfed down a quick breakfast and began taking the rugs upstairs.

In at least one part of Dayton—a Mrs. Mildred Grothjan would recall years later—one man was walking the rainy streets, shouting through a megaphone, telling everyone to flee for the hills: a flood was coming. But nobody, according to Grothjan, believed him, and everyone in the vicinity remained in their homes.

Charles and Viola Adams awakened, not from the Platt Iron Works, although they were within range of the factory, and not from a guy with a megaphone. What made them sit up in their beds were the loud voices of neighbors outside their bedroom window; they were rapping on doors of the houses on their street.

Charles and Viola, hoping their eleven-month-old twins wouldn't wake up, dressed and went downstairs. They had an idea of what the commotion was about. The night before, around nine in the evening, they had left their son and daughter with Viola's sister, Estelle, who had been visiting for Easter weekend, and they took a stroll with their umbrellas to look at the Great Miami River. The water was several feet below the levees, but it was obvious that it was rising. Still, they didn't think it would actually overtop the levee. Just a week earlier, the Great Miami River through Dayton had been 2.7 feet deep, and the levees were designed to hold the river at 25 feet. The highest the water had ever been was 21.8 feet.

At the worst, figured Charles, if the river overflowed the levee, it couldn't possibly go farther than the end of their street, Rung Street, based on what had happened during the last serious flood in 1898.

Still, the concerned couple decided that Charles could check out the Miami again and see what they were dealing with. He put on his overcoat, grabbed his umbrella, and headed out the door, leaving 33 Rung Street to walk several blocks to the river. The rain was unforgiving, and the sky still dark, but Charles didn't feel alone. The streets were full of people coming and going, doing the exact same thing.

Charles surveyed the river. It was as bad as everyone feared. In fact, the river, which was perilously close to coming over the 25-foot levee, would rise to 29 feet. Charles didn't know that, of course, but he was frightened.

Adams hurried back to his house.

Zanesville, Ohio, 4:55 A.M.

The electric power plant stopped working, and the bleary-eyed residents, many of them awake and watching the water outside their homes, were now in the darkness and facing an unseen enemy. Judging from the screams that could be heard throughout the city, some residents were either already in trouble or very, very edgy.

Columbus, Ohio, 5 A.M.

The police stations were now being overwhelmed with telephone calls, requesting help from people whose homes were flooded. Some police stations began calling the fire department, hoping for a little backup.

Dayton, Ohio, 5:30 A.M.

Dayton's city engineer, Gaylord Cummin, reported that the water was at the top of the levees. It was, he calculated, flowing at 100,000 feet per second. He predicted that the water would be overflowing the levees and appearing in the streets within half an hour.

In the northern part of Dayton, the levees began overflowing right about the time Charles Adams returned to his house. He didn't have to convince Viola that they needed to prepare for a flood. Charles's father, who lived nearby, had already come over to help his son's family. Charles's father was named John, and so we don't have images of forefathers in a flood, John Adams shall henceforth be referred to as Grandpa Adams.

Everyone went to work, prepping the house for the flood and developing a plan to leave before it came.

March 25, Dawn, Peru, Indiana

Mayor John Kreutzer, hearing that the Wabash River was rising about a foot an hour and hammering south Peru, asked for bleary-eyed volunteers to brave the rain and help citizens near the river move their belongings or leave for safer ground.

His request for help was heeded. Rescuers were out in force, as they were in communities throughout the Midwest. Sam Bundy had been out in his boat for several hours now, and Glenn Kessler, the man visiting his cousin in Peru who had heard the circus animals all night at the courthouse, was soon another. Indeed, the flood was doing plenty of damage—the bridge near Broadway Street was just about to collapse—and there were plenty of people who needed saving.

Edward Murray and his wife and kids were among them. Edward was awakened by the incessant barking of the family dog. Their pet—whose name and breed is unknown—saw the approaching water and recognized that something was very wrong (the water flooding into the first floor probably clued the animal in). The dog barked repeatedly, hurling his small body against his master's closed bedroom door until it opened. Edward and his wife Mary followed their dog to the windows and must have been flabbergasted and then full of fear. The house was surrounded by water.

By now, their twelve-year-old daughter, Mabel, and Edward's 77-year-old mother, Susanna, were also awake. Or if they weren't, they were once Edward opened the window and began shouting for help.

Their dog shouted, too, in his own way, barking furiously and placing his front paws onto the windowsill.

The Murrays were fortunate compared to many of the neighbors. It wasn't long before Edward, Mary, Mabel, Susanna, and their dog were scrambling into a rescue boat—possibly helped by Bundy, but there were many rescuers out and about—and being ferried to dry land.

Peru's town officials had already mobilized because the Murrays were quickly shuttled into a waiting motorcar. But it was then that the Murrays heard the tragic sound that made everyone sick. Just before the Murrays had climbed into the car, their dog had run underneath the belly of the vehicle, which was almost certainly an inexpensive car, possibly an Orient Buckboard, which had floorboards that were so flexible, they sometimes sagged and even occasionally, if there was enough weight in the car, were split into two. The Murrays, after clambering into the car and onto its floorboards, heard an agonized yelp from their dog.

Their beloved dog, their savior, who had scampered underneath the car, had just been crushed under their collective weight.

Water was entering the cages at the Wallace-Hagenbeck Circus. In the hay barn, where the deer, llama, kangaroo, camels, and other similar docile creatures lived, the river had already made its presence known, and some of the animals that had been roaring and crying out from their cages had already been drowned. The animals that were still alive were picked up by the circus workers and carried to a higher story in the barn, where there were dry cages.

In the room that housed the cats—including lions, a Bengal tiger, panthers, leopards, and a jaguar—the water was a few inches high but hardly life-threatening.

The elephants, on lower ground, would have begged to differ. Elephant trainer John Worden and his three assistants, John Clark, Jack Morris, and Charles Williams, waded in waist-deep water that was flooding the elephant barn, which was a foot below ground level. They apparently closed the door behind them, which was a mistake.

The elephants had been trumpeting furiously, but once they saw their trainers, they stopped. They stood obediently as the men held their breath, dropped under the muddy water, and removed the heavy chains that held the elephants' feet to the floor.

Worden called the elephants to fall in line, just as they had done so many times in rehearsal and for cheering crowds. They marched forward until they reached the barn door.

Then one of Worden's assistants let the big barn door swing open, which released a rush of water into the barn. Frightened, the elephants reversed course, stampeding back away from the entrance, only there was nowhere to go that was safe.

Worden started screaming their names, shouting for Tess, Nellie, Nancy, Bedelia, Josky, Jennie, Diamond, Satan, Baby, Trilby, Pinto, and Jumbo—twelve animals in all—to fall back in line, jabbing them with hooks, trying to steer them outside of the barn. Three times, the elephants did what they were told, only to draw back at the chilly wind. The barn was terrifying, but the elephants sensed that outside was no better.

Worden and his assistants were now in freezing water up to their shoulders. Worden suddenly felt his right leg cramp up, and he started to fall until he saw Nellie put forth her right foreleg, allowing him to climb onto it. He did, and Nellie, with her trunk, lifted Worden up to her back. To Worden's shock, he was able to lead Nellie outside of the barn and toward the two-story brick house where the circus trainers lived. The other trainers, giving up on the elephants, swam after Nellie and Worden.

The trainers all reached the house, on higher ground than the barn but nevertheless filling up with water on the first floor.

Nellie couldn't come inside the house, obviously. She remained outside and retreated back to the barn.

About an hour later, eight of the elephants, led by Nellie, returned to the house and decided that, well, maybe she could come inside. She and the other elephants beat against the doors and smashed apart the windows, but the house was too strong for them—to the utter relief of the seventy-five circus employees inside.

Worden and his trainers handed the elephants a bale of hay that they were going to use for some bedding for the employees, but once they were out of food, the water was so deep on the first floor that they realized they had no choice but to run upstairs with the rest of the circus crowd. From the second-story window, Worden and his crew watched anxiously and helplessly as the elephants splashed around the house in the rain and increasingly deeper water and listened helplessly as they trumpeted for help. After a while, they noticed that there weren't eight elephants but seven, and then six. It was becoming increasingly clear that some of the elephants had drowned. Worden couldn't help but be pleased to see that Nellie, who he would always feel had saved his life, still wearily trudging through the water. He fervently hoped that somehow she would make it.

But the Wallace-Hagenbeck Circus had twelve elephants and not the eight that were encircling the house. The workers couldn't help but wonder: Where were the others?

Some of the people at the courthouse could have answered that. They could see several elephants, running loose through the water and looking for any place dry to go, or at least higher ground. Seven-year-old Mary Jane Ward also saw the elephants. She would grow up to be an accomplished author, her most famous title being *The Snake Pit*, which was turned into an acclaimed 1948 movie starring Olivia de Havilland. Ward wrote shortly after the flood of seeing escaped elephants thrashing in the water and described an altogether surreal scene. The boat took her and her aunt out of their house's bedroom window just as the new piano floated out the front door. As rescuers rowed them to safety, little Jane could see not just elephants but crying monkeys hanging from trees.

Daybreak, West Liberty, Ohio

Phillip Henn, the passenger conductor who had been checking out the bridge over the Mad River when it collapsed underneath him, was still alive. After his fall into the river, he grabbed on to some floating debris from the bridge and was carried about a half mile to another bridge, which he was able to grab hold of. With the water higher than ever, he was able to climb up the bridge—it wasn't a far ascent—and once he was up, he simply sat.

He didn't try to walk off the bridge. For starters, he had a broken leg, and he was weak from the cold and from losing blood. All he could do was sit in a daze and wait to die. But even if he had been able to walk, the river had surrounded the bridge, on each end. It had washed out the middle of the bridge as well, just leaving the railings, one of which he was perched on, above the rushing river.

But as the sun came up, not that anyone could tell with the clouds and rain disguising it, several people spotted Henn sitting on the bridge, including J. Oliver King, a 22-year-old farmhand, and William Leib, a farmer a few days shy of his twenty-ninth birthday, and a man named Coran Grimes.

It would take several hours before they could reach him, and, of course, it didn't help matters when Henn passed out from the trauma, but King and Leib waded onto the bridge while hanging onto a rope, and brought the passenger conductor back to riverbank alive. Both King and Leib would be given Andrew Carnegie Heroism awards, bronze medals and $1,000, for their efforts, and several other rescuers in other communities were also thusly awarded. But there weren't enough medals to go around for the heroism that would be displayed over the next several days.

5:50 A.M., Dayton

Arthur John Bell[*] was the division plant manager and came into his office the night before to be on hand in case flooding started putting telephone batteries out of commission or the power went out. It seemed like a proactive, responsible thing to do, and Bell didn't want to take any chances from a personal standpoint. He had recently been promoted from being a lineman, someone who repaired telephone lines, and wanted to prove to his superiors that they had known what they were doing when they had chosen him for this job.

Bell's instincts paid off because, sure enough, just before six A.M., the power died. The engine room of the power plant flooded, and the streetcars stopped working.

Another important Dayton figure believed there would be a flood. John H. Patterson, president of NCR and recently disgraced executive, had been watching the river much of the night, perhaps thinking of

---

[*]   Often called John A. Bell in the press, probably because his friends and family called him by his middle name, John.

his impending jail sentence. He knew that Dayton was susceptible to flooding, having lived in the area his entire life. His family had been born and bred in Dayton and he and his family understood the power of the Great Miami River and its three tributaries, ever since his grandfather, Colonel Robert Patterson, moved to Dayton in the early 1800s. Colonel Patterson was an impressive ancestor for Patterson, who was born seventeen years after his grandfather's death, to look up to. He was the founder of the city of Lexington, Kentucky, and served with the famed General George Rogers Clark and about a thousand Kentuckians from the Kentucky militia and, among other military engagements, forced Indians from the banks of the Great Miami River in 1788.

In 1805 when the colonel moved to Dayton, he was awarded 2,400 acres of land, land he would pass on to his heirs and that would eventually become part of John H. Patterson's company, the National Cash Register Company.

Patterson had probably heard many tales about the flooding river from his predecessors, but he had also witnessed its power numerous times and once experienced it firsthand. In 1862, when Patterson was seventeen, Dayton had a flood that surrounded a house, and inside there was a family: Joseph Dickensheet, his wife Julia, and their six children, ranging from twelve down to six years of age.

Several neighbors had attempted to reach the house by boat, and all had failed. Stepping out of a crowd that had grown into the hundreds, Patterson and a classmate decided they would give it a try. Bystanders begged them not to go, but the teenagers insisted, and youth won out. Not only did they go, they reached the home, and the entire family was able to lower themselves out the second-story window, or perhaps climb off the roof, and into the boat. As the crowd literally went wild, Patterson and his friend steered the boat toward the shore, and everyone made it back safe and sound.

Patterson would say later of his decision to build the National Cash Register Company on a hill above the low terrain where the Dickensheet family lived, "I had studied the land for years, and I didn't see how the city could escape a big overflow of the Great Miami River. The country the stream tapped would someday provide more water than the river could hold. That's why I built our plant on high ground."

As Patterson watched the river, it hadn't spilled over the levee yet, at least not where he was, but it was evident that the city didn't have much time. The muddy black water, flowing fast, was, in some areas, just five inches from the top of the dam. Patterson hurried back to NCR, a plan forming in his mind.

Dayton, Ohio, 6 A.M.

An extra addition of the *Dayton Daily News* hit the soggy streets of Dayton, warning everyone that the levees were close to overflowing. Later, some people would remember seeing the moment the water started to spill over, but they were so few in number that it did not contribute in any way to advance warning.

Meanwhile, at Dayton's telephone company, the phone lines were jammed with unfounded rumors of levees breaking and the river taking on a life of its own. But as E. T. Herbig, the traffic chief, looked out the window on Ludlow Street and saw the rain still coming down and water filling up the road, he now knew for certain: Dayton was flooding.

Columbus, Ohio, probably about 6 A.M.

Thomas E. Green entered the Columbus offices of the Central Union Telephone Company early. Green, the division toll-wire chief, believed that the heavy rains might cause trouble on the long-distance lines. Better to get in now and try to stay on top of things than come into work playing catch-up all day.

He was testing the phone lines, making calls to Marion, a city about fifty miles north of Columbus, when someone on the line broke in on him. A manager with the last name of Knifflin, who worked at the telephone company in LaRue, a small village near Marion, told Green that two hundred women and children were stranded on the second stories of buildings thanks to the heavy rains. "We must have help, or we'll be wiped out," Knifflin said.

Moments later, more calls came in. And more. All pretty much said the same thing: "Help."

Green put a call through to the governor's mansion, telling him about all of the communities, but making it clear that LaRue needed the most assistance and that if these two hundred women and children didn't get boats as soon as possible, they would die.

It was quite a way for the new governor, James M. Cox, asleep moments earlier, to start the day. Green mentioned that there were boats in Lewistown, thirty-three miles away from LaRue. There were no boats closer, Green said, because at least half a dozen other communities were fighting floods and couldn't spare the boats. Cox issued his order through Green to get the boats to LaRue and then hurried to his office; but with sparse communication tools, there was little he could do but wait for the operator to call him back and tell him how things were faring in LaRue.

Tiffin, Ohio, 6:30 A.M.

George Klingshirn returned to his house to find it surrounded by raging rapids. He must have been crestfallen when he realized his wife and eight of his children were inside, and he was the one who had told them to stay put. His oldest daughter and granddaughter were in the house next door, and they too were stuck.

Approximately 7 A.M., Dayton, Ohio

Many parts of the city already were ankle-deep in water. It wasn't terribly unusual. Sewers often did back up after a particularly heavy rain, and it was still coming down hard.

Luckily, many people now had enough foresight to realize that the backed-up sewers were a warning sign of what was to come. Children in Dayton and across the region, on any normal day, would have been going to school; but most parents kept their kids from walking to school, and soon it would be more than apparent that classes were cancelled for the day. But if the flood had occurred just an hour later, it might have been even more devastating than it was. It's easy to imagine that some parents, trying to be conscientious, might have told their children not to be afraid of some rain and sent them to school. As it worked out, the flood submerged eleven schools in Dayton alone.

Harry Lindsey, a 47-year-old jewelry repairman, lived across the street from Saettel's grocery store and was awakened in the early morning by a shout for help from Oliver Saettel, thirty-eight years old. He was moving his goods out of the cellar. Lindsey threw on some clothes, hurried through the water in the street, and began helping, carrying what they could to the first floor. They—and probably other members of Saettel's family, since he had relatives still over for the Easter weekend—kept working for about an hour, completely unaware of how futile their efforts were.

Charles and Viola, meanwhile, decided it was time to get their twins to Viola's Aunt Fannie and Uncle Ottie's house, just up the next block at 59 Warder Street, on much higher ground. Then Charles could always return and continue flood-proofing the home. They felt that in theory they could wait out the flood on the second floor of their home, but their house had already lost its power, and the thought of waiting upstairs in the cold, without much food or good drinking water for the babies, didn't appeal to anyone.

Charles, Viola, and Stella walked to Aunt Fannie and Uncle Ottie's house in relatively short order. Their uncle and aunt lived uphill, and their front porch was seven feet higher than the street. They would be safe there.

7 A.M., Shelby County, Ohio

The Loramie reservoir collapsed. Not that you'd want any reservoir to collapse on you; but as dams go, this one held plenty of water. The Loramie reservoir was a storage unit; it supplied water for the Miami-Erie Canal. It was a lake six miles long and two miles wide, holding, on average, eight feet of water; but when it was full, it was thirty feet deep. On March 25, 1913, it was full. It didn't help matters any that the western embankment's earthen dam had been crumbling away for years. Local officials of the village of Fort Loramie had made many trips to the state capital, Columbus, to ask for the funding for a stronger, concrete-reinforced dam.

But no such luck. When the dam broke on the west side, it rushed down Loramie Creek, past Fort Loramie, traveling 22.7 miles and a difference in elevation of 72 feet, until it reached the Great Miami River, which cuts directly through Dayton, and Dayton was already in trouble.

And the water from the skies just kept coming. The weather would ultimately bring seven and a half inches of rain, which may not sound like all that much; but as anyone knows who has watched a foot of snow turn into ten-foot drifts, the way rain collects on the ground depends on the terrain, and it always goes to the lowest point in the land. And then there was the spillover from the Miami River's broken levees and collapsed reservoir to contend with.

Near the end of the flood, weather forecasters began tallying up just how much rain had fallen in the Dayton area alone. One estimate making the rounds shortly afterward was that during the four days it rained on Dayton, the amount of water dumping over the city and passing through the streets equaled the amount of water that flows over Niagara Falls in a four-day period.

According to a book published by the Delco Factory, a then-prominent employer in Dayton, the authors stated that the United States Weather Bureau concluded that over 8,000 square miles,* 9 trillion gallons of water fell, weighing 33 billion tons. That seems extreme, given that the respected computational knowledge search engine web site Wolfram/Alpha indicates that 33 billion tons of water is equal to forty percent of all the biomass on Earth. But whatever fell, it was a lot. The Delco writers asserted that a reservoir to hold all of that rain would have to be 174 miles wide, one mile long, and twenty-five feet deep.

The following year, *Popular Mechanics* noted that an expert had estimated that approximately 280 billion cubic feet of water—enough to have raised Lake Erie four feet—fell over Ohio and Indiana during the Great Flood of 1913, in a period of about three days.

Bottom line: this tremendous force of water from the reservoir, the sky, and what was already in the waterways wasn't all gunning toward Dayton; but for those who lived there, it felt like it.

Dayton, 8 A.M.

The 84-year-old father of Dayton's most famous resident worriedly stared out the window at the rising water levels passing by 7 Hawthorn Street. He was understandably anxious. Milton Wright, a bishop in the Church of the United Brethren in Christ, said later in his diary that the day before the flood, he anticipated it, which isn't hard to believe, considering how much rain was coming down. And he was worried.

---

*   The entire state of Ohio is 40,000 square miles, far more than the 8,000 square miles mentioned, and Montgomery County, where Dayton is, is approximately 460 square miles, far less than the 8,000 square miles mentioned, so it's not entirely clear what land mass the bureau was looking at, but it is still clear that the rainfall was unprecedented.

Rescuers came for a next-door neighbor, a Mrs. Eleanor J. Wagner, and they shouted to Milton that he was welcome to get in as well.

Bishop Wright, who already had put his overcoat on, liked that idea. He said that he would but needed to do one thing first, and rushed upstairs. A widower for some time now, Bishop Wright had seven children, five of whom grew up to be adults, although one of his sons, Wilbur, had died of typhoid fever a year earlier. Two of his children, 39-year-old Katharine and 42-year-old Orville, lived with him and were sleeping in their bedrooms upstairs.

Bishop Wright, wanting to let his kids know he was leaving, awakened Katharine and Orville, informed them of what was happening, and then left. That he didn't wake them up sooner, even before the rescuers in the canoe came by, given that the basement was flooding, seems curious; but then again, the flooding had started quite abruptly, and maybe Orville and Katharine really enjoyed sleeping in and the bishop felt he was doing them a favor.

He would have done them a better favor by waking them up. According to Fred Howard's book *Wilbur and Orville: A Biography of the Wright Brothers*, Orville and Katharine spent some hurried moments moving books and small pieces of furniture to the second floor. Then a horse and buggy—a moving van, actually—came by with some neighbors from across the street, the Valentine family, and the driver asked if they wanted a ride, and Orville and Katharine decided they'd better take the opportunity while they had it and rushed out without a moment to spare.

So they climbed into the moving van, which was already quite crowded, especially if the entire Valentine family was there: two parents, James and Mary, who had seven children, ranging from the mid-twenties to ten years of age. The Wrights and Valentines knew each other well; some time ago, several of the Valentine boys had worked in the bicycle shop, which the brothers had closed in 1907, four years after their big day at Kitty Hawk, North Carolina. The media, when they reported about Orville's escape from the flood later, seemed a bit disappointed that Orville hadn't outrun the water in an airplane.

Orville and Katharine were taken five blocks west to some friends of theirs, the house of Edmund S. Lorenz, and then, realizing just how serious this flood was and not knowing where their 84-year-old father had gone, they began to worry.

Charles Adams had returned a couple of hours earlier with Viola's uncle, to flood-proof his home, shortly after his wife and twin babies had settled in at Uncle Ottie's and Aunt Fannie's. Ever since Charles returned to his street, every house was in a flurry of activity. A group of neighborhood men were going from house to house, lifting expensive pianos on tables, so they wouldn't be affected by the river water. Charles, Uncle Ottie, and several neighbors, including a married couple, Tom and Isabelle Hanley, helped move the Adams's belongings to the second floor, notably Charles and Viola's beloved Siberian Cinnamon bear rug.

Charles checked to make sure the windows and doors inside the house were shut tight. He knew that the doors to the bedrooms, closets, and other rooms, if they and the windows were closed, could prevent their home from having raging currents rushing inside the house, surreal and frightening as it must have been to consider. He also noticed their chirping canary and took the cage to the second floor, hoping the bird would be safe there.

Once Charles and Ottie felt that they had done all they could do, they shut the front door and started scouting out the rain-raged neighborhood, looking for others to help, and planning to return one more time to grab a few last-minute things.

Around eight o'clock, the rain still dumping on Dayton, Charles stopped to take a photo of his house. He had grabbed his camera, probably a Brownie, a fairly simple and inexpensive camera that Kodak had introduced to the public thirteen years earlier. There was a rapidly growing stream on Rung Street, which was an unpaved dirt road. It was kind of appropriate that there was water here once again, Charles figured. Only a few years ago, when this land had been a farm, there had been an abandoned trench, powered by a machine called a hydraulic ram. Water ran through the trench—also simply called a hydraulic—to supply the farm with plenty of hydration for crops or livestock. Then later, after the farmer sold his land and houses started being built, a road simply followed the hydraulic. So did the rain.

Charles wanted to get a shot of a boat that someone had already brought up and was passing by his house. He took his picture—which did not survive to today—and then he and Ottie realized that getting back to the house would be almost impossible.

But they did reach it by walking down another street, knee-deep in the water on the sidewalk, and, while Ottie waited behind, Charles scaled a wall against his back yard, wading through the water, and reached his house. The back door was locked, and so Charles raced around to the front and hurriedly packed an assortment of provisions into a basket. He was looking around for what else he might take when he noticed water coming onto the kitchen floor.

Charles made haste for the back door.

Charles was wading through his back yard for the wall when he heard one of his neighbors, Mr. Bach, shouting for him from an upstairs window. Mr. Bach needed help bringing out his wife, who couldn't walk. Charles shouted for him to bring her down, and he and his uncle would help. The water wasn't too deep in the back yard yet, and Charles, Mr. Bach, and Uncle Ottie carried Mrs. Bach to the wall and managed to get her over it and into a nearby apartment building.

Then Uncle Ottie and Charles made their way to Warder Street, where Viola, the twins, Grandpa Adams, and a slew of others were no doubt anxiously waiting for them. But on their way, they saw their first real glimpse of what they might be in for. As they climbed the sidewalk toward Warder, rivulets of water racing under their feet and along the road, they looked back and could see, on Rung Street, a young man hanging from a gas light post. He looked exhausted, as if he couldn't hold on much longer, and was shouting for help. A man in a boat tried to reach him but couldn't; a second boat made the attempt, and the young man, whose grip on the wet metal post was loosening, literally fell into the boat just as his hands couldn't hang on any longer. Charles and Ottie, relieved, hurried up the hill and hoped that their quota for danger and excitement had just been filled.

They could not have been more wrong.

Chapter Five

A Time to Run

Dayton, 8:30 A.M.

The river could not be contained. Some people said that a 350-foot section of the levee broke free, and others said that a five-foot wave of water simply went over the side. Either way, a wave of water, anywhere from five to ten feet high, crested over the levee and then rushed down Third Street, spilling through Perry, Wilkinson, and Ludlow streets. About the same time, the water stormed over the levee and shot down N. Jefferson Street. Before long, nearly all of the roads in downtown Dayton were waterlogged.

As soon as the levee broke, someone at a fire station on Taylor Street pulled the fire whistle. Edsy Vincent, one of Dayton's firefighters, went out on call the moment it sounded. He and a driver hitched their team of horses faster than they ever had before and set off at a gallop. They were met by a wall of water at least ten feet high. The driver turned the horses around and searched for higher ground at full gallop. Somehow they did and avoided becoming a statistic of the flood.

But there was a house on Taylor Street that was directly in the path of the ten-foot-high wave, and the residents couldn't avoid it. C. R.

Meyer, an employee at the National Cash Register Company, saw a woman and daughter in the second story window, there one minute, and gone the next. Meyer didn't stick around to watch more. He was too busy running for his life.

At an upscale, three-story 150-room hotel known as the Beckel House, populated by professionals and some transplants who lived there indefinitely, was Walter D. Jones, a lifelong resident of the nearby city of Piqua and common pleas judge for the Second Judicial District of Ohio. He was an overnight guest after having held court in the town of Greenville. He stepped out of the hotel lobby and into the rain. It was then that he saw water rushing down Jefferson Street. Still, it didn't look dangerous; at first, he thought someone had opened a fire hydrant.

But as the water began to spill over the curb on the sidewalk, Jones went back into the Beckel House and told the clerk that, you know what, he would keep his room a little longer.

The 56-year-old judge trudged up the stairs because the elevator wasn't running, intending to leave his satchel and coat in the room and then return to watch the scene unfold outside. Then he thought better of it and went to watch out the rain-beaten window instead.

He was astonished. It looked like the Atlantic Ocean had suddenly moved inland several states; that is, if the Atlantic Ocean had been a muddy river. But before he had a chance to really digest what he was looking at, there was a crashing sound, the floor shook, and plaster fell into his hair. He could hear women screaming from the nearby rooms.

Jones rushed for his door, but it wouldn't open. He heard men shouting in the hall, and so he called for them to throw their weight against the door. They did, and Jones got out. Someone screamed "Fire," but a guest or hotel worker quickly silenced that person. Walls were cracking and plaster continuing to fall. Whatever was happening, it wasn't good. Jones and the others ran down the stairs, to get their bearings and figure out what was happening.

Meanwhile, guests who were in the lobby were running upstairs. They at first hadn't understood that their city was flooding, even when the water came into the lobby, although some people instinctively started running for the stairs. It was only when the northeast corner of the building caved in, causing a racket, a cloud of dust and debris, and scaring the hell out of everyone, that the guests recognized that they had a problem that wasn't going to go away any time soon.

It was an eclectic group. There was Judge Jones and a fellow judge from Piqua, Squire W. T. Marshall. Melville N. Shreves, a 26-year-old office supplies salesman from Lima, Ohio, later noted that after the caving in, some of the women were screaming and hysterical, but who could blame them, or anyone, for that?*

There was also present a traveling theatrical troupe, actors, a crew and the director, all putting on George M. Cohan and his partner-producer Sam Harris's farce, *Officer 666*. The actors were supposed to perform that night at the Victoria Theatre. With the playhouse in the middle of the flood district, that would no longer be happening, however. Not that this likely concerned them, with everyone worried about getting out of the hotel and escaping with their lives; the phrase "break a leg" now had an entirely different meaning. Later that day, in New York City, Cohan and Harris's executives—whether that was Cohan and Harris themselves, or their staff, is anyone's guess—tried to contact the Beckel House to see how their actors were faring but, like anyone across the country worried about friends, family, and colleagues in Dayton, couldn't get through to the city.

Another person who stood out was the 57-year-old owner of the Beckel House, Clarence E. Bennett. He was ill—had been for some time, although what his malady was isn't clear—and if the staff and guests were to leave the building, as people were beginning to discuss, they would have to take the bedridden owner with them.

For now, the Beckel House guests were simply glad to be inside. Looking outside, they saw madness. Later, Dayton and Springfield, Ohio's papers would run excerpts of a journal written by a traveling salesman, C. C. McDowell, who was staying at the Beckel House. As McDowell remembered the first few minutes of the flood, "Everyone began scurrying to places of safety. People dodged into doorways and onto anything that was higher than the street. Everything loose began to float down the streets; horses were washed off their feet and wagons

---

* To be fair to the women, too, the son of the hotel owner, who wasn't there, later said he had heard that many of the female guests had been far braver than the men when it came to keeping their emotions in check.

were overturned. . . . Great blocks of pavement on Third Street were torn up, many of them being 15 feet square. Plate glass store fronts were broken by the force of the water, which rushed down the street with the fury of a mill race on a rampage," McDowell observed, referring to a stream of water that runs to and from a mill.

"Everywhere was a scurry for safety," McDowell continued. "Horses were unhitched and taken into buildings."

In the Algonquin Hotel, debris quickly started piling up at the front door. A bellboy named Johnny Flynn tried to dislodge it, evidently fearing the door would be crushed and not considering that maybe the first floor of the hotel was beyond saving. Flynn opened the door and was clobbered by a wave of water that rushed inside and swept down the street.

Three streetcars stalled in front of the Algonquin Hotel, and the perplexed passengers struggled to decide whether to run or stay put. Seconds later, they realized they had no choice and began climbing onto the seats and then to the roof of the cars. Someone in a building across from the Algonquin threw a rope to one of the passengers, who tied it onto the streetcar, and everyone was able to use the rope to pass through the rushing water in relative safety and reach the building.

Not that going through the water was safe. Automobiles, pianos, furniture, garbage—it was all speeding through the street.

Boxcars were knocked over on their sides, and one was carried part of the way up a side street. Cattle in two boxcars met a terrible end. The force of the water meant that anything not bolted down to the ground and plenty of items that were, from trees to railroad ties, telegraph poles, furniture and cars, wires, and cables, was being carried down the streets.

One block from the Algonquin Hotel was the Phillips House, a luxury hotel that had opened in 1850, where Adam Harnisch, of Syracuse, New York, was staying. Harnisch was in a shoe store across the street when the water came rushing into the street. He ran across the street to the Phillips House and seconds later saw a young man— possibly the bellboy Flynn—carried down the street.

If it was Flynn, he was carried by the current into the middle of the street, where a whirlpool of muddy water was forming. He managed to stand up, the water only up to his knees, but the currents were colliding, making it impossible for him to push his way through the water, and as if that wasn't enough, rain was pounding him. A young man, a bystander, trying to stretch out an arm and pull him out of the mess, became caught in the whirlpool as well. Harnisch watched all of this from a window or door, terrified, as a police officer, clinging to a lamp post, attempted to stretch a leather strap toward the young men. But it wasn't anywhere near long enough to do any good.

Moments later, both men were gone. Harnisch never learned what had happened to the young man who tried to save Flynn's life, but he suspected that he was killed. Johnny Flynn's body was later found smashed against a tree.

Harnisch didn't have much time to process what he saw. The walls of the hotel lobby caved in, almost taking out the news and cigar dealer, who somehow managed to scramble to his feet and get to a higher floor.

Harnisch did, too.

He couldn't believe what he was seeing. He couldn't be sure yet, but Mr. Harnisch, who like a handful of others had a knack for being in the wrong place at the wrong time, believed he was experiencing something worse than another similar disaster he had survived: the 1889 Johnstown, Pennsylvania flood.

On another street in downtown Dayton, Ray Stansbury, a nineteen-year-old foundry worker at NCR, immediately rushed into the water and started offering to carry women and children from their rickety homes to somewhere safer. He was six foot four, and, at 218 pounds, his physicality instilled a lot of confidence in people. If the numbers reported were accurate, 150 women and children that morning would take him up on his offer.

On the other side of the Great Miami River, in Riverdale, Charles Adams and Uncle Ottie—or more formally, W. Otterbein Fries—reached the house on Warder Street where a whole host of family was anxiously waiting for them, including his Aunt Fannie, Grandpa Adams, Viola and the twin babies as well as Ottie and Fannie's son, Emerson, and his wife, Mary.

Mary was anxious about her parents, who lived in the lower part of Riverdale, and so shortly after Charles and Ottie arrived, Emerson decided to embark by boat and check on them. Charles and Ottie urged him not to—they had seen firsthand what was out there, and to go down to lower Riverdale was to go into the worst of the flood waters and perhaps never come out. But Emerson insisted, joining river-flooded streets that already had quite a few rescuers on them, like Frank A. Schleeman, a barber who worked on the NCR premises. As soon as the river rushed into Riverdale, Schleeman grabbed a boat and, pairing up with a police officer, started rowing up to houses and offering to take people to safer ground.

Another person caught up in the flood was Harold E. Talbott, a 25-year-old whose father was a prominent engineer in the city. Talbott himself was on his way up in life, with his own contracting business. He was driving to it when he found that Fifth Street was under water and horses and garbage were floating past. He turned his car around and drove toward a planing mill,* an idea already coming to him to order some boats to rescue the numerous people he imagined would need help. But before he could get there, the water rose around his car, rising three to four feet. His car sputtered to a stop, and several men—running away from the water—were nice enough to help him push it to higher ground.

Soaked from chin to shin, Talbott made his way to the National Cash Register Company to discuss the situation with Patterson, who knew the young man and his father, Edward Deeds; and after a quick conversation, they agreed. Talbott's instincts—to have some boats made to begin rescue operations—were right on the mark with what Patterson was thinking, and both men believed that the city was on the cusp of a serious flood. While it's impossible to know what exactly was in their minds and hearts, Patterson and Deeds, like so many business leaders then and now, were plugged in to their community and presumably cared deeply about their city. They knew that if they didn't get moving, many people were going to die.

Patterson gave young Talbott full command of his carpentry department, where the men were ordered to start building rowboats immediately. The crew in the cafeteria, it was eventually decided, should start baking two thousand loaves of bread and cook hundreds of gallons of soup. Patterson also ordered that as many cots and beds as possible

---

* For those who aren't up on their mill terminology, a planing mill takes boards from a sawmill and turns them into smooth finished lumber.

should be set up for the refugees who he was certain would soon be coming. He also ordered twenty men on horseback to collect as much food, bedding, clothing and emergency supplies from farming communities in the south as possible. Not all of these orders were issued right away, except for the boats; some of the commands would go out later in the day and days to come. Patterson was starting to morph his company into a rescue and relief command center for Dayton, but he didn't really know that yet.

Still, if Noah of Noah's Ark fame had been around to comment, he would have been proud of Patterson and Talbott's boat-making abilities. Before the day was up, Talbott's operation would make 167 boats with four oars. They were "cranky" and really only safe "for use only in comparatively still water," the engineer Arthur Ernest Morgan would write later, adding, "but there is no doubt that many people owe their lives to them."

Sometime in the morning, Indianapolis

Mischa Elman, a 22-year-old Russian-born American violinist who is still considered one of the best violinists in history, realized that something was amiss Tuesday morning when the bathroom water at the luxurious Claypool Hotel stopped working, and he couldn't turn on the electric lights.* The elevators had stopped running as well. Elman had performed in Indianapolis the night before with Rudolph Ganz, a Swiss pianist. As Elman, Ganz, their unnamed accompanist, and all of the hotel guests would soon learn, they wouldn't be leaving the city anytime soon: for miles, east, west, north, and south, every river, stream, creek, brook, lake, and pond was flooding.

Sometime in the morning, New Castle, Pennsylvania

City officials were still guardedly watching the rivers and blissfully unaware of what was occurring in the state to the west of them. The

---

*   A 1913 issue of *Engineering News* states that the water supply for the city of Indianapolis was interrupted from 12:30 P.M., Tuesday, March 25, until 7 A.M., Friday, March 28. That means that either Elman's memory was faulty, or that the young violinist had a habit of sleeping in and believed it was morning, or that some select places throughout Indianapolis, like the Claypool Hotel, began losing their water before the rest of the city did.

rain was intermittent now, but when it came, it came down hard, and the Shenango River had risen right up to the Erie Railroad tracks. Nobody could remember seeing that before.

Columbus, Ohio, 8:30 A.M.

The police department was overwhelmed. For hours, they had been rescuing individuals and families as fast as they could, including one man in a wheelchair, but they couldn't get officers out to houses fast enough. A little boy with a small dog under his arm pleaded for someone to save his sick mother trapped at their house. A little girl was in tears, begging that a boat be sent out to her mother's home. There were many situations just waiting to become tragedies.

At least one officer manning a boat found himself on the Scioto River in pursuit of a floating boxcar with two hoboes on it. He helped the two men into his river vessel just before the car submerged. Around this time was another frustrating report, this one concerning the body of a male that had been seen floating down the river. Police officers located the body and tried a variety of methods to catch up to it and bring it in—presumably using boats and lassoing ropes—but they couldn't reach him.

Nobody ever learned who the man was.

Dayton, 8:45 A.M.–9 A.M.

More and more people needed rescuing. The water on parts of Main Street, according to some accounts, was now ten feet deep and still moving rapidly. Oliver Saettel and his neighbor Harry Lindsey had abandoned their efforts to save the rest of the goods in the cellar. Lindsey, in fact, quickly recognized that he couldn't get back to his home and raced up the stairs with Oliver and his family.

Lindsey made the right decision to stick with the Saettels and not attempt a crossing. The roads were no longer roads, as many people were discovering. According to several newspaper accounts, a moving wagon with a driver at the reins, and his passengers, a doctor, his four-year-old son, and an African-American maid or nanny, were caught up in the flood. Their horse and buggy was swept into the current until they crashed into a telegraph pole. Just before the van overturned, the doctor, servant, and driver managed to climb up the pole with the four-year-old, where they would remain in rain and snow, trapped, shouting for help that wouldn't come for another thirty-six hours.

Fred Boyer, a high school teacher, was on Main Street when the water rushed over the levee. He wrote about it later, stating that at 8:30, his school decided to close since only ten or fifteen teachers and just fifty students had shown up. The staff had also heard that shops were closing, and that Main Street was underwater. Everyone dispersed.

When at nine in the morning Boyer and five others—it isn't clear if he was walking with teachers, students, or both—arrived at Main Street, much of it was covered with water, but at least where they were, it was nowhere near the ten feet that it was further down the road. About then, a modern-day Paul Revere showed up, according to Boyer: "A man came galloping down the street on a horse, a tall, gaunt, ungainly figure, waving his hands in the other direction and crying, 'The levee's broke, the levee's broke.'"

Everyone began running in the direction the rider was going, including the streetcars, which began backing up, away from where the waters were expected to be coming. Boyer recalled seeing a company of African-American militia, marching up the street from the south, toward the flood, possibly as part of a routine exercise or, more likely, on the scene to see if they could be of help.

But nobody could help. The street gutters were full of water, and suddenly Boyer could see the water coming down Main Street, a wall of water about six inches high in the center of the street. Boyer and his group ran down Fifth Street, where it met Jefferson, but the water was coming there, too.

Miss Flossie Lester, a stenographer, found herself marooned on a horse-drawn moving van when the water rushed through the streets of Dayton. She and several other men had climbed onto the van as the water barreled past them. Eventually, the van tipped over, ripping away from the horses, and everyone went into the muddy water and they were all separated. The van sailed down the street with the horse, Miss Lester, and the men. It isn't known what happened to the men, but Miss Lester managed to stay afloat for a while as the river took her for what looked to be her final swim.

But then she spotted one of the horses swimming near her, and somehow Miss Lester grabbed a dangling strap from the animal and pulled herself up, climbing onto his back, hugging his neck and hanging on. Although thousands of horses were killed in the flood, it was a smart move because this one was a strong swimmer. The horse swam for at least a mile and a half before it navigated to high ground. The horse reached a farmhouse, and Miss Lester, apparently realizing she was safe now, fell off the horse and promptly passed out. The farmer's family took her in and led the horse to their barn.*

Arthur F. Coulter owned a shoe store. When the levee broke, and the river rushed down Second Street, he grabbed the $30 that was in his cash register, one almost certainly manufactured by Patterson's company, and then he dashed outside.

Big mistake. The water was so high that he was swept off his feet, and a telephone pole or some debris hit him, breaking his arm.

Coulter was being carried along Second Street with groceries, grand pianos, pieces of lumber, broken glass, nails, and other parts of Dayton. As he would tell *The New York Times* later, "The water was dark and furious. Everybody was screaming for help, it seemed to me—and there could be no help. I seemed to realize that, and I tried to stop shouting and save my breath. I swam, or rather I kept afloat. I can swim well, but that was of little assistance in that torrent. I don't know how far I went, but I do know that when I was finally picked up by a boat, I was three blocks away from my store."

Coulter escaped Dayton in rapid order and traveled to flood-besieged Columbus, where he was robbed of whatever he had left of his thirty dollars. Then Coulter backtracked to Clayton, Ohio, a village near Dayton where he had friends who were able to give him some money. By the time he reached Cleveland three days after being carried down Second Street, he was able to find a doctor who could set his arm, which had been broken and apparently dangling the entire time.

As miserable as that sounds, Coulter was one of the lucky ones.

---

* Later, Miss Lester told reporters that if the owner of the horse couldn't be found, she would keep him. Whether she actually did end up keeping him is unknown.

While Coulter and other Dayton residents were running and swimming for their lives, John Bell was hard at work. The batteries were submerged in the watery tomb of the basement, but he had managed to keep one wire alive by hooking together several dry batteries that he managed to scrape up. He rummaged around and found a lineman's test set, and with that, he was able to rig up a sending and receiving apparatus. That allowed him to cut in upon the wire on the roof of a four-story building, which connected him with a testing station about eight miles north in Phoneton, Ohio.

Phoneton was a community practically built by the telephone communications industry, as the name would imply. Originally named Tadmor, the AT&T Company built a three-story brick building along the National Road, the first freeway built by the federal government in the 1800s, which currently officially stretched from Ohio to Illinois, though one could take various trails from there to the Pacific. By the time 1913 rolled around and the town's name had long switched to Phoneton, there were houses, buildings, a post office, and other trappings of civilization, mostly to support AT&T's building, where numerous operators managed the switchboards that kept the calls moving over the phone lines across the country.

Once Bell had connected Dayton to Phoneton, no easy and quick task, he explained the situation to the operator and asked to be patched through to Governor Cox's office in Columbus.

In the center of downtown, at the Dayton Engineering Laboratory, which everyone called Delco and employed 1,100 workers, the basement began flooding at 8:50 A.M. A crew of workers was quickly dispatched to remove dynamite from the basement, and while they apparently were successful, two employees did not make it back up. Before the day was over, the water would climb seventeen feet into the concrete plant, just eighteen inches from its second story. Many Delco employees hadn't arrived to work yet and wouldn't, and many fled for their lives or attempted to race back home to their families, but twenty young executives found themselves stuck in the watch tower, watching the city fall apart below.

At the Western Union Telegraph Company station, the workers found that they couldn't open their front door—the pressure of the three-foot-deep water wouldn't allow it. The employees had to escape through a back window and then scale a telegraph pole to the roof.

But it wasn't bedlam everywhere. Not yet, and not at 415 Wayne Avenue, the residence of one Henry Andrews, his wife, his brother-in-law, and a boarder named George W. Timmerman, a foundry moulder who had grown up in nearby Springfield. Timmerman concluded in ankle-deep water that this wasn't a good day to go in to work. Oddly, even as late as 8:45 A.M., with rain still dumping over the city, his neighbors didn't appear to be overly concerned by the flooding, although some people were taking their belongings up to the second story.

This has happened before, after heavy rains, they said.

But fifteen minutes later, the Great Miami River, normally a mile away, came rushing down the street, sending Timmerman and his neighbors running into their homes and upstairs.

9 A.M., Dayton, Ohio

A Western Union operator working with another operator out of Cincinnati abruptly cut off a message he was sending and quickly gave him the news.

Stunned, the operator started spreading the word, and before long it was in morning, afternoon, and evening newspapers around the country. Here's how the first bulletin read, published in the *Akron Beacon Journal* that evening and countless others:

"Cincinnati, O. March 25—It is reported that the Miami River at Dayton has broken and flooded the city.

"At 9 o'clock this morning a Western Union operator working with an operator in this city abruptly cut off a dispatch he was sending, and said:

"'Good-bye, the levee is broken.'

"Dayton is on low ground, and the river levees rise 25 feet above the level of the town. Right in the heart of the city the Stillwater and Mad rivers merge into the Miami and during high water, the levees are in great danger. If they have broken, until loss of property and loss of life has occurred."

Another report in the same paper read: "An unconfirmed report here says that 1,500 people lost their lives in the flood at Dayton today when a levee along the banks of the Miami River went out, and the waters inundated the town."

Word was getting out. Dayton was drowning.

Chicago, shortly after 10 A.M.

Ben Hecht, an 18-year-old cub reporter for the *Chicago Journal*, was jostled awake by a phone call from his editor, informing him that Dayton was being swamped by a flood, people were dying, and a big story was breaking fast, so get out and cover it! Hecht remembered getting the phone call at 5:30 A.M., which would have been 6:30 A.M., Dayton time. Dayton was in a flurry of activity and worry and some flooding by then, but the levee hadn't broken quite yet. Hecht, in his 1954 biography, *A Child of the Century*, remembered the flood as starting on March 18, 1912, over a year off the actual date, so it's also possible he was sleeping in later much in the morning than he imagined or cared to admit*. It's so much more likely that Hecht's editor had seen a bulletin about the levee breaking go on the wire, and that that's when he called the cub reporter.

Hecht, eager to prove himself, listened intently to his editor's instructions. "The cashier's office is closed," said Eddie Mahoney, the assistant city editor. "You will have to get fifty dollars somewhere for expenses." He also told him to catch the train to Indianapolis, and from there he would hopefully find transportation to Dayton.

Hecht lived in a brothel. He spent the next thirty minutes begging his roommates for money, and soon he had forty dollars in cash and was racing for the train station. So were newspaper correspondents from around the country. This had all the makings of a big story.

Hamilton, Ohio, probably around 9 A.M.

Thirty-six miles away from Dayton, Councilman J. Henry Welsh was inspecting the railroad yards when, as the *Hamilton Evening Journal* would put it, he had a premonition that the city was about to flood.

---

* To be fair to Hecht, it was over forty years later when he wrote his biography, and he didn't have the Internet to instantly check things, and he does appear to have had a spot-on memory for the locations that he visited during the flood.

It could hardly be called ESP; after all, it had been raining constantly the previous day, all through Monday and into Tuesday, and there had been that incredible series of tornadoes. A five-year-old who had been following the news and weather might have predicted that Hamilton would soon flood. But in the manner Welsh would later describe it, he just suddenly knew that a flood was absolutely in the making. There was no doubt. He knew.

So he ran from the railroad yards to the police station and asked that they start to ring the fire bells as a warning. Welsh was rebuffed; apparently a hunch wasn't enough for the authorities to go on. Welsh then became an instant modern-day prophet, warning people in the streets that a flood was coming and that everyone should start moving their goods to higher ground now.

9:30 A.M., Dayton, Ohio

George Cleary, an employee at the Apple Electric Company, was walking down Miggs Street when he and a friend spotted a levee on the verge of breaking. They raced to several houses, pounding on doors and telling people that they had to flee now. Either not believing them, or probably thinking it was safer to stay indoors, they wouldn't leave. Cleary and his friend were on the street when a tidal wave came racing toward them.

They sprinted ahead of it for seven blocks until they couldn't run any farther, so they ran into a house that had fifteen other people and began helping everyone move furniture upstairs. But it wasn't long before everyone simply retreated upstairs as the river started coming underneath the doors and swamping the living room.

Meanwhile, the basement of the Bell Telephone Company, where the batteries to the telephone exchange were located, was flooding and the telephone chief decided that the current needed to be shut off before there were electrical shocks and somebody was hurt or killed. The young female telephone operators had been answering the phones, pretty much nonstop, as all of Dayton tried to reach loved ones, but the main fuse was now removed and the phone lines across the city went dead. Dayton residents and workers were officially cut off from civilization, including the twenty women and fourteen men at the telephone company.

9:30 A.M., *Columbus, Ohio*

The levees hadn't broken, but it was just a matter of time. The Busy Bee restaurant, an early chain restaurant—there were three in existence—sent its workers home, and Frank Williams, a cook, hurried to his house to warn his family of the impending flood. Much of his family was there, although explaining his family—a hundred years later—is a bit challenging.

Williams was described in the papers as living with his step-parents, William and Viola Guy, who were married for thirty-four years. It seems likely that one of them was his real parent rather than both of them being step-parents, or perhaps they had both taken him in as a youngster, but no matter: by 1913, Frank Williams was living with the Guy family.

The Guys had five other children, the oldest being Iva, thirty-three, and the youngest Bert, who was twenty-one. Several of the adult children still lived with the Guys. William Guy—at least judging from the 1910 census records—was a factory laborer, and Viola kept the house. Most of the adult children worked in various jobs at a restaurant, possibly the Busy Bee.

Frank told his family that a flood was certain and urged everyone to take their belongings upstairs. Everyone did, but like it would be for so many people, it was a futile exercise. In the midst of all this action, the river came underneath the door, and then underneath the house. It started floating.

There must have been a lot of screaming and shouting and panicking. There were several family members in the house—Frank, William, Viola, their 28-year-old unmarried daughter Nora, and her nephew and William and Viola's grandson, Luther Wolfe. But by the time they reached the roof, Frank's group numbered well over a dozen, a hodge-podge of neighbors, all aware that their houses were floating.

Under a pounding rain, the group frantically scrambled from one house to another, each wobbling and close to being carried away by the rising flood. Everyone finally reached a house that seemed safe, and so everyone settled in, making themselves as comfortable as anyone could be when you think your life might end any moment, and you're in a torrential downpour and looking off the edge of a two-story home and seeing a river where your street once was.

And then it happened: the house, just like the others, came off its moorings. Worse, it began to float away in the current.

There was nothing anyone could do. The group now numbered thirteen. Frank Williams and the Guy family were a part of that thirteen. So was a woman named Mrs. Hunt and her daughter, May. There was a Nina M. Shipley and her daughter-in-law, and Mrs. Shipley's sister, a Mrs. Vine and three boys who were described as Hungarian. All everyone could do was wait and hope that wherever the current took them, it was somewhere safe. But Viola Gay didn't have much optimism. She handed her stepson her bank book, reasoning that if someone got out of this alive, it might be him, in which case he might need it.

10 A.M., Hamilton, Ohio

If his fellow citizens didn't at first believe Welsh that a flood was coming, some minds changed as the evidence kept mounting. Plus, there was a rumor spreading that a dam had broken north of Hamilton, and everyone was pretty sure that the water behind the dam was coming for them, and they were all going to die.

The rumor started in part because of a completely incorrect message sent to Hamilton, about a dam breaking a hundred miles away. It had been forwarded *the previous evening* to a telegraph office in McGonigle, a tiny town about seven miles northwest of Hamilton. The operator passed it on, and apparently not much was thought of it when it reached Hamilton, because no panic broke out. But the McGonigle operator left it on his desk and, Tuesday morning, when the rivers were dangerously high and it was still raining, his replacement saw the message, thought it hadn't been sent, let his imagination go out of control, and then, because the telegraph lines were down, rushed to Hamilton.

Some accounts have said he took an automobile and broke speed records getting there; others later said the telegraph operator hopped on a railroad hand car. Either way, he reached Hamilton and let them know that a dam had burst, and word of mouth spread.

Some people rushed out of their houses, not fully dressed, running for the nearest hill.

But all of the misinformation out there, along with the way the weather was behaving, did spur people to what was ultimately the right decision: school officials decided to send the pupils home and undoubtedly many young lives were saved, including that of J. Walter Wack, a high-schooler. He ran home, plopped his schoolbooks on the kitchen floor of his grandparents' house, and then ran to High Street to watch the Great Miami River.

As he recalled to his hometown newspaper fifty years later, "Trees and small sheds and lots of debris floated swiftly down the river, and much of it struck the underneath beams of the bridge. Then they closed the bridge to traffic."

And as the river grew higher, the garbage against the bridge began piling up.

10 A.M., Washington, D.C.

The telephone bell rang in the office of the National Red Cross at the War Department.

"Miss Boardman, this is the office of the Associated Press," said the voice on the other end of the phone line. "The Miami River is rising in Ohio, and the town of Dayton is partly under water. Other rivers are rising, and it looks like there might be serious trouble."

Mabel Boardman took down the information and sent a telegram to Ohio Governor James Cox, asking if he needed a hand, and then she returned to her main focus: getting help to Omaha.

Governor Cox telegraphed a reply, basically saying thanks, but everything's fine.

But a little later, Miss Boardman received another telegram from Cox, which read something to the effect of: matters were getting worse. Another telegram soon followed: the water was still rising, and there were already many deaths. And another: Ohio would be glad to have the assistance of the National Red Cross.

Miss Boardman flew into action. Their director-general, Ernest Bicknell, was on a train somewhere, on his way to Nebraska, but she knew he'd want to eventually head to Ohio, and so she telegraphed a Red Cross executive, Eugene Lies, in Chicago, to travel to Omaha, and a Mr. Edmonds of Cincinnati to take care of the situation in Dayton until Bicknell arrived.

10 A.M., Dayton, Ohio

It was estimated that the Great Miami River, usually a few hundred feet in width, was now three miles wide.

10 a.m., Columbus, Ohio

Governor James Cox was concerned. He knew about LaRue's flooding problems and had heard of a few more communities experiencing some flooding, but the Red Cross was asking him about Dayton?

The Red Cross *had* to be wrong. Dayton was Cox's hometown. Cox, less than a week away from his forty-third birthday and just over two months into his new job as governor, owned the *Dayton Daily News*, an arrangement that probably wouldn't go over well today. But the people of Ohio, if at all bothered that the most powerful person in the state also owned one of the most prominent media outlets, were impressed with their new governor's business acumen and ambition. Cox had managed to buy a newspaper at the age of twenty-eight, in large part due to a former employer who believed in him enough to invest $6,000 in his quest to raise $26,000 to buy the *Dayton Evening News*. Cox had some money saved up himself, borrowed yet more money, and then managed to raise the rest of the money by selling stock in the paper. If media critics ever questioned whether it was healthy for the governor of a state to own a city newspaper, or if the cozy relationship hurt the *Dayton Daily News*' journalistic integrity, there's no question that during the flood and its immediate aftermath, it was a connection that would end up helping everyone, if only because Cox had made his mark in Dayton and was a passionate advocate for the city.

It seems likely that Cox was spending most of his time checking on LaRue and monitoring the state of affairs in his current residence, Columbus; but as far as his memoirs and other documentation suggest, he didn't yet realize that the state was in serious disarray. After all, he lived in a time before CNN, smart phones, and the Internet, and Dayton's rudimentary phone service was already cut off. Cox would have relied mostly on telephone calls and telegrams, and very few had landed in his office, as the regions in the most trouble had already lost service.

The city workhouse—which held prisoners behind bars for non-violent crimes like drunkenness and embezzlement—was in the process of moving its female prisoners in boats to the county jail while the male inmates remained behind. The river was rising fast, and because of that, about twenty prisoners from the workhouse were ordered to reinforce the levee near the prison. It was a nice but pointless attempt to delay nature. The river not only rushed over the levee, it caught the prisoners and washed them away.

Most of the inmates struggled toward a house and then began swimming from house to house, escaping the flood and, even though it was unintentional, the city workhouse.

At least two men appeared to have drowned, observed Casper Sareu, a prisoner who managed to find a roof to hole up on. Sareu, being dumped on by the rain, trapped on a house that looked as if it would soon be overcome by the flood, was no more free than he had been when he was behind bars. In fact, the prison was starting to look pretty good to him. But for now, he would remain trapped on the roof of a house, sharing the predicament of thousands of other of his fellow citizens.

10:30 A.M., Pulaski, Pennsylvania

Just over the Ohio border, the Shenango River was on a tear, overflowing its banks just under Pulaski's bridge, sending people out of their houses at the crack of dawn. But at 10:30 A.M., Miss Lena Book, a news reporter with the paper, telephoned her editors in New Castle, Pennsylvania, to warn them that the Shenango River was rising rapidly, and that, if they hadn't already, they would soon see flooding.

10:30 A.M., Dayton, Ohio

People were panicking. Someone at the Beckel House once again shouted "Fire," and this time the warning seemed serious, causing the guests to flee into the rain and up the fire escapes onto their roof, and then scamper to the roofs of adjoining buildings. There the scared guests stood, among them Melville Shreves, the office supplies salesman from nearby Lima, and C. C. McDowell from places unknown, drenched as the sky dumped whatever it could on them, and they waited . . . and waited . . . and collectively everyone realized that there was no fire.

Most of the guests retreated back into the Beckel House, while others started exploring other buildings, looking for an escape path to dry land somewhere. Melville Shreves, C. C. McDowell, and a few others, not feeling comfortable staying in a hotel that had its northwest corner collapse, felt that since they were up on the roof anyway, they should attempt to leave.

They were able to cross over from the Beckel House to an adjoining building fairly easily and get into there, but after that their trek became a series of finding windows and doors and fire escapes to help them go from one building's roof to another. In another spot, there was a ten-foot alley between buildings, but with a ladder that they found, they could reach the new Callahan Bank building.

The Callahan Bank Building was just as much an island as the Beckel House, but it was made from concrete and other modern, non-floating materials and was much stronger, and clearly would be more formidable against the flood. It was also twelve stories high, including the first floor, and at the top of the building was a rooftop that had a sturdy wall to look out over, as well as a clock tower adjoining a sign that said "City Bank."

If water covered *this* building, it truly did mean the Atlantic had moved inward, across Maryland, Virginia, West Virginia, and into Ohio. And it wasn't going to fall into the flood. It wasn't going anywhere.

From the roof, Shreves, McDowell, and the others could see the river carting merchandise out of smashed storefront windows and through streets and alleys, boxes and pieces of furniture bobbing up and down, and dead horses, chunks of houses, and overturned buggies floating in the water. It was demoralizing, and the sights gave the guests an idea of what fate they might soon be facing.

Still, the Beckel House across the street had a couple of things going for it that this place didn't: beds and food.

10:40 A.M., Columbus, Ohio

The police and firefighters ordered everyone near the Scioto River in downtown Columbus to leave their homes and find high ground, and fast.

You are not to stop for clothes and valuables, the people were told. In other words, get out of here—now.

Just before 11 A.M., Columbus, Ohio

The downtowners learned just why their police and fire forces were adamant that everyone leave.

A wave of water came over the levee at Broad Street, swamped several buildings, including the three-story brick building of the Columbus Linen and Towel Supply Company. It evidently wasn't all that well constructed. Half of the building collapsed into the water. Fortunately, the employees had already abandoned the place.

A few other nearby structures were ripped off their foundations and floated down the river. "Imagine yourself at the top of a perfectly safe skyscraper looking over ninety square miles of water punctured by thousands of homes—15,000 or 20,000 at least—swirling water carrying them away one by one, or sometimes literally in swarms, and you will have some conception of what we saw in Columbus Tuesday and Wednesday, March 25 and 26," wrote Glenn Marston, a correspondent of the *Chicago Journal* and colleague of Ben Hecht, bound for Dayton. Marston just happened to be in Columbus when the flood began. The skyscraper he referred to was presumably his hotel.

Marston was able to state that, at least at first, this was not a flood hospitable to canoes and skiffs or any kind of vessel. "No boat could live in a moment in the rushing current, which took houses, bridges, railway tracks, telegraph poles—everything—in its overwhelming sweep," wrote Marston.

About the time his fellow city dwellers were running for their lives, Governor Cox received a call from the man who would soon become his favorite phone operator, Thomas E. Green. "We have word from Dayton," said Green.

Cox had been worried about Dayton, ever since the Red Cross had said an hour earlier that the city was destroyed; but soon after, the news started to flood his office. It had been quiet because other communities were having trouble reaching the governor's office through the phone lines. But now he knew that Piqua, near Dayton, was in trouble. Sidney, quite a bit north of Dayton, was flooding, with the electric and gas both out, which was pretty par for the course in almost every community in the state. The city of Troy was also in trouble.

Middletown, too. And Hamilton. From Miamisburg, Defiance, Napoleon, Ottawa, Fremont, Tiffin, Warren, Ravenna, Franklin, Youngstown, Delaware, Zanesville, McConnellsville, Marietta, Pomeroy, Middleport, Gallipolis, Ironton, Portsmouth, Manchester, Chillicothe, Fremont, and on and on came pleas for help via telephone calls and telegrams. In his own city, the Columbus Coal and Iron Company's plant had flooded and then caught on fire. The fire department managed to get the fire out, but, with the waters rising, they were forced to unhook their horses and allow them to run for their lives and leave their water-spraying machines in the buggies.

The entire state was imploding.

"This building was almost a madhouse," Cox said later, "people coming here from every community in the state seeking to gain some information."

Cox, however, at least at first, didn't have any to give. Ninety-four cities and towns, it was later determined, were adversely affected by the flood. Cox would later estimate that in highway and bridge destruction alone, there was $50 million worth of damage, which today would be almost a billion dollars.

So when Cox was patched in to talk to John Bell, on the rooftop of the Bell Telephone Company in Dayton, the governor couldn't be more grateful to get some first-hand information on what was happening in the city.

Bell gave Cox a bird's-eye view of what he saw, and while exactly what was said has apparently never been recorded, it must have been bleak. Water had almost reached the second floor of the Bell Telephone Company. The city streets were under water. Hundreds of people were dead. Maybe thousands.

11:00 A.M., Middletown, Ohio

Two hundred homes, it was estimated, were under water. Residents were seeking shelter in schools, churches, and city buildings.

11:30 A.M., Columbus, Ohio

City officials asked Governor Cox to bring out the national guard to patrol the capital city. Cox issued the order.

It was needed. Columbus was under siege. The city prison was having trouble, having to move prisoners in solitary confinement and in danger of drowning in what were basically holes in the ground to cells upstairs. Meanwhile, 144 men at the workhouse—apparently not including the twenty that were swept into the river—were marooned.

103

One of those prisoners who was swept away, Casper Sareu, found a raft about an hour after reaching a roof and the tops of other buildings, trying to stay dry.* He boarded his craft, aiming it for the workhouse, but the current wouldn't oblige. Sareu was carried right past the workhouse with the superintendent watching him go by. If the superintendent had had a rope handy, he could have thrown it to him, he was that close, and Sareu, not pleased by his situation, would have happily grabbed it.

The North Side Day Nursery was a godsend for single mothers—single white mothers—who were forced to work during the day because their husbands were dead or disabled. From 6:30 A.M. to 6 P.M., every day of the week except Sundays, for just a nickel to fifty cents a day, mothers could drop off their young children, from nine months to twelve years old. Seven kids had been at the nursery when it began flooding; a grocer who worked next door took charge of the youngsters and brought them to an office of Associated Charities, which served the deserving poor.

"It was awful," George W. Davis said later of this period. The water broke through one of the levees near his home on North Central Avenue. "I was standing on my front porch when I saw the water break through," he told a reporter. "It came in a wall ten feet high. The three houses located directly across the street from me were in its path, and they were crushed like eggshells. I saw three little girls run to the porch and fall into the flood. They never reappeared. Everything on the street was washed away clean, and I know that a few minutes before there were several people in them. They couldn't possibly have escaped. I'd rather die than witness such a scene again."

Charles Ford, who worked or owned a laundry, was at his house, trying to save some neighbors, when he realized they would have to figure things out on their own: his own house was breaking apart. He climbed out a window and scrambled to the top of their front porch and started to help his youngest daughter, Mary, eight years old, when the house simply gave way and began moving.

---

* How he found a raft on a rooftop is anyone's guess, but just about anything you wanted was flowing in the river.

The next thing Ford knew, he was swimming in the river for about a block when a neighbor was able to help him into a boat. Ford never saw Mary alive again.

He also lost his wife, Addie, and his daughters, Gladys and Catherine. Several days later, Ford would be missing. Friends believed he was searching for the bodies of Catherine and Addie, who hadn't been found yet, but they were worried because they hadn't seen him. If Ford considered the unthinkable, he didn't do it, possibly pulled back from the brink because he realized how devastating that would be for the one child he had left—his fifteen-year-old son Robert, who was at high school when the flooding began.

Patrick J. Masterson, a police officer, raced home to warn his wife and four daughters that a flood was coming. Moments later, he and his family were racing up the stairs, trying to outrun the river. But soon it was clear that being on the second floor wasn't high enough. They would have to get to the roof.

They did, but before climbing to the top of their house, Masterson had the foresight to grab two objects, and they each turned out to be very handy: a hatchet and a clothesline.

They were useful because almost as soon as the Masterson family reached the roof, the house came off its moorings, began bobbing up and down, and clearly was in danger of floating away; at that point, their fate was anyone's guess. Masterson stared at his hatchet.

He came up with the idea that he would chop through the slate and then the rafters, so that the roof would be a makeshift raft. It was wildly unrealistic to think that he could do this effectively and quickly, but it seemed a better plan than doing nothing and simply staying on a floating, unpredictable house. As he began chopping, he, along with his wife and daughters, shouted back and forth to their neighbors, the Wilcox family. They, too, were on their roof and terrified. But their house hadn't been removed from its foundations.

Fortunately, Masterson didn't have to learn how to be captain of either a floating house or roof. As he chopped away with his hatchet, he noticed a large portion of a floating picket fence. This is where his clothesline came in.

Masterson lassoed the fence and drew it to him.

Once he and his family had the fence, they steered the other end to the Wilcox residence and shouted for the family to grab hold.

They did, and everyone realized what Masterson had done. Their picket fence had become a bridge, stretching from one house to another. Several feet below it was the wild river.

The Masterson family then gingerly made their way across the bridge until they reached the Wilcox home. Before eventually being rescued, they would remain there for the next twenty hours, all the while watching their house float away and marveling how a clothesline had saved their lives.

When he realized Columbus's levees were breaking, Harry E. Keyes, a 43-year-old bookkeeper for the Central Ohio Natural Gas Company, thought of his 85-year-old blind and ill mother, who lived in one of the most flood-susceptible areas in the city.

He arrived just as the water began to overtake his mother's front lawn. He carried her out and hurried down Avondale Avenue and then to State Street. The water was now up to his hips, and Keyes, huffing and puffing, decided to run down Sullivant Avenue. His choice of streets didn't matter. It was flooding everywhere. Running through water and carrying his frail and thin mother was sapping Keyes of his strength. But he ran, undoubtedly trying to shout words of encouragement to his mother, who one can imagine may well have been urging him to leave her behind.

She must have seen so much in her life, starting out in the world in 1827, born in Virginia and eventually moving to Ohio where she and her husband would raise six children on a farm. One can only wonder what went through her mind, unable to see but knowing her son was trying to outwit and outrun a flood.

He couldn't do it. He ran until he fell, stumbling over something—perhaps a fire hydrant—and dropping his mother. The river grabbed Elizabeth Virginia Keyes. Harry hugged some floating wreckage and was carried into a tree. He scrambled up the branches and surely scanned the street, looking for his mother. She was nowhere. Two days later, he laid eyes on his mother once again, this time at the morgue.

Louis H. Mack was a 42-year-old grinder for barber's tools, which meant he was constantly sharpening barbers' blades and scissors. It was an occupation that wasn't considered healthy, due especially to the specks of metal and dust that invariably went into the workers' lungs when they used their tools to manufacture and sharpen whatever they were grinding. But Mack was never in more danger than when the flood began. His house was at least ten blocks away from the Scioto River, but it didn't matter: the water rushed down Sullivant Avenue and as it became clear that their house was going to become a casualty, Mack hurriedly put together a raft made of wooden boxes, and he and his wife, Catherine, and their four children climbed aboard. It didn't look pretty, but it saved the family from drowning.

But it was a wild ride. Soon after, the raft broke apart, with Mack and the oldest son, seventeen-year-old Carl, on what was now a smaller raft, and on the other was Catherine and their other three children: Norman, fifteen, Louis, fourteen, and Lillian, twelve. As Catherine and the kids hung on, going for the ride of their lives and possibly their final ride, they realized that a woman was rushing down the river alongside them.

She was clinging to a piece of driftwood and holding a three-year-old.

"For God's sake, take care of my child," the woman begged, successfully handing off a young boy to a stunned Catherine. "His name is Troy." Then the woman disappeared into the current.

It isn't known if Troy's mother survived or not. That she had the presence of mind to find a family who seemed able to look after her son gives one hope that without having to worry about him, she was able to remain on her driftwood until she was able to reach some sort of dry or secure land. The entire Mack family, and Troy, did survive the flood. At least by 1920, when Troy would have been 10, he wasn't living with the Macks, according to the census records, and so one would presume that he either was reunited with his mother or went to live with his father or other relatives.

The party of thirteen—with Frank Williams, the Guy family, the Hungarian boys and more—were still on top of their floating house. Nobody could quite believe it was holding together in one piece, but it did, despite continually colliding with other debris and wreckage. Still, nobody held out much hope that they were going to get out of this alive.

Chapter Six

Everyone on Their Own

March 25, Tuesday

Animals across the Midwest were doing their best to survive with mixed results. People, passing through Indiana in trains, reported seeing rats and cats on tree branches, taking refuge from the river; days later, passengers would see emaciated cats and rats still stuck in trees.

In West Middletown, a farmer had 276 pigs, waiting to be loaded onto a train. Most of the animals were washed away.

One of the more surreal sights in Logansport, Indiana was a very live cat on a very dead horse, floating downstream.

When they were able, people tried to help animals. One report in a Columbus newspaper surfaced of a blind horse and a pony, which shared several rooms with forty people trapped in a building. Two police officers in the same city reluctantly went back in a boat for a little girl's dog, after she implored: "Please, Mr. Officer, won't you go back and get Brownie? He made such good company for us when we were afraid."

When they couldn't be helped by their human counterparts, the animals were often just as creative at finding a way to survive as the humans. Mrs. C. M. Sipes, the woman who, with her husband, survived the Johnstown flood in 1889, returned to her house in Columbus after the flood to hear her tomcat weakly meowing. He was behind a picture hanging on the wall. He apparently had hung on to the back of the frame for five days.

Aron Dillon, the name of a horse in Columbus, was owned by a man named W. A. Grimes and was an extremely intelligent animal who knew a lot of tricks. His intellect must have saved his life, because when the flood invaded the barn, two colts were swept away, but Aron Dillon climbed up the stairs—possibly it was some kind of ladder—and reached the loft, which was stocked with hay. Five days after the flood began, a humane officer found the horse, alive and relatively happy.

In Dayton, two horses found a cement platform in the back of the Algonquin Hotel and remained there from the beginning of the flood until the end.

In Fort Wayne, Indiana, one man would return home after the flood to discover a cow and thirty-four chickens on the second floor of his house, although the cow admittedly had some help. The man later learned that seven men had led the cow upstairs.

And a terrier named Felix somehow became separated from his owner, a Mr. Rhodes, who was the manager of the Lyric Theater in Richmond, Indiana. Felix managed to stay away from the wrath of Whitewater River and traveled twenty-seven miles due south, dodging flooded waterways like Cedar Falls Creek, until he reached the college town of Oxford, Ohio, which managed to stay high and dry during the flood.

By now, Felix was half starved. Fortunately, some Beta Theta Pi fraternity boys found him, checked out his collar, and then wrote the mayor who passed on the news to Mr. Rhodes. Several days later, Mr. Rhodes and Felix had an emotional reunion in Oxford. Mr. Rhodes pulled up in his car and shouted for Felix. The excited dog ran from the college men and into the arms of his relieved master.

12 P.M., Dayton, Ohio

The rain had stopped, or was at least intermittently slowing down, but the bad news was that the bulk of the floodwater from the river was just getting started.

From the Delco plant, employees spotted two men trying to escape from the Egry Register Company, which made supplies for automatic registers, a relatively new machine that helped business owners make copies of bills of sale, receipts, and other paperwork. The Egry men's boat clearly couldn't withstand the current, so the Delco men threw ropes and were able to bring the men into their building. The executives and workers then heard that the Egry factory held approximately forty-five other people, including a five-year-old boy who the group had rescued from a log.

Before being brought into Egry, the boy rode the log down the wild and wooly streets of Dayton with his father, traveling through a nightmarish maze of debris.

Where was the father? Floating in the streets somewhere. As he was on the log with his son, two pieces of timber came crashing through the current, decapitating him.

About the time the Delco employees saved their Egry neighbors, a house was floating down the Great Miami River and toward a bridge. Panic-stricken people—many of them stranded on their roofs— watched as a door opened, and a man was seen looking outside, squinting in the sunlight and shading his eyes with his hand. His door wasn't opened in the direction the house was floating, however, and he couldn't see the bridge. Behind him stood a woman and, behind them, another woman with a baby in her arms.

People watching from their roofs shouted at him to jump into the water, but the man, apparently not hearing the cries of panic, shut the door as if it were just any normal day, and he was tending to his business inside. A moment later, the cottage crashed into one of the bridge's concrete piers and was smashed into oblivion.

Charles and Viola waited out the flood at the home of their Uncle Ottie, or as the neighbors more formally knew him, the Reverend W. Otterbein Fries. He and his wife Fannie lived in a house with a large tree on the front lawn and, more importantly, with a front porch approximately seven feet above the street level, with a railing around the porch.

Charles and Viola thought that Ottie and Fannie's place was a pretty shrewd one to come to, but at noon, the river was rushing west down Warder Street, marooning them. They had already moved to the second story and knew if they had to, they could wait out the flood in the attic. Charles and Viola discussed finding a new place, however. The cellar was flooded, wiping out their coal-burning stove and heat source. Ottie and Fannie had no drinking water available and little food. The adults weren't worried for themselves, but Charles and Viola were anxious about their babies. Mary, meanwhile, worried about her husband Emerson, who hadn't returned yet.

For the moment, Charles and Viola would stay put, but they kept talking about leaving since the water seemed as if it would be sticking around for a while. In fact, reports—and they would be later borne out to be true—were already spreading that in some parts of the city, the water was twenty feet deep. Two bridges were washed out. They were hearing a lot of things, although a lot of misinformation was getting out as well, although from a safety perspective it was probably better for communities to overhype the flood than undersell it.

"They're dying like rats in their holes, bodies are washing around in the streets, and there is no relief in sight," said Frank Purviance, a Dayton resident and an employee of the Terre Haute, Indianapolis and Eastern Traction Company, which managed railroad and streetcar tracks. He was correct in his assessment that people were dying, and the city was falling apart with few odds of it getting better any time soon, but for accuracy's sake and the sake of not overly panicking the rest of the country, he could have stopped right there.

Instead, Purviance, when asked how many people he believed were dead, in his fear, he answered that it was probably around 8,000. He was off by about 7,000 people, and if one judges the figure by strictly Dayton, he was off by about 7,900.

But that was just the beginning of it. One headline in a Benton Harbor, Michigan, paper early on screamed:

Dayton's Awful Story Lies
Beneath Seething Sea; Even 10,000
May Have Perished
Dayton Is Burning!

But the early newspaper accounts, while wildly off base, were still correct in one respect. Tens of thousands of people may have not drowned, but tens of thousands—really, hundreds of thousands—of lives were threatened by the flood. That more people didn't drown was—take your pick, or perhaps it was a mix of all three—miraculous, a lot of random luck, or a testament to the will of human survival.

Half-truths and wild rumors abounded. A Dayton school building, with four hundred students, was underwater, and "as far as can be ascertained all of these little ones have gone to watery graves," one widely circulated and absolutely inaccurate news report stated. One story that was repeated in the newspapers for a couple of weeks as a tiny item that was apparently used as filler, was an item stating that a commuter train from Loveland, Ohio, to Cincinnati, had gone through a bridge, and all two hundred passengers were killed. Not true, although the Loveland Bridge was wiped out. The entire town of Miamisburg, several miles away from Dayton, and its four thousand inhabitants were washed away, papers morbidly informed their readers. The number turned out to be closer to twenty-five.

People were often listed as dead when they weren't, and at least one of the deceased was mistakenly linked to a prominent name of the era. Esther Jones, a fifteen-year-old girl in Delaware, Ohio, who was being ferried from her home to safety by the Delaware mayor, or would have been if the boat hadn't capsized and she was swept away, was the daughter of Sam Jones, a foreman at a lumber company. However, some newspaper reporter or editor, thinking of the then-well known evangelist Sam Jones, assumed this was the daughter of *that* Sam Jones, never mind that the well known preacher, known for preaching against sin and hypocrisy, died seven years earlier and never had a daughter named Esther.

Newspapers were always hearing it from their readers when they misspelled a name or got a minor fact in the society pages wrong, but now editors and reporters were killing people off left and right.

Springfield, Ohio's paper carried a report that Hamilton, Ohio Police Chief George Zellner came into his house after working tirelessly all day Tuesday and much of Wednesday. He had been assured that his home was out of the flood zone, but instead he discovered it underwater, and his wife's drowned body in the kitchen. Insane with grief, he pulled out his gun and shot himself. None of this was true, however. He actually had come to his house at 2 A.M., on Wednesday, after spending virtually all of Tuesday directing the rescue efforts. He wanted to check on his house and his wife. Finding his house surrounded by water, Chief Zellner waded into it, the water coming up to his chest, and entered his home. His wife was there and doing as well as one could expect.

After a fitful night's sleep, when Zellner woke up the next morning, the river had risen by another six feet, it was estimated, and he realized he and his wife weren't going to be going anywhere. That's when the gossip mill began churning. But Zellner was in good company. Six of his fellow police detectives and officers in Hamilton were, at one time or another during the flood, reported dead, only to turn up alive later.

But it's understandable. The newspapers were only going with the information that they had, and often the people who one would think would know what was going on, didn't. Edward Hazlett, of Columbus, saw his nineteen-year-old brother Claude drown on Wednesday morning after a boat he was in overturned.

A grieving Edward then reported Claude's death to the police, and the local press dutifully reported it. But Claude was found later, very much alive, and lived for many more years to come.

When it was all over, Ohio's Bureau of Statistics would count eighty-three deaths in Hamilton, but it's difficult to know if that number is accurate. In October 1913, a time when one would think Hamiltonians would have a pretty good idea of how many citizens they had lost, the *Hamilton Evening Journal* pegged the number at approximately 250.

Given the destruction, one can hardly blame Purviance or anyone for overestimating the number of deaths in the flood. But Mother Nature was dealing with people, not rats. That there weren't more deaths was due to peoples' ingenuity and the will to use every strategy they could come up with to survive.

In Brookville, Indiana, John Bunz, a 45-year-old junk dealer, was wading through water on the first floor of his home when he lost his balance and found himself underwater. He scrambled to the surface for air and bolted for the stairs as the water chased him. If he didn't quite realize what had happened—his house had been ripped off its foundation and was floating down the Whitewater River—he would figure it out soon enough.

That Bunz and his 78-year-old mother, Margaret, who lived with him, weren't killed seconds or minutes later was because the house came to a sudden stop when it lodged itself into a tree. But after that fortunate break, everything they did was all about trying to outwit or at least outlast the flood. As the water entered the bedroom and began to fill it, Bunz then propped up his mother as high as possible, holding her in his arms, with the icy water eventually reaching his shoulders. He kept her that way for the next seven hours until he realized he had lost her. Bunz was rescued another two hours later.

Grover Brown, a 24-year-old railroad worker living in Cambridge City, Indiana, also floated down the Whitewater River on this day—for sixty miles. Twenty-three hours later, he wound up in Harrison, Ohio, where twelve people reportedly died, and the water was twelve feet deep on the well-trafficked State Street. He spent his time on the river, clinging to the floor of a building that was swept away, and he could have easily died, and by all rights, he should have.

Brown was stark naked for those sixty miles, having taken off some of his clothing to lighten his load when in the water, helping his family escape. Then he lost the rest of his wardrobe from the pull of the river. He came close to freezing to death, and he would have, except that he found some drowned chickens in the water, plucked their feathers, and covered himself as best he could. He was probably too frozen to be embarrassed when two men later pulled him off the roof and away from the water. He couldn't have been too scarred by the experience, though, or at least he must have liked the looks of Harrison. After marrying a woman named Irene Delacroix later in the year, who probably did not see the chicken-feather incident, they moved to Harrison.

James Wrinkle, a wealthy manufacturer of washtubs, created a boat out of his washtubs and was credited with saving 125 of his neighbors. The river had chased him up to the second story of his office building, and as the water swirled around his ankles, Wrinkle found himself staring at a pile of about fifty washtubs. He hastily nailed together eight of them, creating a boat that allowed for seven passengers, and then he grabbed a long pole with a hook on the end, which he normally used for reaching high objects.

With it, he braved the mad waters, using the pole with the hook to grab onto tree branches, pushing him through the river-streets and allowing him to reach houses in his neighborhood. He ended up making thirty trips, taking anyone he saw to high ground.

"Well, I couldn't leave those people to drown, could I?" he responded when a committee of city officials later showed up to thank him for his service. Then he waved them off.

Throughout Ohio, Indiana, and parts of Illinois, Kentucky, West Virginia, and Pennsylvania, many homeowners were collectively preparing a clever flood-fighting tactic that undoubtedly saved many lives and homes. For those who didn't want to leave their house or no longer could, due to the water surrounding them, many people started preparing their homes on the fly. It could be agonizing and against every homeowner's instincts to welcome in the water, but that's what many families did. While Charles Adams was concerned about currents moving through his house, many people willingly opened their front and back doors and windows of their home, and then—most painfully—some even cut a hole in the ceiling of the first floor.

The water was going to come into the house whether the doors and windows were shut or not. Boarding the house and making it water-tight was not only extremely difficult and virtually impossible, it actually just increased the odds that the river would eventually push the house out of its way. By opening everything up, the river could come into the house and—with any luck—let it stay put. The hole in the ceiling meant that if the water rose higher than the first floor, it would continue to have somewhere to go, rather than pushing against the ceiling and eventually destroying the floorboards of the second floor.

That was the scenario at the Zang family in Hamilton, Ohio. Sixty years after the flood, Marie Zang Barnhorn recalled that her father first opened the cellar door so the water would run through the house and not push it off the foundation.

"When the water came up to the second floor, Pop punched a hole in the ceiling, and we climbed up and sat on the rafters," said Zang. "He took the doors off and put them up there so we wouldn't fall through."

Marie and her family were quite comfortable at first. Her mother had already been cooking dinner that morning when they decided to retreat upstairs, and they brought up sauerkraut, potatoes, and pork. It was a feast, but it would be their only food for the next forty-eight hours.

Another strategy that Fred Zang employed was that he hung out the second-story window and kicked logs away from the house, so they wouldn't build up and eventually knock the house off the foundation. One can't argue with Zang's strategy. His family lived through the flood; two neighbors on the same street drowned in their own homes.

Bill Thompson, then six years old, wrote about the experience of being in the flood in Hamilton, Ohio for his company's newsletter in 1959. His family could see a suspension bridge washed away from their home and much more.

"We saw houses and sheds floating down the river," Thompson wrote. "Neighboring houses were broken away as the water kept coming with added depth and speed. As the water began seeping through our second floor, we moved to the attic, using doors across rafters for beds."

Eventually, a floating house leaned against the Thompson home, which turned out to be a good thing. It broke the current. "Folks from that dwelling and another broke through their roofs and climbed through a hole made in our roof," wrote Thompson. "There were about thirty-five praying souls in the same attic by crest time. That crest found the water half way up to the second story windows."

It took persistence and patience to thwart the flood. Another Hamilton resident, Clara Clements, wife of a police detective, would have been on the force herself if this had been another era. She was certainly innovative. Five people, including Mrs. Clements, were upstairs in her and her husband's house, and everyone wanted to escape to the neighbor's house. Eugene Mueller's home seemed far sturdier.

Clara Clements came up with the idea of folding a large carpet into three thicknesses. Then she and her group inserted long poles and, with the Muellers on the other side helping, stretched the carpet bridge over the fifteen-foot gap. Everyone nailed the carpet to the roof on both sides, and Clara and the others safely crossed over.

George Timmerman, the Dayton moulder who was assured by his neighbors that a little ankle-deep water didn't mean a thing, found himself on the second floor of a house when the flood wall came. He was in a neighbor's house, a house he had never been in, seeking refuge with a mother and three children.* Within about an hour, as the water climbed higher, they retreated to the attic, shouting for help. Within about another hour, a rescuer came in a boat. It wasn't easy, and escaping the flood took some initiative and a lot of luck, but a lot of people did it.

That was hardly the end of Timmerman and company's ordeal; rather, it was just the beginning. The rescuer had trouble steering the boat in the current, which wasn't just fast-moving water but a soup of wagons and buggies, dead horses, dead bodies, and driftwood. For a while, Timmerman was sure he, the family of four, and the rescuer would all capsize. But the rescuer steered Timmerman, the mother, and the kids near the top of a porch. They climbed onto that and bid farewell to the rescuer, who felt he could manage the boat, especially now that it was lighter.

Timmerman, the mother, and the children scurried into the attic of someone's abandoned home in an apartment building. It seemed safe enough for the moment, and they even managed to find some food to eat, so they were at least in good company. All of the surrounding homes had people in them, including the building across the street, the one with the sign O. G. Saettel's. For the moment, they decided they would sit put and wait out the flood. Not that they had much choice.

12:12 P.M., Hamilton, Ohio

The Black Street Bridge was the first bridge in the city to collapse. About three minutes later, the High Street Bridge, with high school student J. Walter Wack watching, buckled against the current and the pressing mountain of debris, which was now pinned against the bridge. Then the wires on the bridge began to snap.

"Everyone ran like hell," recalled Wack, himself making tracks for his house.

Elizabeth Hensley Hand, in 1988, told her local paper, "I remember seeing houses floating down the river with people on the roofs waving white sheets for help. Some of the houses hit the bridges and shattered.

---

* He appears not to have met or known them. One would think he would have exchanged names with the mother and children throughout their ordeal, but later, when he recounted the story, he never mentioned their names.

Horses were floating downstream, trying to swim, but drowning, too."
Seventy-five years later, Mrs. Hand said, she would think about the
flood and still cry.

As resident and jewelry store owner Raymond McComb would
write his father: "The water came right through the business section
of town, sweeping houses and barns, horses and cows right through
High Street."

The Great Miami River swamped McComb's store in turn, knocking
over his displays, invading his safe, and destroying the contents.

12:28 P.M., Hamilton, Ohio

A second bridge went down.

In the midst of the chaos, councilman, concerned citizen, and
man with possible extrasensory perception J. Henry Welsh, still in
the midst of warning people, hadn't heeded his own advice. He found
himself caught in the flood despite being quite a bit inland at Tenth
and High Streets and had to swim to a place of safety.

Middletown, Ohio, afternoon

Middletown's residents, hearing about what was happening up north
and warily watching the river, anticipated what was to come.

Daniel Snider, the city's local Ford dealer who proudly displayed
his five new Model-T cars in West Middletown, carefully jacked up
his five cars a foot off the ground and put the cars in a coal shed.
The 36-year-old Snider tied the shed to a tree, fully believing that
at the most, the shed might wind up being a few inches deep in
water. He then went to join his wife, Mae, and their three-year-old
daughter, at the house, which he also assumed was free and clear
of the river.

The tree was destroyed, or perhaps the rope broke, but, some way
or the other, the shed sailed down the river. Snider later retrieved his
cars, but they were in no condition to drive.* Snider miscalculated on
a number of things that day, but he was the only one in the area who

---

* Henry Ford's company sent him replacement parts, and Snider was apparently able to
refurbish them enough to drive; but even as late as fifty years later, Snider would ruefully
regret not driving each car up a nearby hill, where the river couldn't possibly reach them.

had the foresight to own a boat. His parents always owned one and insisted their son did, too, "just in case," they said. Daniel's dad was in the business of making wagons but understood the value of a good boat when living near a river.

When the Great Miami River spilled into West Middletown, Snider made the rounds to houses in his canoe, passing by their second-story windows and taking families to dry land to a home owned by a family named Childs, who must have lived on a hill, for their residence was becoming something of a relief station. But Snider was so busy working to save his neighbors that he almost forgot or couldn't reach his own wife and three-year-old daughter. By the time he arrived at his own house, he was able to paddle through the front door and up to the stairway, where Mae and his daughter were anxiously waiting.

1 P.M., Hornell, New York

Although Ohio and Indiana were suffering the most from the flood, parts of western New York were now seeing their waterways overflowing to dangerous levels. The Canisteo River overflowed its banks north of Hornell, and two hours later, Canacadea Creek, which flows through the city, also left its channel. The waters wouldn't destroy the town or region to the level of what was happening along the Miami River, but one unlucky fellow by the name of Eugene Porter, a farmer on the aptly named Big Creek Road, was surprised by the current and lost his life.

Sometime in the afternoon, New Castle, Pennsylvania

Neshannock Creek, which connects up to the Shenango River in New Castle, remained in its bed. The hundred-mile-long Shenango River, however,began slowly making its way across the main streets of New Castle.

The police force fanned out across the city where they could, helping residents flee to higher ground. Still, the community functioned mostly as normal. School was in session all day. Most people retained power. There seemed to be no reason to fret yet.

Dayton, afternoon

Slowly but surely, John H. Patterson found himself running a rescue center instead of a cash register manufacturing business.

His company's thirty-one cars were being utilized wherever possible throughout the city; and while seven square miles of Dayton was underwater, there were ample rolling hills where cars were able to carry passengers away from the flooding and to shelters. His boats were in high demand as well, and the NCR headquarters atop a hill on Wyoming Street were perfectly situated as a rescue hub. It was already a city landmark, and so word of mouth spread. If you were in trouble, come here.

Some people followed the telephone cables leading up to the campus of office buildings. As was the case around the city, there were often six, eight, or more telephone wires, strung out so that one could literally grab hold of a wire, plant their feet on another, and very carefully walk across the telephone wires. It wasn't terribly dangerous, as long as you didn't fall into the still-rushing current below, or happen to touch a damaged wire.

Realizing that this was going to be the mode of transportation du jour, some telephone linemen climbed up to the cables, carrying tow ropes that were attached to flat-bottomed boats. Their plan was that people could paddle their way up to dry land, knowing that they were securely tied to the telephone wires and wouldn't be swept away. But the water kept getting rougher, and that idea was abandoned. But people who were athletic and daring, or had no choice, still used the cables to travel, clinging to them with their hands while carefully walking the wires up toward the office buildings.

The day wasn't over, and the headquarters was turning into a shelter and rescue center that surpassed anything the actual city government had set up, which was nothing. By evening, the Dayton populace started referring to it as the Cash Register Hospital. For good reason. It was sheltering three thousand people by nightfall, and an emergency hospital had been set up to treat flood victims with hypothermia, broken bones, and burns from fires that were breaking out across the city, for a variety of reasons from electrical fires to broken gas lines, and collapsing buildings, and sheds with paint and other flammable materials.

That night, in the halls of NCR, three women gave birth. Actually, that last part wasn't true but was a rumor that was circulated in newspapers around the country. It isn't surprising that people thought that had been the case. If a pregnant woman in labor had come here and hadn't been able to make it to one of the city's hospitals, odds are, the baby would have been delivered just fine.

Having given up the idea of climbing into any more rowboats himself, Patterson was in the midst of the action, issuing orders and running the business like a command center.

His 21-year-old son, Frederick, however, was commandeering rescue boats and going out into the city, searching for people to help. Patterson's nineteen-year-old daughter Dorothy dutifully stayed behind—whether she wanted to or not, women simply didn't go out and rescue people if there were men around—although she chose a fairly uncomfortable job for herself. She stood outside the National Cash Register headquarters in the rain, greeting flood victims as they were brought over in automobiles.

NCR was one of the few bright spots in the city and state, as overall things were bleak. "I have received reports from my men all along the line that indicate an estimate of five hundred dead is a conservative one," said Frank Brandon, vice president and general manager of the Dayton, Lebanon and Cincinnati Railroad. "At first my men reported deaths at sixty. Later the reports came in so fast, they quit counting. When we are finally able to get the details and the names of the dead, we will find the life loss to be appalling. My men place the property loss at Dayton at six to seven million. The two bridges that were swept away at Dayton were worth half a million dollars each."

Excello, Ohio, afternoon

In a tiny village just south of Middletown and about thirty miles away from Dayton, the river, the canal, and Dick's Creek all formed a united front, overwhelming the farmhouses and some of the residents. Christian Ramseyer, a 45-year-old farmer, had sent his wife, Pearl, and their four youngest children to higher ground east of their farm home.

He and his sons, Walter, eighteen, and Roy, nineteen, and a 39-year-old neighboring farmer, Edwin "Dock" Cassidy, were trying to save their livestock. In hindsight, it's hard not to think that if it wasn't safe for Pearl and the children to be on the grounds, perhaps it wasn't safe for the Ramseyer men and Cassidy to be in the barn either. But in their defense, the water hadn't reached their home yet, and the four men were simply trying to save the animals that kept their farm going. They probably would have been just fine if the nearby levee hadn't broken.

But they made a mistake that many flood victims made—staying behind a little too long. The levee did break, and the rushing water first destroyed the Ramseyer house and then came for the barn where the men were. They didn't have a chance. Cassidy had come on horseback, but even if he had mounted his steed, it wouldn't have mattered. A tidal wave crashed through, and the men and animals were swept away.

Walter's body was found that day in a cornfield. Christian Ramseyer, the father, was found in some brush later in the week. Nine weeks after the flood, Edwin Cassidy was located several miles away in the city of Hamilton.

The bones of Walter's brother, Roy, weren't discovered for another twenty years. He was identified by a Sunday school pin next to his bones, a pin that surviving family members remembered him wearing.

Chapter Seven

That Old College Try

March 25, Tuesday

In a bit of weird irony, a man named Nate Williams, who was a professional diver and possibly worked for a construction crew, which often needed divers for bridge construction, had traveled from the Ohio River community, Portsmouth, at the southern edge of the state, to come upstate to Bainbridge. He was diving in a nearby creek, searching for two men, William Kinzer and John Blackner. They had lost their lives three days earlier, before the flood began, after their boat capsized. But with the flooding, Williams was forced to abandon his search. One has to think he probably soon resumed the search for the two men—and for numerous additional missing men.

Just as with any natural disaster, daily routines ceased to exist when the Great Flood of 1913 showed up. Throughout Ohio and Indiana and various communities throughout other states, schools closed. Businesses shut down. Courthouses and other government agencies either halted or were hampered. Travel by train across the nation was hobbled by the delays and virtual shutdown of railroads throughout the Midwest. Weddings were postponed, or at the very least there was a change of venue. In Indianapolis, on April 2, when Ethel Krouse, eighteen, said "I do" to Christian Anderson, twenty-one, they married on the day they had planned and at the time they had chosen, two in the afternoon; but instead of marrying in their home or church, both of which were waterlogged, they married at the Y.W.C.A., where the bride had been staying, with many of their friends and guests looking on.

The mail for many communities also came to a screeching halt; by the end of the week, the Columbus, Ohio post office would have 250 tons of undelivered mail waiting to go out.

Communication, of all sorts, was severely curtailed. In central Ohio, the tiny village of Zuck was eliminated. In Warsaw, Ohio, several young women, telephone operators, were on chairs, perched up on their knees, trying to do their jobs, as the water washed over the floor. By noon, they were forced to flee their posts or die for the cause.

Newspaper communication was also halted for many communities. In Middletown, Ohio, just about fifteen minutes away from Dayton today by car, the *Middletown Journal* and the *Middletown Signal*, the two city papers of the day, tell the story of what was going on in the city simply by what they didn't write. On March 24, 1913, the town's 18,000 residents had a newspaper featuring on their front page the tornado that devastated Omaha and much of the Midwest. And then, nothing. They wouldn't produce another newspaper until April 1.

And people were going to be sick and dying whether there was a flood or not. The Newark, Ohio paper reported that on March 25, the day the flood erupted, fifteen-year-old Harry Loughman was seized with convulsions, probably an epileptic attack. His elderly doctor couldn't make a house call the normal way, and so a neighbor, Ben Slate, who thankfully was a husky young man, was called in to help. Slate carried the 175-pound town physician on his shoulders for a hundred feet through the knee-deep water to the Loughman family's home.

A three-month-old baby's funeral in Newark was delayed a day, and a Mrs. Charles McNeal wouldn't be arriving in Newark any time soon; the Texas resident, who was coming to town for her mother's funeral, was trapped on her train in Indianapolis, which couldn't make it any farther since so many railroad bridges had been destroyed. Grave diggers in Newark found their jobs next to impossible, for obvious reasons: water kept rushing into their holes. But that was a better situation than the cemetery in Tiffin, Ohio, where coffins were dredged up out of the dirt by the flood and were spotted floating down the Sandusky River. Meanwhile, bodies of missing people, who had died somewhere but hadn't been found yet, were revealed thanks to the flood as well.

The badly decomposed body of James Kearney, a Columbus merchant, would be discovered in a tree on March 29, to everyone's surprise. He had been known to have drowned—several months earlier.

In Peru, Indiana, something similar happened. The body of George Baker, a 53-year-old steel mill worker who had been missing since January, was found soon after the flood began, washed up in a tree. Dead men tell no tales, but people were soon telling them at his funeral, remembering an earlier tragedy Baker had been involved with.

Baker married his bride, a Peru resident, Flora Bannon, on July 6, 1887. He was twenty-seven; she was twenty. Unfortunately, Flora's stepfather, James Christianson, was none too happy about the union and vowed he would kill Baker the first chance he got. That July day, Christianson, stinking drunk, stormed to his daughter's new home and asked her to come outside. She did, and not realizing he was about to demonstrate that she was smart for getting married and leaving his home, he beat her to a pulp. Or he would have, if neighbors hadn't come to her rescue, including a Dr. North, who worked for the Wabash, St. Louis & Pacific railway and just happened to be walking by.

Christianson, realizing he was outmanned, ran for cover and dashed into the woodhouse. Moments later, they heard a gunshot.

Dr. North assumed the madman had realized what a monster he had become and, full of grief, killed himself.

Or at the very least, injured himself and needed medical attention. Dr. North ran to the woodhouse.

Dr. North's assumption was wrong. As he opened the door, Christianson pulled the trigger, and the bullet pierced underneath the physician's arm and went straight into his liver and kidney, killing the good doctor. The neighbors managed to wrest the gun away from Christianson, who was then taken to the jail at the courthouse. By the next morning, a mob had gathered outside of the jail—and by 12:15 P.M., they were storming it. Christianson was dragged to the Broadway Bridge. A rope was thrown over a beam, Christianson was fitted with a noose, and after he was hanged, about a thousand people gave three hearty cheers.

None of this could have been healthy for George and Flora's marriage, for while they had two children, they eventually divorced. In 1899, Flora remarried, and George moved in with his sister and her family. That is, until something happened to him in early 1913 and he went missing, and then ultimately resurfaced, his lifeless body found in a tree. And, in a sense, the entire drama surrounding Baker and his stepfather-in-law was finally finished, for the Broadway Bridge where Christianson had been hanged was demolished in the flood.

Roughly 2 P.M., West Lafayette, Indiana

The timing of the flood couldn't have been much worse for college students, many of whom were on their way home in trains and cars for spring break. Miami University in Oxford, Ohio was on high enough ground that their campus didn't experience any serious flooding, and the flood's timing was such that school's officials forbid the students who were still on campus after Easter Sunday weekend from leaving, thus ensuring their safety, although there were a number of petrified parents who, without telephone access to the University, had no idea if their child was safe on campus or stuck on a flooded train car somewhere between Oxford and home.

Miami University fared well; other colleges did not. In Bloomington, Indiana, the home of Indiana University, the land that hosted the university was high enough that the school didn't fare too badly. The northeastern and southern sections of the city were almost under water, however. The "River Jordan," an amicable nickname for a tiny, easily crossable creek—you can just jump over it in places—that runs throughout the campus, literally became a river. East Kirkwood Avenue, a road leading to the campus, was under more than two feet of water, and the flood was two feet deep in Indiana University's power plant. East Fourth and East Sixth streets were underwater. Indiana Avenue was turned into a lake. Fortunately, it was more inconvenience than calamity, unlike towns around them, like Nashville, where Salt Creek swallowed up and destroyed quite a few homes.

But some universities had serious problems. At Purdue University, most of the students were safe on parts of campus not in the flood zone, but the situation was becoming worse by the hour. Initially, though, the rain and flooding was more a curiosity than anything else, and so students unwisely went on what one of them called "an inspection tour," checking out the Wabash River that separated West Lafayette from its sister city Lafayette.

The townspeople came out as well, among them Paul Wangerin, a cashier at the Burt-Haywood Company, a publishing house. Arnold Herbert, one of the younger owners of Kimmel & Herbert Book Store, was in the mix as well as William L. Oilar, the advertising manager of the *Journal and Free Press*, one of Lafayette's two newspapers. Among the crowd of onlookers, Wangerin, Herbert, and Oilar stopped at the edge of the bridge, discussing the river and how bad the flood might get.

Wangerin then suggested that they cross the bridge to look at the water from the other side of the river, but with the churning water splashing onto and over the bridge, Herbert and Oilar gave it an uneasy look and decided to pass on the idea. Wangerin didn't see a problem, however. This was a modern, sturdy bridge, after all. The asphalt pavement over the bridge, for instance, was an innovation when it had been built just nine years earlier, replacing a wooden predecessor that had lasted for sixty years.

Wangerin started across the bridge and was joined by Charles Burkhouse. Burkhouse, a 44-year-old carpenter who everyone called Charley, may or may not have been friends with Wangerin, but they were both born in Europe. One student would later refer to them as "foreigners," perhaps not unkindly; but as men who were making their way through small-town America, they at least had that bond in common. Wangerin was born in Germany and had moved to the United States sixteen years earlier; Burkhouse originally hailed from Holland.

People, including college students, had been walking across the bridge all morning and throughout the early afternoon. Crossing the bridge may have seemed adventurous, but probably not dangerous.

Back where Wangerin had left Herbert and Oilar, they began talking with William F. Stillwell, president of the Henry Taylor-Lumber Company. The 56-year-old Stillwell, a native of Cincinnati, Ohio, had moved to Lafayette in 1877 and likely brought up the infamous 1883 flood that sent many families and business owners fleeing in West

Lafayette. But, still, the casualty level of the 1883 flood was blessedly low, other than the occasional hapless individual—an eighteen-year-old collecting driftwood around Indianapolis met his doom in the White River. Having seen his share of floods, Stillwell probably wasn't too concerned.

Instead, paying little attention to Wangerin and Burkhouse or the river beneath them, Stillwell and the others were watching their side of the riverbank. The water was chewing up the dirt, and mice and rats were fleeing, following their instincts and doing their best to avoid the rising flood. After observing the adventures of these rodents, Stillwell felt he had better things to do and left. A few minutes later, Herbert and Oilar heard a crash. Rather, they felt it. They said later that it was like being in an earthquake.

At least one pier—the vertical support that holds up a bridge—broke away, followed by two spans—the flat section between the piers that people and vehicles cross on. The bridge, in other words, was collapsing due to the erosion of the riverbank, engineers would later determine, and Wangerin and Burkhouse were both walking on the disintegrating structure.

Like the rats, Wangerin and Burkhouse's survival instincts took over. What was behind them was tumbling into the river, but what was ahead of them wasn't. They broke into a run.

They reached the levee that the bridge was attached to, just as the bridge behind them sank into the raging river.

But they swiftly skidded to a stop. Part of the levee, the part in front of them, had broken apart as well. So there was no bridge behind them, and the river now flowed on all sides of the piece of the levee on which they stood. Wangerin and Burkhouse were marooned on their own little dirt island.

But it wouldn't be an island for long. The river was now rushing past their waists.

The hundreds of horrified bystanders—a number growing exponentially with each passing minute—started screaming, yelling, and pleading for somebody to do something. Confusion abounded. Herbert and Oilar could see two men standing on a broken chunk of the levee but weren't sure if it was Wangerin and Burkhouse or two other unfortunate souls. City officials, now understanding what they were dealing with, rushed to rope off the Main Street Bridge, lest they have people crossing during its collapse. In the chaos, two Purdue students who had come to see the river decided that they weren't going to stand and watch two men die. They grabbed a canoe.

Bystanders warned Leland Philputt Woolery, a 22-year-old freshman from Indianapolis, and George Beckwith Ely, a junior, not to go.

It was too dangerous, and the current was too fast and unpredictable, they were warned, but the young men couldn't be dissuaded by the rational suggestion that they could lose a fight against Mother Nature. Woolery, in particular, may have been on an adrenaline high. He had just been accepted into a fraternity, Phi Delta Theta, and would soon be initiated. His first year of college was going, well, swimmingly.

Leaving the Main Street levee, they rowed into the muddy brown mess that was now sixteen feet deep, with the onlookers fearfully watching. Then, about thirty feet from the new shoreline, a wave crashed into the canoe's side, and Woolery and Ely were pitched into the rushing rapids.

When Ely emerged from under the water, he spotted a roof—of a coal barn, it would turn out—and swam toward it. The crowd broke into cheers, and once he reached it, he fought to hang on to the roof. It took a while, but he managed to pull himself out of the water and scramble up the slippery slope. For the moment, he was safely above the water.

Woolery didn't have as much luck.

As the waves beat against him, he found the top of a tree, but he lost his grip when the overturned canoe crashed into him. Then the current sucked Woolery away from Ely and the coal barn and toward what was left of the Brown Street levee, where Wangerin and Burkhouse watched, incredulous.

Woolery was an agricultural student. It is possible that he didn't know how to swim, or, like most men of the time, couldn't swim well enough to save his life, especially in an erratic current and while weighed down with wet clothes, so it's also plausible that even an Olympic swimmer couldn't have defeated the Wabash River that day.

The thousands of people watching could only stare and shout in terror as Woolery was pulled through the river and then abruptly disappeared underneath the water. When he resurfaced, he seemed to be either unconscious or dead. Then the river took him again.

Later that day, Woolery's father, Frank, received a heartbreaking telegram from one of his son's soon-to-be fraternity brothers. Frank Woolery was informed that at 2:10 P.M., his beloved son Leland had drowned in the Wabash River while trying to save two men.

The rest of the details were left to Woolery's imagination.

On the roof of the barn, meanwhile, Ely was standing on borrowed time. The river was climbing, six inches every hour, and lashing out. Ely didn't fear that the barn would be underwater any time soon, but if a steel bridge didn't have any hope against the Wabash, what were a barn's chances? Any minute, it seemed, the barn would separate into a million splinters, or eventually, given enough time, it and Ely would be swallowed by the Wabash River. Further down the river and still waist-deep in water, clinging to the levee's railing, Wangerin and Burkhouse were worried about the same fate.

By now, Ely's mother had been called, and she watched from the shore with the other residents. She was frantic, hoping against all hope that her son wouldn't meet Woolery's fate, and police captain John Kluth was well aware of her presence. It must have felt surreal. Everyone had been safely watching what was a curiosity, and now, within minutes, Lafayette had lost one young man and three more men's lives were in danger.

But Purdue University was known for its schools of agriculture, pharmacy, and engineering, and Kluth made all of the college's engineering students proud that day.

Kluth didn't feel he could send any of his officers in a boat to bring back either Ely or Wangerin and Burkhouse, not after what everyone had just witnessed. It would be a suicide mission. But Kluth surveyed the situation and thought he might be able to save George Ely.

Kluth noticed that a telephone wire ran from the shoreline to the roof of the office at the coal barn, and then all the way across the rest of the river to the Main Street levee.

First, Kluth directed his men to cut the telephone wire on the shore's end, across the river from the levee. Then an officer tied a rope to the end of the wire, and, shouting to Ely, they made it clear that he was to pull the wire until he had the rope on the roof. Then he was to untie the rope.

Once that was done, Ely had one end of the rope, and the police officers had the other. To the end of the rope that they had, they tied a boat. Ely soon understood. He needed to pull the boat through the waves and to him. Once he did, he could attempt to row back to shore.

It was a clever plan, but the waves whipped the boat so badly that it was soon clear that Ely would need the strength of ten men to pull the boat to the barn.

Kluth had another idea.

Meanwhile, one of Purdue's professors, a veterinary surgeon, Dr. Roy Birmingham Whitesell, determined that someone might be able to row out for Wangerin and Burkhouse if coming from another direction and leaving the shoreline at a point much closer to the two men. The thirty-year-old secured a canoe and embarked into the choppy waters.

Kluth was still putting his plan in motion. Either Kluth or one of the deputies got the boat back to the shore and thus had one end of the rope that led back to George Ely. From there, they tied a pulley to the end of the rope, and Ely was able to bring the pulley through the water and to his roof. Then Ely fastened the pulley onto the telephone wire that led back to the Main Street levee.

Ely climbed onto the pulley, and as Purdue's student newspaper would put it, he "made a slide for life."

As soon as he reached the shore, Ely, assuming the best, asked where Leland Woolery was. Someone broke the news to him that his pal had drowned, and reality came crashing over Ely. He fainted. Then he was carried to a car, with, one hopes, his mother trailing after him. When the car Ely was in drove through some water at the edge of the river, just before speeding away, the crowd broke into a roar of applause and approval.

But the danger wasn't over yet. Wangerin and Burkhouse were still stuck on the Main Street levee, and Dr. Whitesell was risking his life, fighting the waves, doing everything he could to get his canoe to the two men. It took a while, but eventually, he reached them, and the men clamored into the boat. One hopes that they, or anyone else in the crowd that day, never walked across a bridge during a flood again.

2 P.M., Middletown, Ohio

The bridge over the Great Miami River collapsed, after being hammered by house after house hitting it.

2 P.M., *Columbus, Ohio*

On the west side of the city, a plant owned by the Beck Electrical Supply company burned to the ground, but adding to the confusion: for the longest time, firefighters—who were having trouble reaching any fire due to the rivers in the surrounding streets—thought it was the Barch Brothers' Junk Shop that was going up in flames. That alarmed everyone, because residents knew that if the junk shop went down, two more houses next to it would go, and then a carriage factory beside it.

It was a confusing afternoon.

True, most of the 120,000 residents of Columbus were either safe enough on the second story of a building or out of reach from the affected areas, but you couldn't travel far without finding some part of the city that was underwater. Two main rivers, the Scioto and Olentangy, travel through Columbus and meet up just west of downtown, and there were other waterways, such as Alum Creek, Big Walnut Creek, and Darby Creek, to contend with.

For the thousands who were in the water's way, it was a miserable existence. William Bard, a contractor, was rescued by a police officer from the second story of his home; but after their boat capsized, the two men had to wait at the top of a pile of lumber for an hour until another police boat could pick them up.

Albert B. Gore, who isn't an ancestor—not a direct one, anyway—of the future vice president, was a mail carrier and after finishing his morning delivery, he heard that his house was surrounded by water. The 54-year-old postal worker immediately dropped whatever he was doing and set out to rescue his wife and daughter. The only way he could envision getting to his house was to cross the Scioto Bridge, which was in danger of collapsing. Police officers tried to stop him, but Gore crossed and managed to find a boat and rowed six blocks to his house. He took his wife, Flora, and his 23-year-old daughter, Edna, away from their home, but not before promising a girl next door that he would come back for her. Gore brought his wife and daughter to the Rich Street Bridge, which had become something of a landing for refugees of the flood, and then he kept his promise. About two in the afternoon, he went back for the girl.

Flora and Edna begged him not to go back, but Gore insisted and perhaps his wife and daughter felt better when another neighbor or friend, John Hughes, said he would go with him. But the extra help didn't help; Gore and Hughes's boat overturned. Hughes reached the shore. Gore never made it. What became of the girl Gore wanted to rescue isn't known. With any luck, she was able to huddle in her attic and wait out the flood.

Tempers were flaring. One man caught up with the police chief on the Rich Street Bridge directing rescue efforts and demanded that he send some officers to rescue his two sons, trapped in their flooding home. The chief said that they would have to remain where they were until they had rescued some women and children who were in greater danger. Next thing everyone knew, the man and police chief were slugging it out. Several officers pulled the father away, and while they were going to arrest him, they decided, under the circumstances, to just let him go.

But nobody could be rescued fast enough. After their house was destroyed, John D. Underwood, a carpenter, found himself climbing a sprawling elm tree near Green Lawn Cemetery, with his wife, Mayme, and four of their five children: Josephine, twelve, Albert, thirteen, and two more offspring, nineteen-year-old Francis and five-year-old son Edgar. (John Riley Underwood, twenty-one, was out and about, perhaps at work when the flooding began.)

In the same tree was a Mrs. Nicholson and her son Harry, a Mr. and Mrs. William Prewdley, and Omar Clarence Toy and his wife Pauline. It isn't clear how the Nicholsons and Prewdleys wound up in the tree, but the Toys were on a raft, which they constructed before leaving their soon-to-be ruined house. With them was their 22-month-old son, Clarence Omar Toy. At some point, when the water was even more feral and unpredictable than it had been, Mrs. Toy turned to help her husband steer their craft. In that moment, their son toppled out into the water and disappeared.

The Toys reached the tree, distraught.

For the next twenty-four hours, the Underwood parents and their four children, and the Toys, remained in the tree, the rain dumping on them until it turned into snow. Below them was the barbaric, seething current. They had two choices: fall into the river and undoubtedly meet a quick death, or stay in the tree and try to outlast the storm.

Pauline Toy chose death. She hung on to her perch in the tree for some time, but at 1:20 in the morning, exhausted from the freezing rain and snow that had started to fall, and sobbing over the loss of her son, she dropped into the water and let the river do its work.

When the rescuers finally arrived, they were horrified by what they found. John Underwood, still holding Edgar, was insane with grief. Albert was only barely alive, mostly frozen, and he would die shortly after reaching some of the dry land at—in a touch of cruel irony—the cemetery. Josephine, who had been tied to the tree with a rope to keep her from falling, had frozen to death. The rescuer, who had already made several unsuccessful attempts in a motorboat over the course of several hours to reach them, and still very concerned about the threatening current, left Josephine where she was.

As if that wasn't enough agony for the Underwoods, they soon learned that their eldest son was missing. John had gone with a police officer, to check on the police officer's home, and hadn't been seen since. While the police officer later turned up alive, the Underwoods' worst fears about their son were confirmed.

Professor F. S. Jacoby, head of the poultry department at the waterlogged Ohio State University, with 192 acres underneath the spreading Olentangy River, spent much of his day in the basement of the instruction building, trying to save two thousand eggs that were due to hatch in two days. He had put the students to work outside of the building while Jacoby caulked the basement windows—and apparently the doors leading to the basement—with paper and heavy cloth.

Jacoby couldn't have been thinking too clearly, or he didn't realize just how high the water was rising outside, or he would have realized he was effectively trapping himself in the basement.

Outside, the river was surrounding the poultry building. Jacoby's students, unable to come after their professor, ran for their lives, taking with them a slew of baby chicks. As many as 150 hens were swept away by the flood; another 150 managed to fly to the top of their coop and escape the water. But the ducks inside the duck house probably came to an unfortunate end when it was swept away.

In the basement of the poultry building, Jacoby was oblivious, continuing to caulk the windows. But then he heard a creaking above him, and the professor, an otherwise smart man, understood instantly what was happening. The water was collecting on the floor above him, and the ceiling was about to cave in. On him.

Racing up the stairs that had become a waterfall, Jacoby left the room seconds before the ceiling collapsed on the basement and its two thousand eggs. Jacoby reached the attic of the building and remained there for the rest of the day until rescuers, alerted by his students who had escaped to a nearby farm, came and found him.

While most of the professors and students at Ohio State University would get through the day without such a harrowing tale, there were other close calls. Two students capsized in a canoe on Town Street, saving their lives by clinging to a telegraph pole. A police officer made his way to them in a rowboat, but then he also was thrown into the drink. The officer reached the pole, climbing up it and joining the two college men sitting on the top.

From a building, two men threw a one-inch-thick rope to the two students and officer stranded on the telegraph pole. They tied it fast and then, hand over hand, the students and officer dangled from the rope and made their way to the building.

Other people didn't face certain death but were just as resourceful. As the floodwaters crept toward their house, George Roller and his family managed to lead their cow through the kitchen door and then upstairs, where, for five days, they and their neighbors drank fresh milk.

But sometimes, no matter what, all the ingenuity, resourcefulness, or patience wasn't enough. Dr. Robert J. Sharp, fifty-nine years old, in his little corner of Columbus, watched horrific scenes from his house with his wife, Lillie, and their adopted nine-year-old daughter, Dorothy. Their house was safe—eighty-four feet above the floodwaters—but according to a letter he would later send his brother, he saw one man in a tree, holding two children, while his twelve-year-old daughter stood on one of the branches beside him. The wife and mother had already drowned, according to Sharp. They were in the tree all day and night, and by his count, after thirty-five hours of being in the branches, the exhausted twelve-year-old fell into the river.

Sharp—who was never clear whether he witnessed this particular event or heard about it—also shared details of a ten-year-old girl who was seen riding a hen coop, with a stick in her hands, screaming as she was being carried along. A delivery man, or an express man as they were often called, was in his wagon when he saw her, and his horses broke into a gallop. Just as the horses caught up, and the express man had a chance to reach down for the girl and attempt a daring rescue, the undercurrent caught the coop, which disappeared under the water. The delivery man jumped from the wagon, plunging into the waters after her, and they both drowned.

Chapter Eight

From Bad to Worse

March 25, Tuesday
2:12 P.M., Hamilton, Ohio

The Cincinnati, Hamilton & Indianapolis railroad bridge collapsed.

Collapsing bridges during a major flood was as natural and expected as the water itself. On March 22, the day before Omaha's tornado, the fragility of bridges was underscored in Vermont during a train trip from Montreal to Boston. Engineer John Eastman knew the rivers in the area had been overwhelmed and was on the lookout for questionable bridges. When he approached one particular bridge, he noticed that an abutment looked vulnerable, and he slammed on the air brakes.

The passenger cars never touched the bridge, but the train engine stopped on the structure, and as soon as the train came to a halt, it was moving again, downward, careening into the Passumpsic River. Eastman jumped from the engine, landed in the river, and swam to shore. But what really shook up Eastman, his crew, and the 125 passengers was what they learned when they reached the town of Lyndonville, Vermont, to wait for another train to take them on to Boston:

two other bridges behind them had collapsed, shortly after Eastman's train had crossed them.

During the Great Flood of 1913, particularly from March 23 to March 27 but also well into April, thousands of bridges were destroyed, from steel structures to wooden trestles to small footbridges. That even the steel bridges were going down must have been dismaying to many bridge builders, although the concrete industry as a whole couldn't help but feel smug because more often than not, their bridges were withstanding the flood.

In 1913, Daniel B. Luten, an eminent bridge designer and engineer, wrote an article for a booklet published by the Lehigh Portland Cement Company, in which he praised concrete and noted how frequently steel bridges had gone down.

"Concrete is a material which is practically everlasting and when proper and reasonable precautions in construction are taken, will withstand fire, flood and storm," wrote Luten, whereas the other bridges weren't so fortunate: "Steel and wooden bridges went out by the hundreds and thousands. Along the Wabash river in Indiana, two steel bridges were wrecked at Peru, six at Logansport, and two at Lafayette, practically destroying all communication across the river at some of these cities, except for concrete bridges at Peru and at Georgetown below Logansport, both of which remained standing."

He noted that three steel bridges on stone piers collapsed in Indianapolis and pointed out that in Zanesville, Ohio, the reinforced concrete bridge over the Muskingum River, "one of the first large concrete bridges erected in the United States, effectively resisted the flood. The only damage was the destruction of the hand rails which apparently had not been reinforced."

He went on, but his point was clear: the way of the future, at least when it came to building bridges, was concrete. A trade publication in 1913, *Cement and Engineering News*, was quick to pounce on Luten's article once it was published.

Of course, steel-bridge builders were not convinced that steel bridges were inferior to concrete. They still aren't. It's an issue still being debated today. And yet you never knew what bridge might end up holding. In Columbus, Ohio, according to some accounts, the only bridge that wasn't destroyed was the Rich Street Bridge, which fifteen years earlier had been declared unsafe by engineers.

But there was little question that bridges needed improving. During the days, weeks, and months after the floods, train routes were constantly being changed in order to get people from Point A to Point B; in the aftermath of the deluge, one could never easily get there from here. Possibly because so many deaths were associated with bridges lost in the 1913 flood, at least two of the rebuilt bridges became stuck with a haunted label. To this day, it is said, mysterious lights occasionally appear late at night around Ellis Bridge, near Zanesville, Ohio. Everett Road Covered Bridge near Cleveland was allegedly haunted before the flood of 1913—long before 1913, on the previous bridge, a woman trying to cross it during a flood was killed—but the creepy factor wasn't helped when the bridge was destroyed in 1913 and had to be rebuilt.

The bridges going down—and the miles of railroad track submerged under rivers and creeks—created a lot of trouble for Albert E. Dutoit, a train engineer who found himself in the midst of a challenge Tuesday. When the engineer was in Toledo and unable to travel any further, he received a message that read, "Track out at Columbus because of floods," and immediately, Dutoit began worrying about his family.

In a move that could now be declared James Bond-esque, Dutoit detached his engine from the rest of the train—no word on what the passengers, if there were any, thought of this change in plans—and sped ahead on the tracks anyway. At top speed, he spent all of Tuesday on railroad tracks, avoiding suspect bridges and searching for the most direct route from Toledo to Columbus.

Mid-afternoon, Dayton

Things had finally gone from bad to worse.

Not every person in Greater Dayton was struggling to stay alive on March 24, 1913, but it sure seemed like it.

Firemen and policemen were out en masse, saving everyone they could and putting themselves in danger the entire time. Edward Doudna was trying to rescue a family on West Third Street. According to Allan W. Eckert's book, *A Time of Terror: The Great Dayton Flood*, Doudna lost his balance in a boat and plunged into the river. His fire boots filled with water; his heavy clothing soaked up every drop, and the weight of his wardrobe simply pulled him under, and the current and lack of oxygen did the rest.

Some people were seen in the streets, clinging to debris. J. R. Finnell, who worked in publishing, later reported that he saw ropes being dangled from a bridge, in the hopes that the people hanging on to driftwood and floating by would be able to grab the rope. One can't help but think, over a hundred years later, that it sounds like a perverse stunt in a reality show, grab the rope to get out of the rapids and earn some prize money or move on to the next level. Only this was all too real, the prize was life or probable death, and in the half hour that Finnell watched, none of these contestants managed to grab the rope.

But maybe the better analogy for what Finnell and others were enduring is a war zone. A physician, a Dr. G. S. Staub, had just delivered a baby—or as he put it later, in 1913 terms, "I had just delivered a woman in confinement," when a house nearby exploded. Two elderly ladies, seventy-nine and eighty-three years old, were stuck in their home, and when one of them tried to light their gas stove, it blew up and set fire to their house and the women.

In flames, the women jumped into the water. One quickly drowned, but the other caught hold of some wreckage. Dr. Staub and a man named Frank Yenger came up to her in a boat and brought the elderly lady into the boat. Her face was badly burned, Dr. Staub recounted later, and her hands were so badly damaged that her fingernails dropped off. She died four days later.

From the Miami Valley Hospital, deep in downtown Dayton where rescuers couldn't reach anyone, nurses and patients watched, feeling sheer terror but being able to do nothing, as a woman lay on the top of a pointed roof. She clung to the top, called the ridgepole, and then, as the flood lapped at her feet, she climbed back and sat on top of the roof. But the rain was pounding at her, and it was cold—a little above freezing—and she was rapidly losing her strength. She kept losing her footing and would slide down the roof, managing to stop herself just in time and climb back to the top. She did this for more than an hour until finally she couldn't crawl back to the top of the roof and just rolled into the wild river.

At the Beckel House, the guests who stayed behind—and those who retreated to the sturdy bank building several buildings away but returned to eat—were pleased to realize that there was ample food on the second floor waiting for them. Not much to drink, however, and thus many people resorted to collecting rain water. Walter Jones, the judge, was impressed that the staff of the Beckel House didn't make any distinction between the guests and people off the street who had come in for shelter. Everyone was entitled to whatever food was available.

Most of the afternoon, the guests stared outside, at noisy and never-ending currents, at least twelve to fourteen feet deep, as far as Jones could tell. In the front of the hotel, Jones watched the world pass by: driftwood, chairs, counters, shelving, barrels, boxes, crates of fruit from a grocery, pianos, piles of lumber, and occasionally a struggling, drowning horse. That pained him to see, although it was even worse going in the back of the hotel. Horses that had been released from a nearby stable seemed to be cornered in, in the back, struggling in the water, and occasionally surrendering to it.

When he wasn't staring outside, Jones would occasionally go to his room on the fourth floor, just to look at it. The floor was sunken in. In the room below his, the floor was completely gone, having collapsed onto the second and first floor and somewhere in the basement. Jones was told by a jewelry salesman that his trunks, with $30,000 worth of wares in them, had been in one of those rooms and was now floating somewhere in the basement.

Mostly, though, Jones stayed on the second floor with the remaining Beckel House guests, where everyone talked among themselves, the discussion likely sticking with the flood or wondering what family members back home thought of all this. Jones was worried about his wife, Laura, who he had married back in 1879, and their daughter, also named Laura but whom everyone called Lola. He also likely thought about his grandchildren, Randolph and Charlotte.

It seems likely that a nineteenth-century poet and novelist, Jean Ingelow, came up in conversation at one point, either among some of the guests or perhaps between just Jones and Lucia May Wiant, director of physical training for Dayton Public Schools, who lived at the Beckel House. Ingelow had written a well-known poem entitled "The High Tide on the Coast of Lincolnshire," about a devastating sea tide, and both Jones, when he wrote about the flood later, and Wiant, when she penned an article about the flood for an educational journal, mentioned Ingelow's poem. In fact, they each quoted the same passage from Ingelow's 176-line poem:

> ". . . the heart had hardly time to beat
> Before a shallow, seething wave
> Sobbed on the ground beneath our feet.
> The feet had hardly time to flee,
> Before it broke against the knee,
> And all the world was in the sea."

The guests watched out the windows at the muddy sea, climbing higher and higher up the outside of the buildings, and wondered how high it could go.

Jones and his fellow guests also kept a close eye on their own building. Nobody knew why the northwest corner of the Beckel House had collapsed. While the water seemed a likely culprit, the collapse had occurred quite early in the flood, and several people speculated that a small boiler might have exploded in the basement.

"We made and enforced a peremptory order that not a match should be struck in the house," wrote Jones later in a religious newspaper, the *Herald of Gospel Liberty*, published by the United Church of Christ. "From the very first, the dread of fire was on the heart of everyone. One fellow tried to light a pipe but was properly taken care of. We had, as far as I know, no other such creature among us."

Many Dayton residents were afraid—if not for themselves, for their loved ones who they couldn't find. Still having no idea where their father had been taken, or if the canoe he was in might have overturned, Orville Wright and his sister Katharine posted signs in the neighborhood they were staying in that alerted passers-by that they were looking for their father. They also told any stranger they encountered that they were searching for Bishop Milton Wright. But so far, as the day wore on, they had heard nothing.

John P. Foose, then a 74-year-old Dayton resident and the Civil War veteran who sent his daughters to look at the river after being awakened at 4:30 A.M., was certainly worried, if not for himself, for his city. He described what he saw Tuesday from his home in a letter to his brother: "Boats moved past the house with old men and women in the last stages of dejection and despair. Some sat in boats with bowed heads, holding to the sides, expecting every moment to be overturned. Some boatmen were unable to manage the boats for there was a terrific current sweeping past the house. Small and large sheds and stables, even small houses swept past."

Probably only the children managed to enjoy the flood. Dayton resident Rita Rosemary Abel Gabel recalled in her memoirs of helping her father carry books upstairs and then walking on the floorboards, unable to hear the usual sound of her footsteps on the wooden floor and being told that it was because water was right on the other side. Not long afterward, a rescue boat—probably one from NCR—came for her family, and they climbed into it from the second-story window.

"I remember Daddy, the last one into the boat, turning around and carefully closing the window," wrote Gabel. "There we started up the street toward the Main Street Bridge with the man telling us to be sure to duck under the streetcar trolley wires. I, clutching my beloved teddy bear, wasn't the least bit scared, just excited at all that was going on."

2:30–3:30 P.M., Dayton, Ohio

On the roof of the building that housed O. G. Saettel's and William Paterson's saloon, Lydia Saettel prepared to board the boat with her eight-month-old baby, Oliver, Jr., or Ollie, as they called him. Her father-in-law, George, warily eyed the rescue boat and the current and suggested she leave the baby with him.

"No way," Lydia is said to have said, and with the baby and the store's cash wrapped in a baby blanket, left with the rescuers. Her husband, Oliver, had already gone ahead, which sounds a little odd at first—isn't it women and children first?—but the Saettels' thinking was that Oliver could find a place for them to stay and either return or send someone back for them.

George stayed behind for reasons unclear, and so did another two tenants: Caroline "Carrie" Schunk, the 36-year-old wife of a barber, and possibly her baby. It may be that there wasn't room for them, and the rescue boat was going to come back; or, it seems more likely, since

George wanted Ollie to stay behind, that neither Carrie or George liked the looks of the water and felt that they were safer waiting out the flood on the building. It's understandable—climbing into a boat from your second-story window, when the waves are splashing into your home, has to be a terrifying idea. Even so, it was a tragic miscalculation on their part.

For about an hour later, there was an explosion in the building. A neighbor, Lillie H. Kilpatrick, believed it came from the saloon, although some would suggest it was a gas leak in the basement, and still others said Mrs. Schunk was lighting the stove to warm up milk for her baby.

People for miles heard the explosion. George Saettel and Carrie Schunk were hurled into the air, along with burning embers, or wood, which landed in the loft of a nearby stable, still untouched by the water and filled with hay. It quickly caught on fire. Then the flames shot across the street and onto several other homes. That the other homes were damp and drenched didn't matter; they caught on fire anyway. The interior of the buildings' walls, not to mention the second stories, which still had ample carpeting, bedding, clothing, and furniture in them, provided plenty of fuel for the fire.

Incredibly, when Saettel came crashing onto terra firma, he was alive, and he landed on another roof.

A floating roof.

She should have been blown into oblivion, but Mrs. Schunk landed in the water and incredibly had enough presence of mind to cling to a spike in a telegraph pole about twelve or fifteen feet away from one of the buildings. But Carrie Schunk, while alive, was not well. Her clothes were in shreds, and so was the skin on her face and hands. She shrieked for help.

Saettel wasn't much better off than Mrs. Schunk. Like her, he was injured and the roof he landed on wasn't attached to a building. It was a rogue roof, wedged against the building Harry Lindsey lived in and across the street from the grocery store.

Saettel had family members who also lived across the street, and he was about two buildings away from his sister-in-law Mellie Meyer's home, where she, her son Ralph, her niece Norma Thoma and the rest of the Thoma family were camped out. Some of the family and possibly all of them saw the patriarch of their family clinging to the floating roof.

Across the street, George Timmerman, the moulder trapped in an attic with a mother and three kids, had heard the explosion and ran to the window to look across the street and see the walls of the grocery store collapsing into the wild river. If Timmerman and his group saw Saettel and Mary Schunk, and he must have, he didn't say. What his group positively saw was the fire. It quickly spread to a stable and then a stack of hay. It wouldn't take long for an inferno to skip from the stable and mow down the buildings until it had reached them.

Everyone in the immediate vicinity was terrified, and everyone tried something different to escape the burning homes, which burned slowly enough, possibly because everything was so wet from the rain; but by the end, nine homes on the east side of Main Street would go down and then spread to the west side, where four more houses went down in flames. In order to escape, Lillie Kilpatrick and her uncle and some neighbors had to get to a bakery, ten feet away from their own building, which they did by building a bridge made of bed slats. After that, they climbed into a shed and used it as a raft.

Harry Lindsey had thirteen neighbors and family trapped in his home. They all went from building to building until they were able to hail a rescuer in a boat who made multiple trips to bring everyone to safety. After three trips, though, the rescuer pled exhaustion and wouldn't make any more. There was just one more trip needed and three people to save; people pleaded, and after begging and offering the man fifteen dollars, he finally relented.

After shouting unsuccessfully for help, Timmerman and his group quickly climbed up to the roof, where they started going from one building to another. They didn't have a lot of time to waste.

Meanwhile, injured and weak, both Carrie Schunk and George Saettel were still floundering in the water, still trying to stave off the inevitable. Nobody could reach either of them, although two young men got into a boat and rowed toward Mrs. Schunk. The current sent them flying past her, though, and they were unable to catch hold of her, which may have been just as well since their boat capsized. The men swam to the barn, stopping there only for a moment since it was on fire, and navigated their way to a tree and then to another home.

It took about half an hour or maybe even sixty minutes, but Carrie finally lost her strength and became lost in the watery, yellow churn. George Saettel could only hold on to his floating, unsteady roof, which was bobbing up and down violently—and then watch disbelievingly as about twenty horses passed him in the water, struggling to swim and stay afloat, their hooves frantically struggling to find firm footing. Around Saettel and his loved ones and neighbors watching him, the fires only grew in intensity. Making matters worse, other houses, unmoored and floating, crashed into the fire, making the blaze instantly bigger.

Driftwood and debris kept ramming into it, chipping away at the only thing holding the 66-year-old man up. Finally, the roof Saettel was holding on to couldn't hold his weight, and the grocer was adrift again and flowing with the current. He was never seen alive again. His family—and Harry Lindsey, who had been helping his son move his goods earlier in the day—would be haunted by the experience for the rest of their lives.

As Saettel and Schunk fought for their lives, smoke was blowing toward Timmerman, the mother, and children, with the flames closing in, and they were all screaming and crying, running up one roof slope, down another. The houses were close enough, or adjoining, so they could go from roof to roof, but it was an exhausting run across about a dozen roofs, with the flames slowly but methodically giving chase.

And then they suddenly realized they could go no farther. They were out of houses.

Timmerman looked around in the water, hoping to find something useful, like a boat; but all he saw within reach was some driftwood and some hulking figure in the water, possibly a dead horse or maybe a human. There was something else that he found himself looking at, but he could hardly contemplate what he was considering. Telephone wires were jutting out from the home, stretching over the water, and he could see that, far off, maybe six blocks, there were people in buildings. They might be trapped, too, but it looked as if the people were in a lot better control of their situation than Timmerman and his comrades were of theirs. Certainly, there was no fire six blocks away.

But it would be insanely dangerous and impossible for the children to attempt.

Timmerman, however, believed he could walk along the telephone wires, and if he could get somewhere else, maybe he could send help to the mother and child. The mother agreed, although she probably felt she didn't have much choice but to agree.

He started onto the wire, the way everyone did—hands on one wire, and feet on a wire below. If his foot slipped, he would have to hope that his hands could hold his weight. Therefore, he promised himself he would not slip. He walked as carefully as possible and as quickly as he dared. But it wasn't just a nerve-racking exercise; it was actually exercise. His muscles tense, Timmerman sweated in the cold March air, constantly wondering if there would be a point when his arms and legs would simply give out and he would drop into the water.

It became painfully clear to George Saettel's family, once their patriarch was gone, that they couldn't remain where they were.

There was no time to pull a Timmerman and walk along the roofs, looking for an escape route. It was right there in front of them, and they would have to do what many Dayton residents, including Timmerman, as it turned out, were doing: walk across the telephone cables.

Using a wooden plank, sticking out of the window, one end weighted down inside the home and the other end resting on a telephone wire, Mellie Meyer, Ralph, and Norma walked onto the wood. Their feet were planted on one wire; their hands grabbed on to one of the wires above it. Then they began to walk along the cable. Norma's father may have been there, holding one of Norma's younger sisters. Even if that wasn't the case, there are accounts of several parents who navigated the wires, with their young, terrified children hanging on to them.

Norma, like many girls, changed out of her dress and put on men's clothing, knowing that it would be warmer and easier to maneuver in. She and her family carefully made their way down the street on the telephone cables. Below them was the water, rushing past them and between the buildings in downtown Dayton, carrying everything from nails and plywood and dead horses and Model T Fords to fallen trees.

One newspaper account in the *Hartford Herald*, Hartford, Kentucky's paper, described Mellie's maneuvering over the telephone wire: "When just over the boiling torrent beneath, she swayed as though faint, slipped and the crowd stood with abated breath. By a lucky chance her senses came back to her in time and she grasped one of the wires."

George Timmerman kept walking the wires. It was exhausting, and he kept having to try and stop, recalibrating his grip and, while doing so, doing his best to rest. The crowd, six blocks and less away, had now noticed him and were shouting words of encouragement. Timmerman even saw some people he knew and heard them shouting his name. But Timmerman, every step of the way, was sure he was stepping his last. Then his cap blew or fell off his head, and he could hear the crowd gasp, as if anticipating he would go next.

Finally, after six blocks, Timmerman was able to climb down a telephone pole to what was actual dry land, a hill where rescuers were waiting for him. Timmerman had reached the National Cash Register headquarters. By now, Timmerman was described as being in a "semi-hysterical condition," sobbing, crying, and quivering, but he did sputter to self-appointed rescuers that he had left a mother and three children behind who desperately needed saving before passing out. Along with numerous other flood refugees, he was carried into the National Cash Register headquarters.

About the time a boat was being sent for the stranded mother and three children—they were rescued, Timmerman would later be told—Norma Thoma and her family members had walked the wires for three blocks. At that point, a rescuer, possibly alerted by Timmerman to the fact that other people still needed help, was waiting and climbed the telephone pole to help the family down into a boat, where they were carried to safety.

Eventually, the family made their way, like so many, to the NCR headquarters. A reporter captured the exchange that Norma had with one of the workers who was taking the names of the flood refugees.

"What's your name?"

"Norma Thoma."

Apparently, Norma was wearing a hat with her men's clothes because the registrar sounded surprised. "Norma?"

"Yes, I'm a girl," she said.

Ralph Meyer, Norma's cousin, was with her. According to the reporter, Meyer was accompanied by his wife and their three-month-old baby, which would be news to Ralph's descendants. He was only seventeen at the time, and, to the best of their knowledge, not married yet and not a father. Still, even if the reporter got some of the names and information wrong, it sounds as if there was some set of young parents and a baby that day who made their way across telephone wires to safety.

Over on the top of the telephone building, John Bell remained at his post, patching the city's most important people through to the outside world when he could, and keeping both the governor and the occasional reporter informed of what was happening in the city.

Bell could only know what he was seeing, but from the top of his four-story building, he saw enough to know that his city was falling apart. Far off in the distance, he watched buildings on fire. There were at least two going on: the one that started at Saettel's, and another that had broken out at an ice cream factory just outside the business center. Meanwhile, the entire business section of Dayton was like a stormy lake, at least ten to twelve feet deep, he told a reporter listening in Phoneton.

Bell was wet—it began raining again—and he was exhausted from lack of sleep but supremely grateful to be on a building that didn't seem to be planning on going anywhere. His gratitude expanded whenever he saw someone who would have given anything to have traded places with him. He watched two men rowing a boat, desperately trying to keep it afloat. They were unsuccessful. They managed to grab a lamp post, however, and clung to it for half an hour before someone managed to throw a rope to them. The men were pulled into the second-story window of the nearest building.

Bell saw quite a few objects floating past the building that looked like bundles of clothing. He eventually came to the sickening realization that he was seeing bodies.

But what must have been even worse, the stuff post-traumatic stress is made from, was the sight of a woman and a child on top of a house floating by. The woman was screaming and begging for help while her child lay still at her feet. Bell watched from afar until the house was carried over a dam and he could see them no more.

Chapter Nine

Desperation

Casper Sareu, the workhouse prisoner who was caught up in the flood and then a passenger on a raft, was coming to the end of his travels. For a while, he had drifted among voting houses, which were popular in cities and were just what they sound like. They were small houses built for the express intent of voting for elected officials; they began to go out of favor as the population grew, and communities started using schools and other public buildings more frequently to give a place for people to vote. The voting houses had easily come off their foundations and were bobbing up and down, menacingly. They were small buildings, but they were still buildings, and they came close to crushing Sareu.

From there, Sareu's raft took him past a butcher's shop, where stranded men unsuccessfully tried to throw ropes to him.

After Sareu's raft took him between two floating houses, which threatened to flatten him into a human pancake, he began to lose any hope of being rescued. His luck started to turn, however, when he floated near the car barns, or garages that housed the streetcars and where maintenance workers did repairs. Some of the car men saw

Sareu and threw a rope. He grabbed it, but knowing he lacked the strength to hang on to it if they pulled him in, he tied it around his waist. They did reel him in, and Sareu spent the rest of the day and night with his saviors—with very little food among them. The next morning, a boat picked him up and took him to dry land, where Sareu would give himself up to an incredulous police officer.

3 P.M., Dayton, Ohio

The residence of Aunt Fannie and Uncle Ottie Fries, where the Adamses were hiding out, now had a few inches of water making its home on the first floor of their house on Warder Street. The road itself, which was always a bit of a trench, being four feet deeper than the front yards, was now a swiftly moving river itself, six or seven feet deep and getting deeper by the moment.

Fannie and Ottie's furnace was long submerged, and of course the gas and water supplies were shut off. As the Adamses had discussed for the last few hours, it was going to be a cold night, with no food, and they had two babies to consider. The last thing they wanted their children to catch was pneumonia or to be thirsty and hungry. So they shouted until they were able to hail a rescuer in a boat, which thankfully were plentiful in this part of the city. The rescuer's first name was Carl. His last name was the unfortunately prophetic Sinks.

Charles told Carl Sinks they wanted to go to what was now known as the Geyer Street landing, or to a rescue center that had been set up at Forest and Grand Avenues, all around two or three blocks away. That proximity between their house and the rescue center may have given Charles and Viola a false sense of security.

The babies were both wrapped in shawls, and the grownups were in heavy overcoats. They climbed into the boat, rocking in the current. Once they were all in, Carl Sinks pushed the boat away from the porch railing, and like a roller coaster lurching forward, the current caught its coaster, whipping it forward—and into the tree in the front yard.

The boat flipped over. Everyone fell into the water.

In her heavy overcoat, Viola screamed "Hon, I'm drowning," as the waves ripped her baby son from her arms. Grandpa Adams lunged for Christopher, Jr., scooping up the baby, as Charles, holding on to Lois, reached for Viola.

In doing so, Charles somehow—he was never sure how it happened—loosened his grip on Lois, who was sucked into the current. The girl, just a month shy of her first birthday, disappeared into the rapids. He would never forgive himself for that.

But there was no time to even think about what had just happened. In nine-foot-deep freezing and muddy water, Charles was fighting to save his wife's life; Grandpa John Adams, holding on to his grandson as tightly as possible, was trying to gain footing on a terrace or porch that he felt beneath him, but couldn't and found himself swept down the current; Carl Sinks, too, was swept away.

In the background—not that Charles, Viola, Grandpa Adams, and the others could hear over the river—frantic neighbors screamed, unable to do anything, although across the street from the Fries' home, a neighbor, Dr. Charles Whitney, remembered an old pistol that he had in the house. He searched his house, found it, and fired his revolver into the air, a known signal of distress. His hope was that someone would come with a boat or a rope. Harold Miller, a rescuer in a boat too far away to do anything useful, began shouting as well. Bill Chryst, a neighbor and an engineer, came running when his wife shouted for him, and right away he knew he had to try to do something.

Viola and Charles managed to each get an arm across the upturned boat and swam with it to a small tree sapling about a hundred feet away, where Grandpa Adams and Carl Sinks had landed. They were each hanging on to a branch, desperately trying not to be carried off.

They let go of the boat, which had sunk but lodged itself into the tree, and with his right hand, Charles hung on to a tree branch and with his left tried to steady Viola. Their long, soaked overcoats, weighing them down, made survival even harder, but somehow they kept glued to the slight tree. As much as he could, Charles braced himself with one foot in the underside of the boat, but his raincoat kept getting in the way of his feet.

Once they seemed to be able to stay put for the moment, Viola asked the question she must have been terrified to ask but had to: "Where are the babies?"

"I have one," said Grandpa Adams.

"Which one is it?" Viola asked.

Grandpa Adams wasn't sure—they were twins, after all, and they were being rained on and struggling to hang on to a tree—but he turned the baby's face to their parents. Charles, Jr. Both parents forced themselves to look downstream. Just below them, in the branches of another tree near their own, was a white shawl, dangling in the water. There was no Lois inside it.

Just then, Charles, Viola, Grandpa Adams, and Carl Sinks could see Bill Chryst wading toward them. It became too deep, however, and everyone realized he was risking his life as he started swimming toward them. Chryst wasn't much of a swimmer, but he reached the tree. It was probably about then that it occurred to him that he had no rope, no boat, and no way of getting any of these tree-bound people back to shore, but he was nonetheless a big help. Chryst's energy hadn't been sapped by the cold water—yet—and he was able to help the others stay tethered to the tree.

It seemed like hours that they hung there. The shouting didn't stop. There were more gunshots. The roar of the river was unceasing. It kept raining. But eventually Charles saw a man rowing a boat, a man he recognized, John Ryan, a fellow member of the Knights of Pythias, a club that they both were members of and an organization that had been around since 1864. Charles shouted like he never had before, and was certain, as the boat was rowing away, that Ryan hadn't heard him.

But Ryan had. He was trying to figure out a way to reach them in the formidable current. Once he arrived, Bill Chryst and Charles Adams helped Viola into the boat. She then asked for the baby, and Grandpa Adams carefully handed over her son.

Viola gratefully accepted the baby, and then, from Charles's point of view, she suddenly disappeared. Bewildered, Charles realized when Viola had reached for Charles, Jr., she had tipped the boat slightly, and waves flooded it, knocking it over. John Ryan lunged for one of the tree branches, but Viola and her baby son weren't as fortunate. They had been swept away. Just like that. One moment they were near death and then almost saved, and now they were gone again.

Charles would later remember the memory only vaguely, like looking at a faded negative of a film. "I can just dimly see them sinking into that seething river," he would write.

Charles held on to the tree, but only out of instinct. He was aghast and empty. His father could see it.

"Hold on, my boy, don't let go," Grandpa Adams kept shouting.

Charles kept trying to think of reasons why not to let go. His wife and babies were gone. He had been supposed to watch over them, and he had failed. And there was no boat to save him. Why hang on?

He probably would have let go, but almost immediately another boat arrived. Two firemen, Jack Korn and Warren Marquardt, had heard a gunshot, brought their boat to the tree, and pulled in Charles and Grandpa Adams. The other men—Bill Chryst, Carl Sinks, and John Ryan—would be safely rescued soon after.

Once Charles rolled into the boat, he lay on the floor, shivering and teeth chattering and barely able to move, except for his shaking. The conversation—in the rain and wind and with the backdrop of the roar of the river—must have been a jumble of shouts and confusion. Following instinct more than anything else, Charles told Korn and Marquardt to take him back to the house of Reverend Fries, where he had started this journey of death. They obliged, somehow steering the boat through the current toward the house. While Charles lay in a heap, wanting to die, Korn and Marquardt interrupted his thoughts and informed him that his wife and son had been rescued.

Viola Adams couldn't shed her overcoat, which may have been what kept her alive. It was suggested later that the coat, spread out over the water, kept her buoyant. Still, as she fought the deadly current, she kept going under and swallowing water. But somehow, a man named Dudley Artz, manning a boat and rowing against the current on Warder Street, spotted her and came to her rescue just as Viola was going under the water for a third time.

If someone was going to be drowning and seconds mattered, you couldn't pick a better person to scoop you up. Artz was a charter member of the nearby Stillwater Canoe Club, and neighbors watching reported that he somehow rolled Viola, waterlogged overcoat and all, into his boat without any significant water going into the craft.

Once ashore, a Dr. D.E. Miller took immediate charge of Viola, but after it was clear she didn't have any water in her lungs, Dudley Artz and Miller had trouble finding anyone to take the young mother into a house, where she could get warmth and rest. Artz's brother ended up accepting her.

Charles, Jr., meanwhile, had been separated from his mother and, like a ragdoll being carried by the current, washed down Warder Street and onto Geyer Street, and that should have been that for the little baby, but he had a guardian angel in another rescuer in a boat, an Elbert Riley who had two women in the back of his boat. Riley was fighting for his and his passenger's lives, trying to steer clear of a whirlpool that was creating an island of lumber and debris. Just as he was clearing it, someone from some apartments—the Folsom Apartments—shouted: *"Get that baby out of the water!"*

That voice, which would never be identified, saved Christopher, Jr. Riley looked down into the water and for a second, he could see an object under the surface, sinking and heading into the whirlpool. Taking an oar out of its socket, while trying to avoid being sucked into an eddy, was an incredibly brave and risky move, but Riley decided to chance it. He stretched his oar right where he thought the baby might be. When he raised the oar, he discovered it had caught the baby, scooping him up, flat on his stomach.

Riley pulled the baby and oar into the boat and quickly dumped the wet, dying infant into the laps of the women, who screamed.

Riley shouted at them to hold the baby in their laps, so that the baby was face down, allowing any water to possibly spill out of his mouth and lungs. Then he threw the oar back into its socket and rowed as hard as he could, trying to keep them all from crashing into the whirl-pool and its pile of debris.

When they reached dry land, Elbert Riley and his passengers must have been stricken. The infant he had fished out of the water wasn't breathing. But Dr. Miller was nearby and feverishly began trying to get the water out of the lungs of Charles Otterbein Adams, Jr. For what seemed the longest time, Miller kept at it, while a miserable crowd watched. Then suddenly the baby offered a little cry, and for the doctor and crowd, it was the happiest sound imaginable.

Stunned to hear that Viola and Charles, Jr. were alive, Charles pushed himself up, enough that he could look over the side of the boat. About a block away, he could see a woman in a boat, wearing a black coat, whom he assumed was Viola. What shape she was in, he didn't know. He didn't see Charles, Jr., but he took the men's word for it that his son had been rescued. The idea of asking the men to take him to his wife and son apparently didn't occur to Charles, or, more likely, everyone recognized that they just couldn't, given the current and Charles's current condition. He was in no shape to do anything.

Grandpa Adams was just as wet and cold as Charles but probably drew strength from seeing his son exhausted and then euphoric again and knowing that Viola and Charles, Jr., were nearby and alive. Grandpa Adams told Korn and Marquardt to take him on to the landing on Geyer Street. He would find them.

At Uncle Ottie and Aunt Fannie's house, it became a group effort and family activity to get Charles warmed up. Uncle Ottie gave Charles a rubdown with liniment. He also put some liniment in some water and gave it to Charles to drink. It would never be advised today to drink liniment, a liquid often used to help muscle fatigue, but back in the day, ads for products like Sloan's Liniment would suggest: "For growing youngsters, give 10 drops of Sloan's Liniment to ten youngsters in half a pint of moist mash twice a week only. Put five drops of Sloan's Liniment in every quart of drinking water."

The ingredients in Sloan's Liniment included turpentine.

It didn't seem to hurt Charles, however, who remarked that what he really needed was a shot of whiskey. The family then got Charles, who was shaking violently, into a bed between woolen blankets.

It didn't work, he soon realized. He couldn't sleep. His mind was likely too littered, wondering where Viola and Charles were and thinking about poor Lois. His legs were also in pain and still freezing.

Charles climbed to his feet and tried to walk, hoping to improve his circulation. But his pacing did little good. He soon decided to climb back into bed.

March 25, 4 P.M., Delaware, Ohio

There was one bit of good news that papers were able to report to their readers. Mayor Bertrand V. Leas of Delaware, Ohio was seen marooned on the second floor of a building surrounded by water. He wasn't dead, as had been believed. Rescuers were doing what they could to reach him. He had, at this point, been sitting on the roof of this building for the last fourteen hours.

March 25, 4 P.M., Indianapolis

The water had risen enough that streetcar service and water service had ended, and, because there was no water, the city would have to do without fire protection as well. Fire Chief Charles E. Coots eventually would resort to bringing a cistern, which is often used to catch rainwater, and, with a machine called a pumping engine, his men could pump water from the cistern through a hose. It was a crude way of fighting fires, but it was better than nothing.

But all in all, Indianapolis was holding its own. It had stopped raining earlier in the day, and while the rivers, particularly the White River, were rising, the streets weren't yet flooded.

The electric and gas were still on, although many people worried that if there was, say, a gas explosion, that lack of a functioning fire department might be a problem. If there was good news for anyone in the city of Indianapolis, which had an estimated six square miles of its downtown underwater, it may have been for the hotel owners. By nightfall, due to an influx of residents driven from their homes, the hotels were now full. Their existing guests, the ones who had come before the flood and who weren't going anywhere, tended to book for another night as well.

One hotel guest who wasn't happy to be spending the night was Ben Hecht, the cub reporter from the *Chicago Journal*. He had arrived in Indianapolis only to be told that the trains weren't going anywhere remotely close to Dayton, which was about 115 miles to the east. So Hecht found himself holed up at the Claypool Hotel, sitting in the barroom with a crowd of other reporters. Train service was expected to resume the next day. For the moment, the reporters drank, and Hecht listened to tales of adventure from other, older journalists.

He was frustrated to be trapped in a hotel, but he enjoyed the stories. Hecht admired his fellow journalists deeply and idealized his chosen profession. As he wrote years later, "No other profession, even that of arms, produces as fine a version of the selfless hero as journalism does. . . . A good newspaperman, of my day, was to be known by the fact that he was ashamed of being anything else. He scorned offers of double wages in other fields. He sneered at all the honors life held other than the one to which he aspired, which was a simple one. He dreamed of dying in harness, a casual figure full of anonymous power; and free. For the newspaperman, the most harried of employees, more bedeviled by duties than a country doctor, more blindly subservient to his editor than a Marine private to his captain, considered himself, somewhat loonily, to have no boss, to be without superiors and a creature always on his own."

Hecht, listening to his fellow journalists, came to a decision that he kept to himself. He was going to Dayton, train or no train.

Approximately 4 P.M., Tiffin, Ohio

Jacob Knecht, a fifty-year-old sausage maker who worked at the Beckley Meat Market, was trapped on his house with his two sons, Clarence, a 25-year-old with a promising future at the U.S. Glass Company, and Wilson, fifteen years old. Jacob's son-in-law, George Schwab, twenty-two and just four days shy of his twenty-third birthday, was also on the roof.

For many people, the roof could be a sanctuary; but as people in Tiffin were finding out, many houses only had a matter of time before they were washed into oblivion.

Rescuers had determined that they couldn't do anything for Knecht and the young men. The icy water, they calculated, was moving at sixty miles an hour.

The force was too much. People from dry land and from their own homes watched in horror as the Knecht house cracked from its foundation. The entire house exploded into splinters, wood, debris, and memories. Only the roof remained as anything recognizable: it had turned into something of a raft. All four men began screaming for help that their neighbors couldn't give.

They didn't have much chance to ponder the surreal turn of events or to try and enjoy the ride. Up ahead, they could see their fate.

They were headed right for the Huss Street Bridge.

It was dismal luck. Later, the bridge would wash out, and if it had washed out earlier, maybe things would have ended differently for at least some of the men. But because it was there, all four men realized that they didn't have much of a chance if they smashed into it.

So about twenty feet before that alternate fate, the men jumped off. Nobody ever saw Clarence, Wilson, and George alive again.

Jacob Knecht, on the other hand, emerged on the other side of the bridge alive and embraced the top of a willow tree and remained there.

Just outside the United American Mechanics' National Orphans' Home, the man in charge of it, a Mr. Simpson, tried to swim to Knecht, but the water was either too cold or too evil-looking to spend any real time in it. He quickly returned to the riverbank.

Adolph Unger, a West Point cadet, tied a rope around his waist and charged into the freezing water. He attempted to swim, but either his line was too short or the water too wild. He couldn't make it closer than 150 feet and returned to land, a chilly, wet mess.

Men gathered along the shore, throwing out every idea they could come up with to reach Jacob, but fifteen minutes after grabbing the willow tree, freezing and weak, the sausage maker knew he was about to succumb to the inevitable.

"Thanks, good-bye, boys, I'm—" and then the water forced its way into Knecht's mouth, obscuring his last words. He was swept into the river.

After the Knecht house went down, the people watching the Klingshirn house, mostly full of children, became even more determined to somehow get the family out. Considering the Klingshirns could see the Knecht house go down, they must have been even more frantic afterward. Tiffin residents Harry Houck and Don Souder embarked in a boat, with a rope tied to it, to help keep them from losing control and being sent down the current.

Everyone watched, excited as Houck and Souder showed everyone how a rescue was done. They were fighting the waves with their oars, paddling with everything they had, but it was working. Their rowboat was forty feet away from the house. Then thirty. Then twenty-five.

At twenty feet, the rope snapped, and Houck and Souder were sent downstream. Fortunately, they managed to steer themselves to safety.

Houk's son and another neighbor then took off in another rowboat, with another rope tied to them, and approached the house next door to the Klingshirns. They reached the Hostler house, right next door.

Everyone began cheering as the two young men reached the second-story window. Mary Hostler climbed into the boat, holding her baby,

Madeline, swaddled in a heavy blanket. Then they successfully made the perilous journey back to land and into George Klingshirn's arms. Watching them reach land must have been encouraging to the Klingshirns and Ray Hostler watching from next door. Mary and Madeline were Ray's wife and daughter, and Theresa Klingshirn's oldest daughter and granddaughter.

But Houck's son and O'Connell could not navigate their way to the Klingshirns. Even though they were right next door to the Hostlers, in the manner that the current ricocheted off their house, it was too powerful for anyone to reach. George Klingshirn, watching all of this, was visibly horrified, but since he didn't climb into a boat himself, he must have recognized the futility of trying to reach his home. Everyone would have to hope that the foundation of the Klingshirn house was stronger than the Knechts' home.

March 25, late afternoon, Peru, Indiana

The river was four feet deep in the streets surrounding the courthouse and nearby businesses, which might not have been so terrible had the rapids not appeared to be moving as fast as a locomotive. Actual trains, as it were, weren't able to get within two miles of the city; in fact, the train dispatcher for the L. E. & W. Railroad, reported that his office was unusable due to the high water inside: the tables were floating.

Residents, meanwhile, were doing everything they could to ensure the tables were turning. Frank McNally, a 37-year-old butcher, brought his canoe up to a fast-submerging house where two seventeen-year-old cousins lived, Icea Hesser, and Georgia Delight Shields, who had just moved in. Shields's mother, Mattie, was in the house, as was the head of the household and her mother's employer, Thomas Lovatt, a 68-year-old wealthy manufacturer of farm plows, and possibly his seventeen-year-old son, George. It was a complicated household: Lovatt had had an affair in 1896 behind the back of his wife Louisa and kept up his dalliances for several more years until she had had enough and divorced him. From there, he seems to have hired Mattie, who was herself a divorcee, to manage the household.

At first, for a few years, Delight (nobody called her Georgia) appears to have been living with her father, Emery, an insurance salesman—but shortly before the flood, she took a job as a stenographer with Antrim & McClintic, a law firm and moved into the Lovatt house, which by now wasn't just a home to Lovatt and his son George but Mattie and her 66-year-old mother Frances. Mattie's niece, Icea Hesser, who had lost her mother two years earlier, also lived with them.

The community seems to have accepted Lovatt and Mattie's unusual relationship. In the census records, they were never listed as husband and wife. In the 1910 census records, Mattie calls herself Lovatt's daughter, despite her being very much the daughter of William Lovatt, an Ohio farmer, and by 1920, Mattie was referring to herself as Lovatt's "partner" in the household. Whatever their relationship, and it may well have been platonic, in 1913, everyone was referring to Delight as Lovatt's step-daughter. Peru was a small town in an age when gossip spread freely, but that the 68-year-old Lovatt was the richest man in town may have made him impervious to anyone criticizing him for having left his wife and being in a relationship with a woman thirty years his junior.

When McNally came to the house, it was decided that his first two passengers would be Delight and Icea. If the teenage girls were worried about their chances in the boat, McNally wasn't. He had rescued seventy-five people over the last two days.

McNally steered them over Franklin Street, some twenty feet below them, and toward dry land, just as he had dozens of times.

Only this time, something went wrong.

The boat crashed into a house's front porch, shattering into pieces. McNally, Hesser, and Shields were instantly in the river and separated. McNally immediately shouted to the girls to grab something substantial, like a tree or the porch. Then McNally, a strong swimmer, swam toward a tree that Icea had been swept directly into. She grabbed the branches. Delight wasn't so fortunate. The current carried her away from the house and into the street.

Screaming for her didn't help bring her back. She was nowhere to be seen. McNally and Hesser, both distraught, clung to the rain-soaked tree.

Late afternoon, Dayton, Ohio

Grandpa Adams walked along the shoreline of Warder Street, asking everyone he found, who seemed as if they might know, if they had seen a mother and a baby boy sailing by, and if anyone knew what had come of them.

Late afternoon, Columbus, Ohio

Many mothers gave birth during the flood in less than ideal conditions. One woman, who the papers referred to as a Mrs. J. E. Gonschrlitz, gave birth to twins on the second floor of her home, with the first floor flooded, but she had a doctor who was able to get to her and help her and, compared to some of her fellow mothers, she had a pregnancy picnic. On the west end of the Rich Street bridge, improbable as it sounds, a maternity camp was set up and run by a Dr. S. J. Goodman. During the flood, at least ten mothers gave birth here.

But every mother who has gone through natural childbirth should stop what they're doing right now and pay homage to a Mrs. Olmstead. Sadly, her first name, and thus her age and everything else about her, seems to have been lost to history, although the *Columbus Evening Dispatch* reporter apparently did his best, printing the first name of her family physician, Dr. Robert Drury, and the patrolman, Edward E. Shaw, and Fred Masters, the detective, who took Mrs. Olmstead to the hospital. But Mrs. Olmstead is just Mrs. Olmstead, a woman who lived about a mile west of the Rich Street bridge.

Given all the indignities a mother goes through in the delivery room, perhaps it is somehow oddly fitting that the woman who had one of the worst deliveries in all of history doesn't actually get to be fully remembered by history. So as for Mrs. Olmstead—she was pregnant when two male rescuers picked her up in a boat, but not pregnant when she landed at the Rich Street Bridge. That's right. She gave birth in the boat—in a drenching rain, in a frail rowboat knocked about by the waves, which was then caught in a whirlpool until the men fought and kept them all out of it. It was as "natural childbirth" as it gets.

Mrs. Olmstead was met at the bridge by Shaw and Masters, who both must have heard from other boaters that a mother was delivering. Drury ordered the rescuers to take her to either the Protestant or Grant hospitals. She arrived at neither, leaving everyone to believe the mother and baby had gone to a private home, which wouldn't have been unusual under the circumstances.

But as wretched as the circumstances were when Mrs. Olmstead delivered her baby, at least she had a happy ending and something she could hold over her child for the rest of his or her life ("You can't find a few minutes every once in a while to call your own mother and say hello? Well, let me tell you about the time I gave birth to you . . ."). Mrs. Olmstead's experience makes the labor of a woman known only as Mrs. McSweeney seem charming in comparison. Mrs. McSweeney is said to have delivered her baby alone in a tree, with rain or snow pelting her and the psychotic waters below her.

Not long afterward, rescuers reached Mrs. McSweeney, but it was too late to help her baby. Several days later, a doctor in Columbus would estimate that the city had seventy pregnant women who lost their unborn babies due to the hardships that they were put through during the flood.

The party of thirteen was still on their floating house, but as light started to give way to darkness, the house was splintering, and their roof was growing smaller. Everyone began saying what you say when you think you're never going to see each other again. Mrs. Guy gave her stepson instructions on what to do if she died and he survived. Frank Williams was struck with how calm his stepmother seemed.

"I kissed her and we said good-bye," said Williams later, between wrenching sobs, referring to his stepmother. "Then the timbers groaned and cracked, and the entire structure went to pieces."

Williams told reporters that he ended up on a portion of the side of the house, clinging to it with Mrs. Vine, Mrs. Hunt, and her daughter, as the waves tossed them. At some point, the three Hungarian boys clambered aboard. On a separate chunk of the drifting house was Williams's stepfather, William Guy, and his step-sister, Nora, three-year-old Luther, and Nina Shipley.

As for Mrs. Guy? "I saw my stepmother floating away on a frail piece of timber," Williams said. "I never saw her after that."

Williams and his fellow survivors realized that the river was taking them toward Green Lawn Cemetery, which must have been disconcerting. But it was nothing personal; the cemetery was in close proximity to the Scioto River. Their part of the house became stuck in trees and bushes, and they would be rescued later in the night. The remaining guests of the doomed party of thirteen weren't so fortunate.

4:30 P.M., Dayton, Ohio

The Beckel House served a hot dinner. Word got back to the guests who were camped out at the National City Bank, and they used their ladder to make the trip across the alleys until they reached the Beckel House. The guests had eaten food at noon, just four and a half hours earlier, and now everyone was having dinner, so everyone was eating well. But, really, what else was there to do? Stare out the window and watch the fires or terrified-looking people on the roofs of their two-story homes?

It was still an apocalyptic mess out there. In C. C. McDowell's journal, he described the scenes outside.

"The scenes on the streets are something terrible," McDowell wrote. "Horses are screaming and fighting against the flood and finally having to give up and drown. On Main Street, a large building used as a cafe collapsed, and we have every reason to believe that many people went down to their deaths in the wreckage of this building. Up Third Street, another large building collapsed, but we have no way of knowing how many were killed. While we are waiting for rescue, we sit about and wonder what the outside world knows about our plight. How many anxious hearts walked the floors in all parts of this country all of last night wondering as to the safety of their loved ones who were known to be in Dayton at this time?"

Everyone's nerves were on edge, and consuming food was something positive to do.

After dinner, most of the hotel guests, including the ones who had been at the Beckel House all day, took their blankets and either walked across the ladders leading to the more secure Callahan Building or stayed at one of the buildings in between. Judge Walter Jones hunkered down in a building owned by an insurance company, where five employees were trapped. "They were very kind to me, as I shall never forget," wrote Jones later.

Jones took a chair and slept in it. Not that Jones or anyone in his vicinity would really manage to sleep that night, listening to the roar of the river outside and able to see at least one fire from their windows.

As C. C. McDowell, a traveling salesman, later wrote in a journal that he kept during his hotel stay, "Very few people had any sleep, except one man from New York who snored all night like a buzz saw in a planing mill."

TOP: April 6, 1913. With the Mississippi River rising a foot an hour, a gang of workhouse prisoners builds a levee in Memphis, Tennessee. BOTTOM: Also in April 1913, in Memphis, on Main Street. The sign "Boil Water Before Drinking" reminded residents that while the Mississippi was normally considered safe to drink, it wasn't now, not when the river was full of car tires, dead cats, and drowned rats. *Both images courtesy of Memphis and Shelby County Room, Memphis Public Library & Information Center.*

TOP: Again, April 1913, Memphis. Horses and carriages make their way down Washington Street, before the water levels get any worse. BOTTOM: April 1913, Memphis. A tent city is erected alongside some floodwaters. *Both images courtesy of Memphis and Shelby County Room, Memphis Public Library & Information Center.* OPPOSITE TOP: Survivors survey the wreckage shortly after the March 23, 1913 tornado in Omaha. OPPOSITE CENTER: Another look at Omaha after the March 23, 1913 tornado. OPPOSITE BOTTOM: Tornadoes have a way of making everything look the same. These are the remains of a home destroyed in Terre Haute, Indiana. *All three images courtesy of The National Oceanic and Atmospheric Administration/Department of Commerce, archival photography by Steve Nicklas, NOS, NGS*

TOP: Still (barely) standing. The March 23, 1913 tornado that hit Terre Haute, Indiana and pulverized this home was part of a storm system that brought forth numerous tornadoes and, of course, the flood. BOTTOM: Late March, 1913. Fremont, Ohio, experiences the flood up close and personal. *Both images courtesy of The National Oceanic and Atmospheric Administration/Department of Commerce, archival photography by Steve Nicklas, NOS, NGS.*

TOP: Late March, 1913, somewhere in New York state, along the Hudson River. *Courtesy of The National Oceanic and Atmospheric Administration/Department of Commerce, archival photography by Steve Nicklas, NOS, NGS.* BOTTOM: At Forest Avenue and Palmer Street, in Dayton, Ohio, an oarsman takes some people to safety. *Courtesy of Dayton Metro Library, 1913 Flood Collection.*

TOP: It looks calm here, in Troy, New York, but on March 28, 1913, when the worst of the flooding hit, fires broke out and hundreds of people were made homeless. BOTTOM: The flood, which hit Watervliet, New York, was said to have infected the wells in the area and the general drinking water and may have been responsible for making residents sick. Eleven people died in the aftermath of the flood of typhoid fever, double the amount of deaths from the disease in the years before and after. *Both images courtesy of The National Oceanic and Atmospheric Administration/Department of Commerce, archival photography by Steve Nicklas, NOS, NGS.*

TOP: In Youngstown, Ohio, many of the residents lived on hillsides and were spared the wrath of the Mahoning River in March 1913. The industries in the valley, however, weren't so lucky. *Courtesy of The National Oceanic and Atmospheric Administration/Department of Commerce, archival photography by Steve Nicklas, NOS, NGS.* BOTTOM: The mustachioed man in the dark clothing, evidently watching boatmen doing their rescuing, is John H. Patterson, the founder of the National Cash Register Company (NCR) and a Dayton, Ohio legend for his efforts in saving his fellow townspeople's lives. *Courtesy of Dayton Metro Library, 1913 Flood Collection.*

LEFT: Nelson "Bud" Talbott, son of Harold Talbott (the man in charge of the boatmaking at NCR) and Frederick Beck Patterson (right), son of John H. Patterson, pose for a photo. It was said that, together, Talbott and Patterson rescued 162 people from their homes in a canoe. BOTTOM: On the first floor of the National Cash Register building, a kitchen was set up to feed flood refugees. In the center is John Patterson's nineteen-year-old daughter Dorothy. *Both images courtesy of Dayton Metro Library, 1913 Flood Collection.*

TOP: Some Dayton, Ohio citizens watch as flood survivors "walk" the telephone wires until they reach dry ground. A few citizens below aren't even watching the ongoing scene above them, suggesting that by now the escapes were becoming commonplace. BOTTOM: Another shot showing just how precarious these walks along the telephone wires in Dayton, Ohio were. That there seem to be no reports of people slipping and falling to their deaths seems like a minor miracle. *Both images courtesy of Dayton Metro Library, 1913 Flood Collection.*

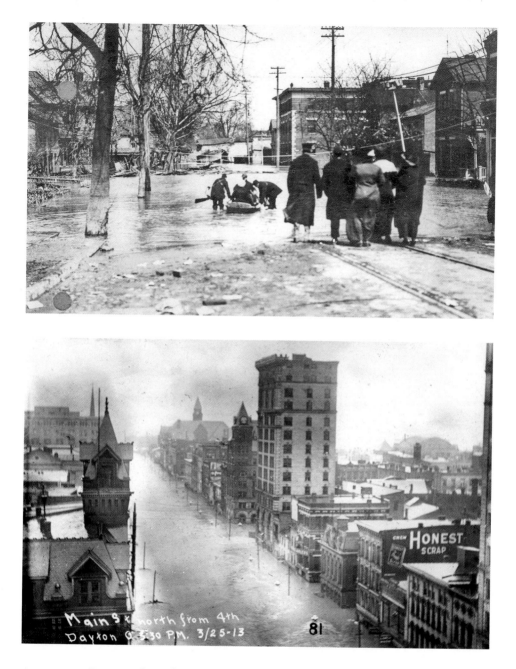

OPPOSITE TOP: Dayton, Ohio, after the flood. A familiar sight: the ruins of a flooded house. OPPOSITE CENTER: Another familiar sight: that of a piano being washed away. OPPOSITE BOTTOM: An unidentified barn or house, destroyed in the flood. TOP: Rescue operations such as this one were ongoing in Dayton and communities across Ohio and numerous other states, including Indiana, Pennsylvania, Kentucky, and West Virginia. BOTTOM: A look at Main Street in Dayton during the flood. Someone has scrawled on the photo that it was taken at 3:30 P.M. on March 25, 1913. *All five images courtesy of Dayton Metro Library, 1913 Flood Collection.*

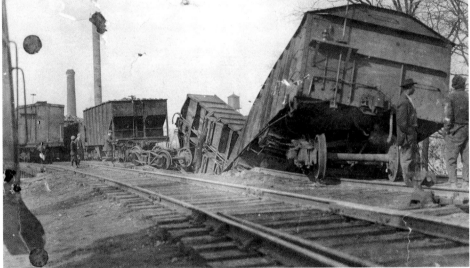

TOP: After the flood: the ruins of the Lowe Brothers Paint Store Company (and no, there's no connection to Lowe's, the home improvement chain). The rubble of the William D. Huber Furniture Company, south of the store, is also in the shot. Both businesses were taken out not by just the flood but by fire too. BOTTOM: What it looks like: railroad cars tossed aside by the flood. OPPOSITE TOP: One of the many sad and not unusual scenes in Dayton after the flood, on North Ludlow, near Second Street and the First Presbyterian Church. OPPOSITE CENTER: Someone took this shot either during or shortly after the flood—in one of the untouched, dry parts of the city—of Dayton savior John H. Patterson and Edward A. Deeds, a high-level executive at NCR, who, like Patterson, was also looking at a year in the clink for violating the Sherman Antitrust Act. OPPOSITE BOTTOM: A musical graveyard: It seems likely that in this neighborhood, people came back to their homes after the waters receded, found their ruined pianos, and began tossing them here. *All five images courtesy of Dayton Metro Library, 1913 Flood Collection.*

OPPOSITE TOP: One of many flood refugee camps, this one at the northeast corner of Main and Stillwater in Dayton. Behind the people is an apartment building. OPPOSITE CENTER: Flood survivors are walking past the courthouse in Dayton, carrying, yes, someone who didn't make it. OPPOSITE BOTTOM: All we know about this photo is that it was apparently taken during the days of (or perhaps shortly after) the flood. The man in the center is James M. Cox, the governor of Ohio. *All three images courtesy of Dayton Metro Library, 1913 Flood Collection.* TOP: The woman standing left of the bicycle is Lydia Saettel, who wisely took her baby with her instead of leaving him behind with her father-in-law, who remained at his building, which later blew up in an explosion. The man next to her is her husband, Oliver. BOTTOM: The Saettels' grocery store—the man with the apron is probably Oliver Saettel. This photo was presumably taken before the flood. After the explosion, however, the building was rebuilt. The grocery store finally closed around 1970. Fire and flood couldn't take it down, but supermarkets did. *Both images courtesy of Elinor Kline.*

TOP: These homes along Main Street in Dayton, Ohio, were destroyed by fire and flood. *Courtesy of Dayton Metro Library, 1913 Flood Collection.* CENTER: A house on the edge of the flooding in Mentor, Kentucky, taken by the author's great-grandmother, who lived in this town. BOTTOM: The same house as the one in the previous photo, taken almost a hundred years later, in 2012. If you look down the road, past those trees is a sprawling field that looks to be as long and wide as a couple of football fields, and past that is the Ohio River. *Last two images courtesy of Jim and Rita Williams.*

Chapter Ten

Heartbreak

Late afternoon, Fort Wayne

It was melee. People were shouting to other people in their homes to evacuate as quickly as possible, by any means necessary. It was getting dark, but the police tried—mostly by shouting—to make it clear that they would take anyone away on a boat if residents would just shine a light in their window, alerting them that someone was still there.

Herbert Snow, a stranger in town, volunteered himself as an expert oarsman and said he'd be glad to help out. Someone mentioned Snow to city attorney Harry Hogan, who had also volunteered his services, and suggested that they go out on a boat together. That sounded good to Hogan, who climbed into the boat with Snow, a 28-year-old who looked strong and capable; but it wasn't until they were in the water that the attorney could smell trouble, not to mention his fellow passenger's breath. Snow was drunk.

Snow was also not an expert oarsman, at least not in his current state. Snow first started paddling down Main Street, decided that was no good, and turned to try another road.

And then some water splashed into the boat.

Snow panicked, which must have panicked Hogan. Even more so when Snow jumped out of the boat and into the freezing, muddy, fast-moving, and very deep water.

Hogan shouted for him to get back in the boat.

Snow climbed back in, or attempted to, anyway, pulling the side of the vessel downward, allowing water to rush in.

Physics quickly did its thing.

The boat sank.

Hogan shared a frantic look with Snow. Then Hogan, weighed down by heavy boots and an overcoat, decided it was time to swim for shore. Snow must have had the same thought, but he apparently wasn't an accomplished swimmer. Hogan was, or enough that he was able to reach a tree.

Snow wasn't so lucky. Hogan never saw him alive again, although some bystanders saw Snow go underwater and struggle back up, go under and then raise his head over the water once again, before disappearing completely. Other bystanders said that moments after the boat sank, he simply did too.

Meanwhile, as Hogan reached the tree, he grabbed a branch, which immediately snapped off.

Then he struggled in the water until he was able to find a limb he could climb onto. Fairly certain he wouldn't die now, Hogan shouted for help, catching the attention of Albert Abbott, the brother of Fort Wayne's chief of police, and another resident, Austin W. Stults, who were both in a boat. Hogan yelled out to look for Snow. They found nobody, although much later Snow's body was found with grappling hooks, just a few feet from where the boat had overturned. Inside his pockets were letters from a presumed girlfriend in Elkhart, Indiana, and it was observed that perhaps under the water, in his final seconds of life when he was desperate to somehow save his life, he made a futile attempt to grab something that might save him—a bush or the ground—for there was grass and straw clutched in his dead hands.

But all Abbott, Stults, and Hogan could see was river water, moving very fast. After it was clear that Snow had drowned, Hogan asked if they wouldn't mind picking him up. They obliged, and Hogan, after making it to dry land, hurried home to change into dry clothes and then rushed off to a city council meeting where he and several others strategized about the best way to save their city.

As for Snow, Fort Wayne officials later learned his name was actually Ralph Templin, thanks to a small personal identification card found with the body. Templin had left his home in Sturgis, Michigan after an argument with his parents and five brothers, who all felt Ralph had a serious money problem. He wasn't a saver but a spender, and evidently one of his last purchases was some alcohol. He actually was a good oarsman, his family informed everyone. Templin had often rowed and trapped in a creek near their house. But, they said, he never did learn to swim.

It was now clear that the children at the Allen County Orphan's Home should be moved somewhere safer. The kids were all in the second story of the building, and the water was still less than a foot high in the first floor of the house. Nobody was too concerned that the river would swallow up the house, but they were now worried that the house might not remain standing indefinitely if the currents continued to gain strength. Two men arrived in a very small boat and concluded that it would take thirteen trips to get all of the children out, and, as people were becoming aware with this flood, being in a boat didn't guarantee safety; capsizing was always a risk. For now, everyone who had a hand in the matter decided, the orphans would stay put.

5–6:30 P.M., Indianapolis

Some people couldn't be persuaded to leave their homes despite it being more than obvious that the levees were going to fail.

Not going wasn't always due to a fear of drowning somewhere, but more or less a fear of what would happen if they survived. There was the sad case of Mary E. Smith, a 76-year-old widow for the last year, ever since her husband fell out of a wagon and into the street and was killed. Mrs. Smith had two daughters, one living in St. Louis and the other in Los Angeles, but apparently she felt that moving in with one of them, if she needed to, wasn't an option.

"Oh, I can't," Mrs. Smith sobbed when one of her neighbors, Ella Fanning, begged her to leave her house on River Avenue. "My things—they're all that I have in the world. If I leave them, they are lost and without them, I, too, may as well be lost."

Other neighbors pleaded with Mrs. Smith to no avail. About half past six, Mrs. Smith had lost her chance to leave. Four-foot-high water came storming down Oliver Avenue and began dispersing to the other streets. About a hundred people, working on the levee at Oliver Avenue, and bystanders were stunned to see that the river wasn't coming up over the earthen dam they were working on—but down the road from behind them.

Everyone dashed into their homes or ran down the street until they could scurry over the Oliver Avenue bridge, where it seemed safe. And it was a secure place for the moment. But as residents would eventually find, there were very few places in Indianapolis—on the western side, anyway—that could be considered safe.

But the good news was that it was only one levee that had failed, and that the others were holding up for the moment. They wouldn't last—everyone seemed to know that—but people had just bought some extra time to escape. Not everyone necessarily used that time wisely.

The *Indianapolis Star* later reported that there were several flood refugees holed up at the YMCA Building, chuckling over a story making the rounds about a man who owned a fancy breed of chickens. He had fifteen and was trying to save them. Animal lovers may understandably admire the guy, but what struck people as really funny was the man's misplaced priorities. While he raced around the chicken coop, trying to rescue his prize poultry, strangers in a passing boat rescued the man's wife and children.

Nobody telling the story was sure if the chickens had been saved, since apparently nobody stuck around to find out.

As for Mrs. Smith, later that night, people reported hearing a faint sound of what sounded like a woman screaming, although nobody could be positive who it was. The next day, people thought they heard a voice coming from her home, but with the water and piles of debris surrounding the house nobody dared try to reach the place.

When three police officers went to her house on Saturday, a good five days after the flood, they found Mrs. Smith on her bed. Best as they could tell, judging from the height of where the wallpaper was ruined and from the position of her body, Mary E. Smith had been standing on her bed, with her chin just up above the water. She had done this, it was surmised, for about eighteen hours, until finally she couldn't take it any longer and sunk to her knees, the fight all sapped out of her. Her problem was that she kept asking the wrong question. She shouldn't have wondered what would become of her if she left and her belongings were destroyed. She should have considered what would become of *her* if she *stayed*.

6:30 P.M., Sugarcreek, Pennsylvania

The elements were worsening one state to the east of Ohio. Ethel Weaver, a nineteen-year-old, was clinging to her second-story window, waiting for rescue boats to get her. Her parents' house was going to go any time; it was a victim of being in a low spot near not only Sugar Creek, but also French Creek, which Sugar Creek emptied into.

Several men in boats, bouncing and bobbing furiously in the water, had rowed up to the house, and one of them was just below Weaver.

Poised for a dramatic rescue, the men shouted for her to jump, and she did, right at a moment when the water pushed the boat away. She fell into the water and was never seen alive again.

Sometime in the evening, Columbus, Ohio

Everyone was feeling desperate, particularly at the workhouse. The 144 men were panicking and made it clear to the warden—at the first chance they got, they would try to escape their compound, not because they wanted to break the law, but because they wanted to live.

George McDonald, the superintendent, responded by letting the men know that the guards could use their guns if anyone tried to leave. Not that he was trying to be a cruel and vindictive man, stressed McDonald. He believed that anyone who climbed into a makeshift raft or tried to swim to another building would be dead within minutes. Frightening as it was to be surrounded by water and for the first floor of the workhouse to be deluged, he knew it would be far safer to stay.

8:30 P.M., Dayton, Ohio

The rescue efforts near the NCR headquarters continued. Ray Stansbury, the foundry worker who had saved 150 people in the morning, kept at it through the afternoon, though his progress was getting slower as the waters became deeper. He had saved twenty-two lives, according to bystanders, still using his method of carrying people on his back and shoulders, through the water until he reached dry land. But he was getting tired.

Allan W. Eckert's 1965 book, *A Time of Terror: The Great Dayton Flood*, is a fun read in which the author admitted there were some creative flourishes throughout the nonfictional account to make up for not knowing exactly what had happened during the flood (over fifty years later, at the point Eckert wrote his book). But whether he was using his imagination or not, Eckert probably got it about right when he described Stansbury's final moments as a rescuer.

Stansbury's "hands were punctured and gashed in a dozen places where they had encountered bits of glass clinging to window frames or nails or other sharp objects encountered beneath the muddy surface," wrote Eckert. "Three times nails had driven through the soles of his shoes and into his feet, but it hadn't stopped him. His back and shoulders were sore where dozens of boards and branches and other floating matter had bumped into him."

That may explain how Stansbury lost his balance, falling into the water and getting caught up in the current.

Given what a life-ending move that usually would be, Stansbury should have died, and would have, too, if he hadn't managed to grab a guy wire, which helps structures like telephone poles stay planted in the ground. The nineteen-year-old was caught in an eddy, more commonly known as a whirlpool.

It didn't take long for people to notice Stansbury floundering in the water as he hung on for dear life.

Patterson made his way to the crowd, according to some reports, and may have assisted in the rescue. However he got out, Stansbury was pulled from the water unconscious and taken back to NCR where he was soon revived, although it may be that he had a more difficult recovery than he should have had. There's one anecdote out there of a Dayton youth who rescued many people and then almost drowned— which sounds like Stansbury—and so a well-meaning bystander gave the young man whiskey. So much whiskey that the young man "was in a state of delirium," according to a news wire report, which added: "He nearly died, but will recover."

A little after 9 P.M., Pittsburgh, Pennsylvania

The Allegheny River was rising, along with every other river in the region. The *Pittsburgh Post-Gazette* reported that a "negro may have perished," stating that witnesses watched a black man in a skiff coming down the Allegheny River, but when the boat passed under the bridge, it was caught in the undercurrent and capsized. It looked to them as if the man and his boat were sucked underneath a barge. Newspapers were often tinged with light and heavy racist remarks, and near the end of the short news item, it mentioned that "it was ascertained later that a skiff had disappeared from the Dougherty boathouse, situated above the Sixth Street Bridge."

The article doesn't come out and say it, but by putting that item at the end of the story, it does seem to leave the idea hanging there that the man may have stolen the boat. One may also easily suppose that, fearing for his life, he took the boat as a way of trying to escape the flood, but being 1913, it seems doubtful that many readers came away with that conclusion.

Tiffin, Ohio, probably around 9 P.M.

Occasionally Ray Hostler, the husband to the eldest daughter of the Klingshirn clan, Mary, lit a match to show their neighbors that they were still in the house and hadn't somehow magically been spirited away. It was a hopeless attempt, really, to remind everyone that they still needed saving. Water was on the second floor at this point, and everyone was standing on furniture placed on beds, trying to keep their heads above water.

The Klingshirns kept shouting for help.

Crowds of neighbors, strangers, and potential rescuers remained on the riverbank, refusing to leave the Klingshirns but unable to do anything to change the equation. The Klingshirns were in the middle of the river, but there might as well have been an ocean between them and the waterlogged citizens of Tiffin. The rain hadn't stopped, the river hadn't slowed, and potential rescuers were blinded by the night. It is possible that several of the townspeople had their trusty Eveready flashlight, a product that had been mass-produced since 1902 and could be bought in a general store for about a buck or two, depending what type of model, but one or two flashlights wouldn't have been any competition against the darkness. Even if they could turn night back into day, there was the river, which was moving swiftly. What they needed was a motorboat, but there were none nearby, and even motorboats were prone to tipping over in these currents.

Inside the Klingshirn residence, there was no electric, no flashlight; just the matches. Every once in awhile, spectators would see Ray lighting a match to show everyone that they were still there. Horror movies existed in 1913: *Dr. Jekyll and Mr. Hyde*, starring King Baggot, was making the rounds in theatres across the country. But nothing on the screen could compare with the chilling light-flickering sight of Ray, William, and Mrs. Klingshirn, holding Helen, and the children, all standing on furniture, trying to keep their heads above water.

10 P.M., Dayton, Ohio

Before retiring for the night, Governor James Cox ordered the entire state's National Guard to mobilize. It was too dark and unsafe, even for the military, to travel to Dayton and throughout the state at night; but in the morning, first thing, they would head to the communities throughout the state that were in trouble, which was just about all of them.

10 P.M., Indianapolis

The levee on the north side of the Morris Street Bridge crumbled under the pressure of the river. Minutes later, the water was as high as ten to fifteen feet throughout much of downtown Indianapolis. The city was now officially under attack.

Inside homes and buildings, at least those not touched by the flood, the people of Indianapolis still had electric light and could plan their rescues without squinting. The police superintendent ordered trucks sent to all corners of Indianapolis that could still be reached, where boats were believed to be, including a sporting goods company that furnished thirty canoes, and carpenters began building boats and oars. But a lot of the rescuing was directed by ordinary citizens mobilizing and realizing that if they didn't do something right away, no one would.

Once outside, rescuers truly were on their own. Although some streetlights may have been operating, attempting anything was mostly a matter of using a lantern and hoping for enough moonlight. But at least the rescuers had a boat. That was more than the victims had.

Philander Gray and his oldest son, William, were wading toward Morris Street when the second levee broke, and a wave of water came rushing for them. They were caught by surprise but had been well aware of the flooding, and really never should have been there. Philander had taken his wife, Laura Jane, and the rest of their children to safety, leaving his sixteen-year-old behind at their house to move furniture to the second floor. Then the 41-year-old father, who put up wallpaper for a living, went back for his son and helped him move more belongings and valuables to the second floor.

According to an account written by John R. Repass for the West Indianapolis Historical Society, around 10 P.M. they were swept off their feet but grabbed onto a railroad switching tower, which was on the northeast side of some tracks. They were able to scramble up the tower for a while and presumably could have remained there. But it was dark, and it was obvious that the flooding wasn't going to get better any time soon. Repass speculates—and he's probably right—that Philander and William heard the screams from a family—a mother, father, and two children—in a house just across the street from the switching tower. (A rescuer, I. C. Huddleston, reported seeing the bodies of the four, so the screams were emitted just before a terrifying end.)

Those shrieks may have been the impetus for the father and son to leave the tower and try to make their way to dry, higher ground, which in this case was the corner of Harding and Morris Street. They didn't have all that far to go—about a block—and they fared pretty well, or so it seemed. They half-swam and walked and waded together, in the darkness, shivering and frightened, and as William emerged from the water, rescuers swarmed him and took him to a shelter. William believed for days that his father was at another relief station. But once he learned the truth, he realized that somewhere in the last few feet of their travels, his father must have tripped or been knocked off his feet. Obviously, Mr. Gray meant well and was trying to do the right thing by his wife and kids, but as Repass astutely observes, "The family of eight children was left destitute because of a futile attempt to save household furniture."

And yet—you can hardly blame Philander Gray and so many other flood victims for trying to save their belongings and not wanting their family to lose everything they had. Flood insurance did not exist in the United States.

Flood insurance was first sold by a company in Trieste, a city in Austria that is now part of Italy. The company soon gave up the product, though, and then some French companies tried again in 1865, but they, too, soon stopped, citing lack of demand. In 1897, in Toulouse, France, three more companies made the attempt—France was infamous for its floods—but once again, lack of demand killed the idea. That same year, a stock company in Cairo, Illinois, a city well accustomed to flooding, began selling flood insurance to homes and businesses in the Mississippi Valley. But then there was a flood in 1899, and so many claims were filed that the company went out of business—and to add insult to injury, the insurance firm's head office was flooded.

So by 1913, no company in the United States had made the attempt to sell flood insurance again, and the only business in the world selling flood insurance was the Swiss National Insurance Company in Basel, Switzerland. Nobody in America would try again until the 1920s. The basic problem, as insurance carriers saw it, was that there were too few consumers interested in flood insurance. The only ones who bought it were those who knew that there was a good chance their home might be flooded, and then of course the insurance companies did not want to sell to them. Someone miles away from a river or creek had no incentive to fork over money whereas with tornado insurance, that was another matter. As long as your state was routinely in the path of a tornado, it made sense for anyone to buy it, and since the demand was there, and odds were good a tornado would be more selective in its number of victims, it made financial sense for an insurance company to offer it.

There may been other specious reasons. One unidentified insurance agent interviewed by the *Indianapolis Star* in a story that ran on March 27, 1913 tried to explain the reluctance to insure against the river in this way: "When a flood destroys property, everything is swept away, and if flood insurance were written[,] the company would be forced to take the property owner's word for the amount of loss. This arrangement would be very unsatisfactory to any insurance company, and for this reason the writing of flood insurance is not practical. In the first place, the people do not fear floods, and for this reason there is little demand for insurance to cover damages done by high water."

The insurance agent was right. As a general rule, people *didn't* fear floods, but they sure did now. The insurers wouldn't bite, however. They knew that flood insurance was a losing proposition for them.

The rest of the country . . .

For anyone in a safe, dry part of the country and reading the evening papers or going to bed that night, it must have felt as if the country was washing away, from the center outward.

In Milwaukee, almost four hundred miles away from the ground zero that was Dayton, the rain turned the streets into miniature rivers while a tornado-like gale blew down seven of the city's biggest coal conveyors, shattering the massive steel frames into shrapnel. A sign on the top of the city's famed Majestic Building, which was supposedly the largest one-word sign in the world at the time, was hurled off its foundation, the steel frame landing on the roof of a nearby hotel while hundreds of electric light bulbs smashed into the street.

In Racine, a hotel was wrecked, barns were blown apart, trees uprooted, and forty windmills and twenty silos destroyed. Nobody had seen anything like it since the Cyclone of 1883. Heaven help you if you or your home were in the path of any one of these flying objects.

And in Fond du Lac, Wisconsin, the flooding was at the highest level since 1881. Schools were closed, businesses flooded, and homeowners ran for the second flight of stairs or fled for higher ground altogether.

Just outside of Erie, Illinois, yet another tornado ensured that nineteen-year-old Lulu Ellison, asleep in her home, came to an untimely end when her house collapsed onto her.

In St. Louis, the River Des Peres rose out of its banks, seven feet higher than anyone could remember, and flowed through the neighborhood of Forest Park. While the city came through the flood with minimal damage, ten blocks of houses were submerged and one person drowned: William J. Ross, a 54-year-old African-American carpenter. It was 6:30 in the evening when Ross decided to attempt to wade the current that had surrounded his house. It isn't known if his wife, Lizzie, forty-eight, was inside the house, but she worked out of the home as a laundress. Perhaps Ross decided to pick her up, given the storm conditions, or he may have been used to seasonal flooding and not been worried. Ross lived in a neighborhood known as the Bottoms, historically an area of the city known for flooding—and poverty.

The water wasn't deep, but the current was powerful, and Ross was knocked off his feet. Whatever came next—drowning or a head injury—his body was found just an hour later.

In Arkansas, in the villages of Leslie and Rumley, approximately ten people were killed by a tornado. One was killed in the town of Clarksville, a little over five hundred miles away from where the first tornado had touched down two days earlier in Omaha.

"The most terrific rain storm in years combined with a heavy thaw played havoc with railroad systems all over the state Sunday and swelled local rivers and creeks until they are well past the flood stage," reported the *Grand Traverse Herald*, the paper of record for Traverse City, Michigan.

And all the while, it kept raining.

11 P.M., *Tiffin, Ohio*

Sometime during the night, Theresa Klingshirn prepared for the worst. She made a rope out of clothing and tied it around the waists of her two-year-old, Helen, and Catherine, who was four, and possibly eight-year-old Richard. She hoped her children's bodies could be found more easily if they were all together.

The family was prepared for the inevitable but not going down quietly. Across the river bank, George Klingshirn could hear his wife and children shouting and screaming for help.

Then it happened. The house disintegrated into the river. The cries from the wife and children stopped, and the shouting from the crowd started as everyone searched for signs of survival. But there were none, and it was over in a matter of seconds. Somewhere down the river was almost everyone that made up George Klingshirn's life: his wife, his nine children, his young son-in-law, and a future daughter-in-law who was only eighteen years old.

And over the bystanders' din, everyone could make out George, who released an agonized wail that didn't stop.

WEDNESDAY, MARCH 26, 1913

Chapter Eleven

Fighting Back

March 26, Wednesday
Midnight, Indianapolis

Ben Hecht, the cub reporter out of Chicago, was still stuck in a hotel in Indianapolis. But at midnight, Hecht pretended to be tired and said he was going to retire to his room. Instead, he slipped out of the hotel and into bone-chilling temperatures. If it was still raining, it would soon be snow.

Shivering, Hecht walked along the White River, looking for a place to cross.

After midnight, Cleves, Ohio

Hecht wasn't the only one going for a walk that night. Edward Woods, a 25-year-old machinist living outside of Cleves, a village outside of Cincinnati, went on one himself. The water, as it seemed to be doing everywhere, was rising, and so he and his wife, Katie, made the calculated decision that they couldn't wait until sunrise. They needed to get out of their house, and fast. Corny, but it must be said: the Woods escaped through the woods.

Katie took the hand of her four-year-old son, Richard, and Edward carried Nellie in a container called a half-bushel chip basket, which was usually used for their produce.

The family trudged across swampy hills covered in forestland, and often were, without warning, walking and then wading through knee- and waist-deep water. If they had had a flashlight, lantern, or some sort of light source, it wouldn't have made much of a difference. They were blindly making their way across the land.

That's how Edward came to stumble and fall into some stream of river water, dropping the basket containing Nellie, which moved away from him as if he had just placed it on one of Henry Ford's conveyor belts. The current seized it. Terror-stricken, Edward scrambled through the water, chasing after Nellie, who was crying and drifting away, traveling off somewhere in the darkness. Edward kept racing after Nellie, undoubtedly tripping and stumbling in the darkness, all the while listening for her crying until eventually she was crying no more. Then Edward realized that he wasn't sure where Katie and Richard were, either. What had seemed like a smart, preventative, and proactive decision had turned into a parent's worst nightmare. Both of his children and wife were lost.

Distraught and thinking Nellie was dead, Edward hurriedly tried retracing his steps, searching for Katie and Edward. Rain-soaked, he wandered aimlessly through the forest and swamp for the next two hours, shouting for Katie and Richard, to no avail. And then he heard it. A baby crying.

He later realized he was half a mile away from where he had first dropped the basket. Following the baby's wailing and poking through the bushes, Edward finally found his baby daughter in her basket, wedged in the lower branches of a willow tree. Nellie was wet and uncomfortable, probably hungry and certainly frightened, but she was alive, and she looked okay. Edward, holding his daughter in a tight embrace against his chest, started hiking again. When he reached the village of Cleves, he found Katie and Richard waiting for him.

After midnight, Dayton

For many people, there was no going to bed between Tuesday evening and Wednesday morning. Arthur John Bell, the intrepid phone operator in Dayton, was giving interviews or at least passing on information, telling a reporter in Phoneton, Ohio, that the water was still rising, that he estimated the depth of the water at nine feet, and that the current was running strong. Bell had been on the job all day, but if he wanted to sleep, either his adrenaline or commitment to keeping the phone lines open and active wouldn't let him.

Columbus, Ohio, shortly after 1 A.M.

The Broad Street Bridge that spanned the Scioto River finally collapsed. It was the last link between the eastern and western halves of the city, and the Scioto River was still rising. For Albert Dutoit, the train engineer who had spent much of Tuesday traversing railroad tracks to reach the city, it was vexing. He couldn't cross the river on his own, and the one bridge—the Rich Street Bridge—that hadn't fallen was being guarded by police officers and soldiers with the National Guard who wouldn't let him or any resident on it. The only action they allowed on the bridge was for automobiles to travel over it one at a time if they were carrying victims who had been rescued. Rescue workers were also allowed to go over, and that was about it. Besides, it was too dangerous to go downtown, officials no doubt said. But that precisely was why Dutoit wanted to go downtown, of course. His family was there, and, for all he knew, in grave danger.

Peru, Indiana, around 1 A.M.

It began snowing. If you've ever been stranded on a rooftop, freezing and wondering if your house will be swept away and what it will feel like to drown, you can begin to understand how discouraging the sight of snow was for many people, including the rescuers. And yet many people freezing on their rooftops were also dehydrated but hadn't dared drink from the filthy river. The snow gave many Peru residents their first actual fresh, safe drink of water.

Sam Bundy and several other men were still navigating their boats—with nothing more than lantern light to guide them—to houses and trees and picking up people. Bundy was going on twenty-four hours without a break. A lot of people started to notice, full of awe, admiration, and appreciation. A reporter for Huntington, Indiana's paper wrote a fawning piece about Bundy that was syndicated in a couple other papers in the region. As the nameless reporter said, accurately, Bundy's accomplishments were "a tale of calmness and courage, of strength and skill, of nerve and nobility, of a clean-limbed body and a clear-eyed soul. A tale that will be worth the telling to one's children, and to one's children's children."

The account noted that Bundy's physical prowess far outmatched the white rescuers. "And those white boatmen were not to be sneered at," the *Huntington Press* stated. "They had grit, and muscle and stout hearts and capacity for endurance beyond most men, but at the end of twenty-four hours, they had to give up. Some of them were enough rested after twelve hours to go back. When they returned, Chief Bundy was still on the job."

1:30 A.M., Indianapolis

It was snowing so hard that rescuers could no longer see, and those without gloves and proper clothing were at risk of developing hypothermia. Listening to the screams and crying from people on rooftops, slowly freezing to death themselves, the reluctant rescuers were forced to row back to dry land until sunrise.

Indianapolis, 2 A.M.

Ben Hecht found his way across the White River. It was a high railroad trestle. The river was lapping against the bottom of it and would soon overcome it, but for the moment it looked passable. Hecht lurked about, searching a nearby shack until he found a lantern. He lit it and headed toward the trestle.

Hecht saw a figure approaching him. He held up the lantern and immediately felt the defeated feeling of knowing he wasn't going to get his scoop. In front of him was Christian Dane Hagerty, the Associated Press's former legendary foreign correspondent who now was the director of the AP's Chicago bureau.

Hagerty, according to Hecht's memory, was fifty-five years old now—actually, he was only thirty-seven, but to an eighteen-year-old he probably seemed like he was in his fifties. The legendary Hagerty had also witnessed enough history to give him the gravitas of an older statesman in journalism. He had covered the Boer War, the Russo-Japanese War, the Boxer Rebellion, the Spanish-American

War, and a score of other notable calamities. He once traveled across the country, from New York to San Francisco, by car—in 1906, when traveling by car for even a couple of hours was something of an adventure—with another reporter, in an unsuccessful attempt to set a world's record, most likely fastest cross-country trip. He was on his second marriage and would have a third in the next few years. He had spent time in a Mexican prison on more than one occasion, and legend had it that in the autumn of 1911 in western Chihuahua during the Madero revolution, he was ordered to be shot at sunrise. But as the joke went, Hagerty never woke that early, and so the execution didn't take place.

He was something of a colorful character.

According to Hecht, Hagerty was fat,[*] "his waist line gone, his voice hoarsened by the river of whisky that had flowed down his gullet. His eyes were bloodshot." But there he was, a clear threat to Hecht's plan to scoop the other reporters.

"I'm going to cross the bridge," Hecht told him. "I don't think you'd better come along. It's risky. You can see it's shaking already."

"I've been following you for an hour," Hagerty informed him. "I yelled at you a few times, but you're evidently deaf."

"I'm not deaf," said Hecht, who likely hadn't heard him over the incessant rumbling of the water.

"Glad to hear it," said Hagerty. "I knew a deaf newspaperman in Africa once. Wore my fingers out talking to him. Get going," Hagerty then said, "and keep the lantern raised."

Hecht obeyed, miserable and suddenly frightened. The river was definitely rising, and just a few feet away was instant death if he slipped. He walked quickly on the trestle with no railing whatsoever, but carefully, holding the lantern so he wouldn't make a misstep, and listened to Hagerty wheezing behind him.

When they reached the other side, Hagerty pointed and said, "Dayton is that way. Get going."

They walked, following railroad tracks, and Hecht listened to Hagerty panting, coughing, and spitting out phlegm. Hecht was hoping

---

[*] At least one account, if you're wondering about his girth, puts him at 210 pounds, which for 1913 standards was probably pretty hefty. Hecht himself was quite lean, and so everyone looked heavy to him.

Hagerty might give up the idea of going to Dayton, which was, after all, over a hundred miles away. Neither man wore an overcoat. They could have used one.

"Want me to carry the lantern?" Hagerty asked.

"No, it's my lantern," said Hecht.

Hagerty laughed. "I saw you steal it."

The two kept walking.

Indianapolis, 3 A.M.

As the night wore on, the crying and shouting had become less frequent, and by now, people who had been listening noticed that it was eerie quiet, as if many people had been silenced by the flood. And perhaps some had.

Middletown, Ohio, 3 A.M.

Not that anyone noticed except the weather watchers, but the Great Miami River started to fall, ever so slightly.

The middle of the night, somewhere in Indiana

Chris Hagerty was in the middle of a long anecdote when, as Hecht would recall in his biography, "two Italians were on the roadbed ahead of us trying to lift a handcar onto the tracks."

They were going to Dayton, and they agreed that Hecht and Hagerty could come along if they helped pump the handcar. "I looked at Hagerty in the lantern light," wrote Hecht half a century later. "His face was purple. He looked frozen, spavined* and on his last legs."

Hagerty told them, "Go ahead. You start, and we'll relieve you in fifteen minutes."

Sometime in the middle of the night, Brookville, Ohio

While Hagerty was doing his best to get the Associated Press to Dayton, a nameless Associated Press reporter in another city had

---

* Hecht had an impressive vocabulary. Spavined means to be marked by damage or ruin, but since it was a term often used with horses, he was probably trying to suggest his comrade looked like a dying animal.

established contact with a telegraph operator in a tiny town, twenty miles northwest of Dayton. The telegraph operator, whose name didn't appear in the report, spelled out what the city was facing:

"Practically half of Dayton is under water from thirty to forty feet. At the lowest estimate 200 lives have been lost. The city is without electric lights, street car service or water service. It is impossible to estimate the damage. There is much suffering and the people are in need of food and clothing. All bridges have been swept away. There is no communication with the outside world. Many persons were caught in their homes with all avenues of escape cut off."

As if that news wasn't bad enough for readers of the next day's morning papers, the telegraph operator concluded with a final, not-so-cheery thought for everyone living in the Dayton area: "The water is still rising and a heavy rain falling."

Rain wasn't the only thing falling. Temperatures were, too. It was challenging enough to be trapped on a roof, without food, without worrying about freezing to death. But for thousands of families and individuals, that's exactly what people were facing.

Middle of the night, Dayton, Ohio

Charles Adams couldn't sleep. In the early evening, after he had rested a bit and warmed up, he wanted to go find his wife and son, but his family begged him to wait until the morning, when it would be daylight and perhaps the flood waters wouldn't be so rough. Charles reluctantly agreed. But he couldn't sleep. Whenever he shut his eyes, he saw little Lois, floating away.

His sister-in-law, meanwhile, was frantic because her husband, Emerson, hadn't returned from checking on her parents. She imagined he might also easily be floating face-down somewhere.

It was a long, miserable night for the Adams and Fries families. Even if Charles and his sister-in-law Mary were able to occasionally forget for a few minutes or seconds about their loved ones, there were constant reminders of what was happening outside, such as the sounds of debris crashing into their house with a thud and the cries of help from people who weren't in a house as sturdy as the reverend's seemed to be.

4 A.M., Mayfield, Michigan

John Hawthorne was the engineer of the plant overseeing the dam that provided electricity to several towns in the area, like Mayfield and Kingsley. The dam itself was forty-five years old, just about three years younger than Hawthorne, who possibly chose the night shift to work, since he wasn't married and apparently did not have a large family, other than a sister in Canada and a niece in Elkhart, Indiana.

He was alone when the wooden dam, and the water behind it, came careering two hundred feet downward and into the power house, splitting it into two, and carrying off its occupant.

The sheriff and coroner, after locating Hawthorne's body early the next morning in the daylight, tried to piece everything together, particularly why Hawthorne was completely naked. They surmised that he realized what was about to happen and was afraid his clothing would become caught in the machinery surrounding him. He must have removed some of his wardrobe and then the rest was ripped away in the flood.

Or else the water disrobed him completely. Such was the relentless fury and power of the flood.

March 26, 4 A.M., Indianapolis

Maybe he was worried about his family. Maybe by experiencing that wave of invincibility that got a few other young people his age in trouble, he underestimated the risks. Maybe he was simply tired and not thinking clearly. Maybe his co-workers begging him not to go wound up making him more determined than ever to give it a try because he decided he was up for the challenge. Whatever was on his mind, nineteen-year-old Chester Arnold should not have attempted to swim home.

Even at the best of times, no one should have ever attempted to swim the White River. It was a cesspool, a waterway filled with butchered entrails and dead hogs, along with human excrement dumped out from outhouses and industrial waste. The Indiana Engineering Society had issued a report seven years earlier, stating, "The odor is distinct for 40 miles down the river. Animals will not drink it. It cannot be used for the laundry or other domestic purposes when the cisterns and wells go dry."

Arnold lived in a city that serviced eighty passenger trains, and it was on this early morning, at the Indianapolis Belt Railway Company, that he stood on elevated railroad tracks that were for the moment still above the White River. He had been trapped by the water at a shop that he worked at, but he and his fellow workers managed to get free, but not so free that Arnold could make it home. So he decided that he could swim from the Peoria & Eastern Railroad tracks and then reach the Vandalia Tracks. From there, he must have believed he could walk the rest of the way to his house. And when he jumped in, he obviously believed he could swim the currents between the tracks. But he couldn't have been more wrong.

Two men would later tell the local paper that they tried to rescue Chester Arnold, but with no tree branches to try to bend his way, with no life preserver tied to a nylon rope or any other equipment handy that might have been helpful, their rescue attempt was probably mostly screaming and jumping in the air and willing him back to the railroad tracks.

A few minutes after 5 A.M., Tiffin, Ohio

Chester Arnold's fatal mistake was taking a hugely unnecessary risk, but some people found themselves in trouble because they were afraid of taking *any* risk. They just wanted the flood to go away. Addline Axline, born Adison J. Alexander, was one such person. From the beginning of the deluge, she wanted to remain in her house. Almost twenty-four hours earlier, her husband, William, a few months away from his sixty-third birthday, left for work at the *Tiffin Tribune*, where he was the foreman of the printer's department. It was a demanding job, in which the successful printers needed both a mechanical and business mindset, since, being a low-profit-margin industry, one needed to work fast and efficiently. A foreman often found himself covered in printer's ink, and yet the newspapers needed to be clean and tidy.

William undoubtedly had a busy day on Tuesday, with the paper covering the flood, and while he was gone, neighbors beseeched her to leave. Citing all the familiar excuses—where would she go; she wanted to at least wait for her husband—Mrs. Axline stayed put. But then when her husband came for her, she still didn't want to leave. She refused. So in the end, Mr. Axline, who had been married to his wife since 1877 and stuck with her through good times and bad, determined that he would stay with her. They had no children, only each other. It must have seemed impossible to imagine leaving her behind.

But now the Axlines' worst fears finally began to come true. There was a series of ear-splitting cracks. The home ripped from its foundation. The Axlines were adrift.

William and Addline must have had, at first, a stab of hope. After all, the house was floating upright, flowing with the current down Washington Street. This was much different than their fellow Tiffin citizens, the Knechts, whose house left its moorings but soon split apart, and the tragic Klingshirns, whose home splintered apart immediately.

If the river parked their house on dry land, they'd be able to walk out of their home without a drop of water on them. And their luck held. The house dodged a mountain of metal that was once the Monroe Street bridge, and it kept going.

But then the Axlines' home floated toward the Baltimore & Ohio railroad bridge. Spectators were on the steel bridge, and according to reports, some of them, as the house made its way toward the bridge, incredibly didn't leave. This bridge was not going anywhere. Some people couldn't watch, and yet others couldn't turn away, for what they saw unnerved and encouraged them.

The Axlines were standing at the window on the second story of their house. Addline's face was buried in William's shoulder, and he was patting his sobbing wife on the head. He kissed her. Some spectators swore that they saw a rope tied around each of their waists, in the hopes of staying together once they were in the water.

The house slammed into the bridge, and then appeared to duck underneath the bridge because the current pulled it directly underneath.

Except for the roof, which was shorn off. The windows exploded, and the siding almost came off but somehow hung on. Several townspeople on the bridge, watching the house, would never forget what they saw next.

The house was still upright and floating down the river.

What's more, inside the bedroom were William and Addline, standing, hugging each other, miserable and terrified. But alive.

The house traveled another fifty feet. The Axlines were still beating the odds.

And another fifty feet.

Then the two-story house without a roof did the unthinkable and ruined this feel-good survival story.

It capsized.

The house tore into fragments. Moments later, William Axline could be seen, being pulled through the current, clutching driftwood and holding on to Addline. Moments later, William let go of Addline, but she, too, clung to some of the debris that may have been one of the floorboards in their bedroom or kitchen. Then a few minutes later, two blocks from Washington and now over Minerva Street, William and Addline were separated.

Addline's body would be found some time later on Abbotts Island, a land mass in the Sandusky River, five miles north of Tiffin. William Axline's body wouldn't be found until early May and was the last of the nineteen Tiffin residents to die in the flood. He also was located at Abbott's Island, which is where most of the victims of Tiffin were dumped by the river. Dutiful husband to the end, around his waist rescuers found a rope.

Addline's hair was so entangled with the branches and garbage that it had to be cut in order to remove her body, observed at least one newspaper. Oddly enough, it's difficult to imagine a detail like that being shared with readers today. While the mass media today reports many intimate details about people's personal lives that someone in 1913 would have found astounding, editors and reporters often resist painting too gruesome a picture of how a victim, whether of a natural disaster or at the hand of a gun, looked when their bodies were located or discovered, among the reasons being that it's unnecessary sensationalism and upsetting to the grieving victim's family. It may be that reporters in earlier times wanted to gin up their articles and make them more exciting to read or satisfy readers' innate curiosities. Probably all of that is true.

But there may be another reason papers easily offered up grim details of how a body appeared when it was found. This was an age when you could easily find your life snuffed out by a flood, when a raft of diseases from measles to typhoid fever to whooping cough could end your life prematurely, in a time when stillbirth deaths were frequent and childhood mortality from a variety of diseases (which we are vaccinated against nowadays) was rampant. If you were alive into adulthood during the early 1900s, it was almost a miracle. Mellie Meyer, one of the flood refugees who walked the wires after the Saettel grocery store blew up, could have told anyone that. Her husband, William Meyer, a jeweler, had died six years earlier in a freak accident at thirty-eight years old, after stepping on a match.

In 1907, many matches were still made of phosphorus, but that type of match was losing its appeal as a household product because the fumes were known to cause bone disorders in the workers manufacturing them. The initial appeal when they were first invented, however, was that these matches were "strike-anywhere" matches. All one needed to light one of these phosphorus matches was a bit of friction.

William's shoe, stepping on the match, was just enough for the phosphorus, and the spark it produced might not have mattered had it not been for the pan of gasoline that happened to be on the floor near him. A fireball erupted, catching William's clothing. He ran out of his jewelry store, down the street, and into a grocery store, probably Saettel. Then he fell onto the floor, shrieking in agony, while everyone inside the store did what they could to extinguish the flames. But they couldn't do enough.

In 1913, you could be doing just about anything and find yourself in mortal danger. It may be that reporters offered grim facts about the flood's victims to spell out that but for the grace of God, what happened to this person happened to you.

Chapter Twelve

Waterworld

March 26, Wednesday
Early morning, still dark, close to 7 A.M., just outside of Dayton, Ohio

Ben Hecht and Chris Hagerty bid their pump-car companions farewell before the sun peeked out over the watery horizon. The Italian-Americans wanted to go down a different track away from Dayton, and Hagerty knew that a telegraph station was nearby and, with Hecht, started lumbering down a road leading to a faroff building illuminated by some electric lights, an oasis of power on the edge of a darkened city. Hagerty's age and physical condition were showing, but when Hecht asked if he needed to rest, he was met with a hoarse "Keep going!"

Suddenly, a gunshot ripped through the air. There were several more shots, close enough that bullets sprayed snow down on them.

Hagerty dove off the road and into a snowbank. Hecht jumped in after him. Wet and shivering, they could hear voices.

"What the hell are they shooting at us for?" asked Hecht.

"Deputies," Hagerty said, breathing hard. "Shooting down looters. They don't know that we're not a pair of 'em."

"I'm going to tell them," Hecht said.

"You goddamn dumb cub," Hagerty said, "stay put. And keep out of sight. If they see us, they'll pinch us and throw us into the can—either that or the morgue."

It should be noted here that with the benefit of hindsight and a broader knowledge of the state of law enforcement in Dayton during the flood, it seems virtually impossible that deputies would be shooting at Hecht and Hagerty. There were indeed some deputies in Dayton who were on the lookout for looters, but not in these early days of the flood when most of the force was focusing on search and rescue. It's also unlikely because Hecht and Hagerty were on the outskirts of the city, away from shops. Dayton was becoming something of a No Man's Land, so it's possible that farmers or well-meaning but misguided citizens had taken it upon themselves to shoot first and ask questions later. However, it is most likely that Hecht and Hagerty heard gunshots from people on roofs in distress, trying to attract someone's, anyone's, attention, or even worse, a rare but occasional occurrence during the flood: someone ending their own life.

Whatever happened, about fifteen minutes later, Hecht and Hagerty began walking again—this time through deep snowbanks, away from the road—and the bullets.

"It's about another mile," said Hecht after a while. Then he looked at Hagerty, who had stopped walking.

"Go on, kid," said Hagerty. "You've lost me. I can't go any farther."

Hecht felt sorry for him and elated at the same time.

"Go on," Hagerty repeated, casting a long look at the city below them. "It's your story. That's Dayton down there. It looks like quite a flood."

"I'll send somebody back to get you," said Hecht.

Hagerty nodded. Hecht couldn't help but think his road companion might be dying. "But he did an odd thing for a man dying," wrote Hecht. "He walked to a telegraph pole and started climbing it. I stood watching him, sure he had gone mad. I watched his paunchy, exhausted body lift itself foot by foot up the pole."

Hagerty, as it turns out, had been a telegraph repairman before going into journalism, and was able to nimbly scale the pole despite his otherwise weakened condition. He removed a pair of pincers from his pocket and, after a few moments, Hagerty slid down the pole and passed out in the snow bank.

Hecht was baffled. It was only later that Hecht would learn what his friendly nemesis had been up to, and that at six A.M., in the Chicago office of the Associated Press, a bulletin arrived, via Morse Code through a telegraph wire, and that bulletin tersely offered up a one-word update on the flooding and scooping Hecht: "Dayton, Ohio—A.P. Everywhere. Hagerty."

Hecht and Hagerty were not the only reporters rushing to Dayton. Although many communities had their share of reporters coming to cover the flood, as the most affected city, Dayton was where reporters from all corners of the country wanted to be, and they were willing to do almost anything to get there.

The day before, two *Cincinnati Times-Star* reporters, a photographer, and an Associated Press reporter piled into a car and set out for Dayton. It wasn't easy driving in the rain to Dayton—the dirt roads were mud pits—but the machine, reporters wrote later, "splashed, slid, skidded and bumped splendidly until Muddy Creek," a waterway between the towns of Mason and Lebanon. About two hundred yards of the road was covered with Muddy Creek, and in the middle of the road was an old, dilapidated wooden fence. The men were pretty certain their car could get through the road with the two feet of water, but the fence needed to be moved.

Two of the reporters took off their shoes and socks and waded into the icy water—the rain was still pouring down, too, mind you—and moved the fence. Then they hurried back into the car, and onward they went.

In Toledo, Dwight F. Loughborough, another Associated Press reporter, was told to make tracks for Dayton. He was refused a ticket on a relief train full of food and rescue supplies being sent to Dayton, so Loughborough volunteered to work as a train employee if they'd just let him on. They did.

When Arthur J. Peglar of the *Chicago American*, an afternoon paper, reached Toledo, he was refused passage on the relief train but sneaked aboard anyway. He was soon discovered by a captain in the National Guard and thrown off. He then managed to get a phone call from Toledo through to Xenia, a town sixteen miles east of Dayton, where he talked to the editor of the local paper, interviewed him, and filed his story with his editors in Chicago. From there, he managed to find a train to Springfield, just twenty-six miles from Dayton, and from there made his way to the beleaguered city.

St. Louis sent its star reporter Carlos F. Hurd, a 36-year-old who had gained local and national fame the year before by being the only reporter on the rescue ship *Carpathia* when the *Titanic* went down. Hurd, who was on the *Carpathia* taking a vacation with his wife, quickly recognized that he had stumbled on the story of a lifetime, but he was forced to do his interviews in secret, writing down notes on any random piece of paper he could find, including toilet paper, because the *Carpathia's* captain, figuring the *Titanic* wasn't going to be good publicity for the shipping industry, refused to help Hurd and did what he could to stop him from writing about the sinking ship. Hurd was banned from using the ship's telegraph, and the stationery from the ship's staterooms was taken away.

Nevertheless, when *Carpathia* reached New York Harbor, Hurd threw the five-thousand-word manuscript—sealed in a cigar box and buoyed by champagne corks—over the railing to Charles E. Chapin, city editor of New York's *Evening World*, who was waiting in a lifeboat with other eager reporters anxious to interview the *Titanic* survivors, and that's how the first in-depth news of the now-infamous sinking reached the general public.

For Hurd, Dayton's flooding would have seemed almost hospitable. The survivors of Dayton and the Miami Valley were anxious to tell their stories and get the word out to friends and family in other parts of the country, who were just as eager to learn what was happening in the heartland.

But once the reporters arrived in Dayton, there was no telegraph or telephone to relay information; and so once the journalists had conducted their interviews, they scattered to the nearest working telegraph station. For the journalists—the *Cincinnati Times-Star* reporters, anyway—that meant traveling to the town of Lebanon, twenty-seven miles away, one way, along muddy highways through rain and snow—and then driving back to Dayton to collect more information. A United Press journalist later reported that he and two other reporters traveled to Lebanon in a car that broke down.

They hired a horse and buggy to take them the rest of the way, but the buggy became stuck in the mud. The information highway in 1913 was slow and fraught with peril.

Dawn, Peru, Indiana

Most of the men who had started rescuing people the day before stopped to sleep, having been hard at work for twenty-four hours, giving others a chance to take over. Sam Bundy, or Chief Bundy, as they called him, was the only original rescuer who still hadn't taken a break, still rowing in his canoe, plucking out children from attic windows, stopping for frightened mothers on a roof, and helping men clinging to tree tops. His endurance was superhuman, and dozens of people now owed their lives to him.

Early morning, Dayton, Ohio

Judge Walter Jones awakened in his chair at the insurance building, unsure if he had actually slept. He decided he'd try returning to the Beckel House, in hopes that the hotel was serving some sort of breakfast. To his surprise and pleasure, they were. He and the guests received what he described as "cold meat and fried potatoes," and, to everyone's utter relief, they were given a glass of water and a cup of coffee.

That was about the only good thing they experienced. Outside, they could tell that the water had dropped a little, but it hardly made a difference, as the current was still moving fast, and at every window they could see people looking back at them. Nobody was shouting for help any more. Everyone knew that nobody would be coming.

Some guest or staff member came by and took Jones's name and added it to a list. There were about two or three hundred people in the hotel, Jones learned, including those who had come from the street the previous morning. Someone nearby quipped, "May be useful when it comes to identifying remains."

Several people grunted a laugh, and then the room, except for the roar of the water outside, became quiet as everyone suddenly understood. The guest wasn't joking.

Charles Adams had hardly slept and, by the time light started to emerge, he was looking out the second-story window, searching for a boat. He was a jumble of so many mixed emotions. He was still euphoric that his son and wife had been saved, but the re-realization that his little baby girl Lois was gone forever, and that he would never hold her again, never make her laugh, never see her grow up, hit him hard. It was a long, miserable night.

But it was morning now, and it wasn't long before he spotted his two rescuers, Jack Korn and Warren Marquardt. He started to flag them down, but as it turned out, they were coming for him anyway. "Come on, Charley," said Marquardt, "your wife and babies are up at my house."

Charles stopped short. He must have heard wrong. "Babies?" he asked.

After Lois Viola Adams had been pulled by the current from her father's grasp, she had floated downstream, the water filling up her lungs. Two rescuers, Bob Whyte and Howard Ooly, turning onto Warder Street from Brightwood Avenue, spotted a woman waving frantically at them. The woman—whose name the Adams family never learned—had been looking out her window from the Folsom Apartments—the same place where someone would later spot Charles, Jr.—and saw Lois hurtling downstream. She shouted at the men to grab her. The perplexed men spotted the floating baby, snatched her up, and rushed her to the shoreline, where they found a policeman who had just taken a course at the Y.M.C.A. in life-saving techniques. He went to work trying to revive her.

Lois was blue and, according to eyewitnesses, had swallowed her tongue. The police officer removed her clothing and began rolling the water out of her stomach. Once Lois began breathing again and emitted a cry after an interminable amount of time—some accounts say an hour, which seems ridiculously long, but clearly it was a long and agonizing wait—the officer wrapped her in a woolen blanket and took her to a nearby cottage belonging to a Mrs. Young. Not long after that, it was also Mrs. Young's home where Lois's twin brother Charles was brought.

Grandpa Adams soon caught up with both Lois and Charles. But he had to do some serious talking to get the woman watching Lois to give her up. Mrs. Young was convinced that Lois's mother had drowned and planned to keep the little girl as her own. Eventually, she relented, though, and agreed that Grandpa Adams could take her with him to the rescue station, where he found Viola.

"What do you mean, babies?" Charles asked.

"Both babies and your wife are up at my house, and they are all well," said Marquardt, who must have enjoyed the shock and joy registering on Charles's face after all of the dismal news that had engulfed the city. "Get your hat and coat, and we'll take you up to see them, and you can stay up there."

Silently praying and vocally shouting to his family that Lois was alive, Charles threw additional clothes on, concluding that they might come in handy later, and he practically jumped into the boat with Marquardt and Korn. Thankfully, it was a smooth enough ride, and the firemen were able to get Charles to the land without any problems. From there, it was a mile to Marquardt's house. The two firemen then bid Charles good-bye and went back to looking for people to save.

As he walked underneath a canopy of clouds and some rain, it struck Charles that on the thankfully mostly-dry street that he had to travel on, there were no streetcars functioning and no cars to be seen. They had either been called into service to help rescue people, to transport them from shoreline landings to hospitals, and, with most of the city's roads impassible, there wasn't much incentive to have a car on the streets.

His three-and-a-half-foot stride always had worked out well for him, but this felt like the longest mile Charles had ever traveled.

But eventually he reached the Marquardt house and, as he walked onto the porch, he saw Charles, Jr. and Lois peering out the windows, and the two twins, just a couple weeks shy of their first birthday, started toddling toward the door to meet their father.

"Viola was the first to open the door," Charles wrote later, "and the joy of our meeting was felt no more keenly by anyone than I, with my arms full of babies and wife. Father soon came in, too, and to say that we were thankful to all be together again is putting it entirely too mild."

There was another happy reunion of note on this day in Dayton, although the exact timing is unknown. A neighbor of William Hartzell, a carpenter whose last name was Siler, recognized Bishop Wright and contacted Katharine. Siler told her that her father was at Hartzell's house. Orville picked him up and brought him back to the friend's house where he and his sister were staying.

Soon after, however, Orville and Katharine took their father to the house of Lorin Wright, one of their brothers, and camped in with his family. It was a new home, which he and his family had just moved into a week earlier. Orville, Katharine, and Milton would stay with Lorin and his family for the next three weeks and a day.

Approximately 7:30 A.M., just outside of Dayton, Ohio

Ben Hecht reached the Miami Junction telegraph station, which was manned by twelve men. Hecht told them about Hagerty, and three men went after him. The remaining telegraph operators were busy sending messages out to an anxious country.

Hecht talked to the head operator, hearing amazing stories for the first time, of horses swimming into second-floor windows and houses floating away with families on the roofs. Hecht asked the head operator if he could file an entire article about Dayton to the *Chicago Journal.* Hecht was given a firm "no."

Because of all the messages going back and forth, the head operator had been given instructions that no message any longer than two words could be sent out by any sender, who was also allowed to leave their signature. Most of the messages being sent out from the telegraph office were "am safe" messages from family members and even the stymied journalists, who figured that their editors might want to know they had reached Dayton alive.

"Can I use your typewriter?" Hecht asked.

"It's no use," came the reply. "You can only file two words."

Hecht started writing his article, and after about an hour, Hagerty arrived. Hagerty did not collapse into a corner and lie on a bed recovering, which is what Hecht would have liked to see. Hagerty managed to secure his own typewriter and convince the operator to let him send it out. "He was not a man to be trusted to stay silent," wrote Hecht.

But Hecht soon produced his own story, six pages of double-spaced copy.

"Just read it, even if you can't send it," said Hecht to the head operator, who began to protest.

The head operator read the article and suddenly started fighting back tears. He reddened. "Some have dropped from exhaustion. The Western Union men, who were the first to break into the city, haven't slept since Tuesday. 'Safe.' 'Safe.' The monotonous words of rescue and death have jammed the wires since the first one opened," read Hecht's article in part.

As Hecht describes it in his memoirs, his article was about the heroes of the Miami Junction telegraph station, telling readers about "the twelve men who had sat for thirty hours without leaving their posts, without knowing if their own families were alive or drowned, and tapped out the thousands of happiness-bringing 'Am Safe' messages to other relatives. The names and descriptions of each of the twelve heroes were in my story."

"Take a rest, Jim," the head operator called out, and a few moments later, he was tapping out the article, sending it out for the rest of the world to read.

Morning in Columbus

A police skiff, after a lot of difficulty, rescued two families hiding out in a house in the middle of the city. A railroad track was near the house, and from the accounts that exist about the rescue, it sounds as if a wire was tied from the train to a boat, and once the train began moving, it—with the wire attached—began dragging the boat with two families in it through the current.

But before that could happen, there were two telegraph men who had to bring the coil of wire to the train, and they were now stranded on the other side of the riverbank. They and a *Columbus Citizen* news reporter managed to climb up one telegraph pole, and use the wire to cross the river and climb back down the other side of the river. They then gave rescuers the wire. It was tied to the boat, and an oarsman took it to the house where the Eis and Cooke families were.

The families were sick with fear. The previous day, Esther Eis had been talking to her neighbors who were no longer among the living, as far as the Eis and Cooke families knew. Thomas Wey and his wife Catherine and their four children were in a house next door along with another family, James and Catherine Griffin and their eight offspring, ranging from twenty-seven to nine years old. Esther remembers one young woman nursing a baby, probably the Griffins' 24-year-old daughter Cathrine Engle, and she was out of her mind with fear.

"She seemed almost crazed," Esther said later. Everyone was terrified, Esther included, and at one point the Weys and the Griffin children told Esther that their house seemed to be moving.

Esther tried to be encouraging, telling them that the house would be just fine. But in the middle of the night, Esther could see that her neighbor's house also looked like it was floating. She called everyone who was awake in her home to the window. They soon saw that the house with the Wey and Griffin families inside indeed was bobbing in the floodwaters.

Then without any further warning, the house completely collapsed. They never saw the occupants inside, and Esther and her comrades assumed the families were lost. According to Ohio's death records, however, most of the Griffin and Wey families miraculously survived. Of the Weys, only Catherine Wey and her 21-year-old daughter Anna didn't make it. Of the Griffins, the three youngest, two girls and a boy, ranging from nine to fourteen, perished, but the rest of the family somehow survived, including Cathrine Engle and possibly her baby, for there are no Engle infants listed in Ohio's death records in March or April 1913, nor do any Engles appear in Ohio's official death tally.

But the 1920 census records show that Cathrine Engle had young children, none who were alive during the flood, so if her baby survived the collapse of the house and the current, he or she may have not lived for long, succumbing to another one of the countless day-to-day hazards of the era.

Albert Dutoit, the train engineer racing through Ohio in search of track line to take him to his family, emerged at the Rich Street Bridge this morning, without his train, which he left behind once he could go no further with it. Police officers stood guard at the bridge, refusing to let people cross it into downtown, which was becoming something of a water wasteland.

Surveying the situation, Dutoit noticed a group of workhouse men who were helping with the rescue effort—and they were crossing the bridge. Dutoit slipped into the group and pretended to be one of them, and then when he was across the bridge, he slipped away without being spotted.

From there, he managed to make his way to his house, which was surrounded by a vast body of water. Dutoit caught up with some *Columbus Dispatch* reporters with a motorboat and persuaded them to help him rescue his family.

Knowing a good story when they heard it, they probably didn't need much convincing. Minutes later, he was soon helping his wife, his eight-month-old baby, and three sons out of their second-story window.

Meanwhile, the National Guard was ready to start fanning out across the state. Colonel H. G. Catrow and a party of military officers were under orders from Governor Cox to spare no effort to get to Dayton; but the Scioto was one to three miles wide, and Catrow's motorboat, like so many vessels before him in the region, overturned.

Catrow, the military men, and the newspapermen with them all survived—another boat picked them up—but it was clear that they couldn't cross the Scioto River. It was just another indignity Mother Nature heaped on the government.

Still, later in the afternoon, Catrow and a group of newspapermen waded across the Fifth Street Avenue bridge and, unable to get any trains, evidently located a car to make an attempt to travel on the muddy highway toward Dayton.

It was not an easy trip. Fred Ward, reporter for the *Columbus Citizen*, made the journey from Dayton to Columbus, a distance of seventy-one miles, leaving on a Wednesday and getting there on a Thursday, taking twenty-five hours to do so. First, he left in an automobile, reaching Jamestown, twenty-nine miles away, in two hours. He switched to another car and traveled for another hour, making it to the community of Washington Court House, twenty-one miles away. So far, not too shabby, considering that these were 1913 cars on extremely muddy roads. He spent the night there and the next morning hired, rented, or somehow found a third car to use, apparently taking a couple of hours to reach Mt. Sterling, a mere fifteen miles away.

At Mt. Sterling, all of the bridges except for a railroad trestle were destroyed, and so he borrowed a railroad handcar and, with the help of two men, got it as far as Orient, nine miles away. In Orient, Ward hired a driver to take him via horse and buggy to Grove City, another nine miles away and closing in on Columbus. The postmaster in Grove City let Ward borrow his car, and he finally reached his newspaper's office at 4:30 P.M. Catrow and his crew were ready to see some action.

8 A.M., Indianapolis

Indianapolis residents were waking up to discover that the previous evening's nightmare was real. The Washington Street Bridge over the White River was no longer in existence. The Morris Street Bridge was still up but closed. The Kentucky Avenue Bridge was impassable but still standing. The Oliver Avenue Bridge was closed since part of the structure had disappeared into the current. A number of bodies, including those of young children, were occasionally spotted drifting in the water, like that of a woman whose body, face down, floated under the Morris Street Bridge around eight o'clock in the morning. Thousands of people were being sheltered in churches, hotels, and, at least in one case, even a dog pound. Thousands more were also trapped in factories, taverns, rooftops, trees, and on telephone poles.

Somewhere in this chaos was Dr. Fletcher Hodges, who had a patient in Haughville, then a village west of downtown Indianapolis and now a part of the city. He wanted to check on him but was refused passage on the Oliver Avenue Bridge.

Fletcher wasn't pleased, since there were no other bridges he could cross. Unless. . . .

An idea forming in his mind, he decided to do what reporters Ben Hecht and Chris Hagerty had done the night before and cross along a freight bridge. He went to the Vandalia Railroad Bridge, which was in danger of collapsing at any time, despite empty railroad cars having been pushed on the edges, along the land, to strengthen the foundation.

Dr. Hodges walked on the top of the railroad cars and then climbed down onto the bridge and made the trek across it. The police and government officials had considered allowing people to evacuate on the bridge, but everyone was worried that people would look down the spaces between the railroad ties, lose their balance or mind, and fall in.

The doctor escaped that fate, eventually treating his patient. In between crossing the bridge and returning to the same bridge, Dr.

Hodges reported seeing the waters enveloping freight cars filled with pigs; saw a rooster atop a house surrounded by water; and encountered an old man who appeared insane with grief, unable to find his relatives.

But Dr. Hodges made it back to the bridge and carefully crossed the rickety structure, moving from railroad tie to railroad tie, with the White River raging beneath him. Moments after crossing it and making an argument for the creation of a hall of fame solely for doctors who pay house calls, the Vandalia Railroad Bridge sank into the water.

Hodges was certainly a better physician than whoever was watching over West Indianapolis. It may be the stuff of folklore, but one of the local papers told a story of how there was only one doctor who was accessible and available to attend to sufferers. This doctor was also the victim of a morphine habit. The doctor successfully helped a woman deliver twins in the Methodist church, but the pressure of attending to his patients, and not being able to get morphine for them or himself, was too much. The physician lost his mind and, after making three unsuccessful attempts to jump out of a window, was placed in a straitjacket.

9 A.M., Peru, Indiana

Benjamin Wallace, the circus owner, was going out of his mind with worry. He had heard plenty of gossip and innuendo about what had happened to his circus animals, and surely he wondered about his employees, but he had no way to get out of downtown and travel the few miles to the circus headquarters and investigate. He put up a $5,000 reward for anyone who would take a boat out to the circus farm, brave the torrent, and bring back a true report of what was going on out there. He had no takers.

Early morning, across America

In the morning papers, which Ben Hecht and Chris Hagerty contributed to, an appeal from President Woodrow Wilson went out to readers across the country, asking them to help the flood sufferers:

"The terrible floods in Ohio and Indiana have assumed the proportions of a national calamity. The loss of life and the infinite suffering involved prompt me to issue an earnest appeal to all who are able in however small a way to assist the labors of the American Red Cross to send contributions at once to the Red Cross at Washington or to the local treasurers of the Society.

"We should make this a common cause. The needs of those upon whom this sudden and overwhelming disaster has come should quicken everyone capable of sympathy and compassion to give immediate aid to those who are laboring to rescue and relieve."

There was, in fact, a flurry of activity in the Oval Office on the 26th day of March. Wilson fired off a letter to both Senator Thomas S. Martin and U.S. State Representative John J. Fitzgerald, stating:

"I am directing the War Department to extend the necessary aid to the sufferers from the floods. May I assume that I will have your approval in seeking the subsequent authorization of Congress and the necessary funds?"

They heartily approved.

Wilson also dashed off identical letters to both the Ohio governor, James M. Cox, and Indiana's governor, Samuel M. Ralston, simply saying, "I deeply sympathize with the people of your State in the terrible disaster that has come upon them. Can the Federal Government assist in any way?"

Cox thought so and promptly replied that day with a telegram reading:

"We have asked the Secretary of War this morning for tents, supplies, rations and physicians. In the name of humanity see that this is granted at the earliest possible moment. The situation in this State is very critical. We believe that two hundred and fifty thousand people were unsheltered last night and the indications are that before night the Muskingum Valley will suffer the fate of the Miami and Scioto Valleys."

President Wilson promptly replied. "Your telegram received. Have directed the Secretary of War immediately to comply with your request, and to use every agency of his Department to meet the needs of the situation."

Governor Ralston didn't reply. He couldn't. He had no idea that the president had contacted him. President Wilson's telegram couldn't get through to Ralston due to the floods. While the telegram could be transmitted almost instantly—it was the e-mail of its day—someone had to actually physically deliver the telegram from the office to the recipient, and on March 26, getting a telegram from the telegraph office to the governor's mansion was a challenging feat.

That technology was failing or not working the way everyone was accustomed to was disconcerting. At least one newspaper columnist at the time lamented that perhaps the influx of communicative devices, from telegraphs to telephones, was making the nation soft since, suddenly, going without them was sending so many people into a panic, almost suggesting that maybe the country would be better off to go back the way it had been, when nobody could reach each other and everyone was more self-reliant.

As the *Cambridge City Tribune*, the paper for Cambridge City, Indiana, lectured its readers in an April 3, 1913 editorial, "Now you know how it was to live in this country in the days when there were no railroads, no daily newspapers, no telegraph, no telephone, no furnaces, no roads, no bridges. In this age, a few days' isolation is a great hardship."

And when telegrams could get through, they may have done more harm than good, in terms of making the public anxious.

In Zanesville, an Ohio city in the Muskingum Valley that Governor Cox worried about, a telegraph operator sent out a final message: "Entire city under water. It's coming into our office. The building next door has just collapsed and I am compelled to leave now for safety. . . ."

The message then abruptly ended, and an *Indianapolis Star* reporter, in relaying the contents to the readers, speculated, "It was assumed by officials here that the operator was forced to swim from his post."

The Midwest was falling apart, and with everyone seeking higher ground, telegraph poles were in danger of becoming more useful for their height than as instruments for communication. It was extremely frustrating to Governor Cox, not just seeing his state in disarray, but not being able to procure any hard facts about what was happening. Before he bought the *Dayton Daily News* in 1898, he had been a reporter himself. One story about the governor places him on the scene of a terrible railroad accident, and while the other reporters naturally made their way to the destruction, the future governor first went to the town's only telegraph office. In a move that would have impressed Hagerty and Hecht, he hired the telegraph operator to transmit the Bible to his newspaper. He did that, knowing that the current laws dictated that once a message began, it couldn't be interrupted by other people.

Then Cox covered the accident and wrote his article. He came back to the telegraph office, which was full of impatient and angry reporters all waiting to use the telegraph. Cox handed his article to the telegraph operator who transmitted it, allowing the future governor to scoop all of the other reporters.

But now, Cox was governor of the state and was virtually single-handedly relying on his Columbus operator, Thomas Green, and his Dayton operator, John Bell, to patch him through to others or furnish him with the scant flood information that was out there.

What Cox was hearing about Dayton was alarming. Over a hundred thousand people were estimated to have sought refuge on the second floors of buildings, many of which seemed in danger of collapsing. At the city prison, sixty prisoners were without food and water and, behind bars, were promising the superintendent that if they escaped, he and his family were as good as dead. The superintendent, probably through John Bell and the city's only working telephone line, got word out that he needed the national guard's help, and he needed it now. Three hundred people in the Algonquin Hotel were trapped, with the water up to its third story; men, women, and children stuck their heads and arms out windows, begging for rescuers to bring their boats and save them. No one did, unable to manage the currents or figuring the hotel seemed sturdy and probably fearing a riot if they brought their tiny vessel to a crowded window.

What Cox didn't know as he ran the relief efforts from the governor's office, but could imagine, were the tales of individuals who were suffering. In Dayton, John Gartley, his wife, and three young children sat on the roof of their house with nine neighbors. They had two loaves of bread and rainwater to subsist on for about thirty-six hours until they were rescued.

Also in Dayton, Marcus Furst, his wife, and nine-month-old daughter all sat on a roof. The only food that they had was a box of crackers that Marcus had retrieved, just as the floodwaters hit their kitchen.

Those crackers were hard fought, too. Furst barely got out of the kitchen alive. But he did, dashing upstairs, where his wife was nursing their baby, and at that moment Marcus realized that he wouldn't be eating any of the crackers. His wife needed them, and in return, their baby would get them. What he couldn't have realized was that they would be trapped on their roof until Saturday with nothing else for his wife to eat. For a drink, he and his wife stuck their hands into the muddy water lapping their roof and sucked on their fingers.

But that was more nourishment than Dorothy Wright, her parents, and her 96-year-old aunt Anna Caise had. They were trapped in their attic in Dayton for fifty hours with no food or water, very little ventilation, and no warm blankets or warm clothing. By the time they were rescued, they had all virtually given up hope.

In Richwood, Archer Vaughan, his wife, and their eight-year-old granddaughter sat on a bed on the second floor of the house, the water lapping up against the mattress. For the next three days, they sat there, without food and drinking the muddy water to survive. Mrs. Vaughan, meanwhile, was haunted by what had happened before they were forced to climb onto the bed.

When the water had been rushing by their house, the levels right up to the second-floor windows, Mrs. Vaughan had spotted one of her neighbors struggling against the current. As he came past the window, he screamed for help, and she had reached out toward him, missing his hand by a few inches. Later, she would learn that her worst fears were founded; he had drowned.

In Columbus, the papers told of a mother, Mrs. Fanny Turner, and her daughter, handing over some of what little food they had, on a pole, to a neighbor with a baby. Mrs. Turner and their daughter hoped the neighbor's baby would be all right, provided her mother could eat food and then nurse the infant. There was, indeed, a happy ending in that everyone lived, but Mrs. Turner, her daughter, and the neighbor were stuck on their rooftops from Tuesday until Friday night.

These were the types of people Cox, the Red Cross, and the National Guard were powerless to help.

Intermixed between the hunger and fear was boredom. The residents of the Algonquin Hotel were hungry, but the staff had collected enough rainwater so thirst wasn't a problem. So, hungry and bored, but not fearing for their lives, a number of guests amused themselves by making fishing rods out of their room's brass curtain poles. They then attempted to fish what they could out of the swift current. Among the items they caught: boxes of cigars, panama hats, automobile tubes, ladies' hose, and boxes of handkerchiefs.

In Middletown, Ohio, John McLaughlin, a superintendent at the W. B. Oglesby Paper Company, stayed at the factory longer than the other workers and found himself trapped, alone. For the next twenty-four hours, he drank river water that he ran through a piece of felt as a filter and ate oats that he found in a stable. The 55-year-old attempted to catch a hog that floated through a window, but the hog didn't appreciate that and escaped. McLaughlin himself eventually managed to make a break from the factory in a boat.

At 10 A.M., Governor James Cox did what he probably should have done the day before; but like many people of the era, any era, he hated to admit that he needed help. He fired off a telegram to the Red Cross's Mabel Boardman. His telegram read:

"Latest advices are that the situation at Dayton is very critical; more than half of the city is under water to a depth of 5 to 9 feet; horses have been drowned in the business section; the entire downtown commercial district is under water.

"At this time there is no means of knowing the extent of human loss. Piqua, Hamilton, Sidney, and Middletown also badly in need. The maximum of our military strength is being used in different parts of the State. We have appeals from some parts by telephone to the effect that women and children in the second story of their homes await rescue.

"Boats are being rushed overland by wagon, as railroad traffic in flooded districts is practically suspended.

"We greatly appreciate the interest and cooperation of the Red Cross."

Mabel Boardman didn't need to hear any more. She immediately—or as immediately as possible in 1913—dispatched T. J. Edmonds and C. M. Hubbard, of St. Louis, who were currently working in Omaha on tornado relief, to get to Dayton as soon as possible. Not long afterward, the mystery of Bicknell's location was cleared up when a telegram arrived at the Red Cross. For the last six hours, he had been stuck at a train station in Wellington, Ohio, far up north in the state, about 170 miles away from Dayton. He was hardly alone, of course. Hundreds, if not thousands, of people were stuck, trying to get from one place to another. One story that made the rounds in papers was that of a Miss Wilkins, a nurse who traveled to Jacksonville, Florida, to visit a sick sister. While there, she heard about her family—in Omaha—and how her mother had been seriously injured. She took the train to go see them but became held up for an interminably long time in the flood chaos.

And as horrific as the situation was throughout Ohio and Indiana and its surrounding states, people in Omaha were still suffering. Before Wednesday, March 26, was over, two more people had died from their injuries sustained in the tornado, and another man, Thomas Barron, 48, was reportedly despondent after the destruction and, in the privacy of a hotel room, with a gun, he ended his life.

Chapter Thirteen

Greed

The morning of March 26, New Castle, Pennsylvania

The city slowly came to a standstill. The Shenango River didn't rush onto the streets like the Miami River rushed into Dayton and other towns, but it came nonetheless. School was called off, the electric light plant was flooded, the city water had been turned off, and just as it was unfolding in communities throughout states in the Midwest, Northeast, and Southeast, people were stuck on second stories and roofs without food and clean drinking water. It was estimated that at least one thousand homes were flooded, and police, firemen, and volunteer rescuers were manning boats and trying to help people to safety.

But some police officers had a funny way of helping people. It wouldn't become public knowledge until later, but at some point on Wednesday, a few officers apparently decided that their salary wasn't high enough.

Constable William Kerr asked resident John Standard, who lived on Mahoning Avenue, dangerously close to the river, for two dollars before allowing him on his boat.

"I only have one dollar," said Standard.

"All right, give me that," said Kerr.

Standard, who must have been fuming inside, fished a dollar out of his pocket and handed it to a red-haired police officer at the front of the boat who then gave it to Kerr, at the rear of the boat. Standard was far from the only person asked to pay passage before being ferried to safety. Peter Kowalcruck, also of Mahoning Avenue, was also told he needed to fork over money. He and five other men asked Kerr for a ride away from Kowalcruck's house and was told: "If you have got a dollar, we'll come back and take you out." The officers came back, and the six men gave them six dollars.

Walter VanHorn, a 37-year-old Mexican or Spanish immigrant who is said to have not known much English, was told the going rate for being saved from the flood was five dollars, a whopping sum for someone of his socioeconomic status. VanHorn, who worked as a steamfitter at a steel mill, paid up. He had a wife and three kids to worry about.

Dominick Dimucco of Center Street also paid five dollars, to a man who didn't have a uniform on, in order to get his sister, her husband, and their seven children out of their house. He claimed it was a fireman and one other man who insisted on receiving money for transporting his family, although in court he would acknowledge that the fireman himself didn't take the money and may have been unaware of what was going on around him.

Whoever was receiving the money, profiteering was a sad reality. William Kerr and several other men of authority were benefiting, particularly from ethnic minorities and women, who they believed wouldn't speak out, and the price kept going up with the water. It later came out that on Preston Avenue—which is no longer in existence—people were being charged twenty-five dollars each before being taken out of their flooded homes in boats provided by the city.

Naturally, some people, honest and not, used the flood as an excuse to make a buck. The Morris Bros., a store that specialized in selling candy, ice cream, magazines, and newspapers in Van Wert, Ohio, began advertising their souvenir postcards of the flood on March 28 when much of the community was still underwater. The ads appeared on page three of the *Van Wert Daily Bulletin*, three columns over from the daily column with the headline DEATHS AND FUNERALS. Readers could learn how Mrs. F. A. Ward was fifty years old and a victim of the "terrible flood," and of how the body of Nolan McElroy, who drowned with Charles Morris and two horses in a flooded quarry near Ada, Ohio, had just been found. Then, if they were feeling nostalgic, they could go over to the Morris Brothers for some of their famous oysters and some postcards featuring flood scenes.

Nobody in town was particularly surprised that the Morris Brothers would find a way to profit off the flood. After all, J. W. Morris, the oldest of the brothers, had been in trouble with the law, complete with a warrant for his arrest, just a few years earlier for making some sales on a Sunday.

In May of 1913, in Titusville, Pennsylvania and undoubtedly other papers in the area, the First National Bank of Warren ran an advertisement, noting that when their city of Johnstown, Pennsylvania had its nefarious flood "24 years ago, the 31st of May, many people who saved their lives not only lost their household furniture and personal effects, but their money, as many families had money hidden about the house. In the recent flood here," the ad continued, "in our own state and in the states of Indiana and Ohio, there was a smaller percentage of loss of currency, but a number of cases have come to our notice where money secreted about the home was washed away or destroyed."

So the bank was literally trying to use the flood to drum up business, but at least their message—your money is safer in the bank—had the virtue of being true.

Picture houses, in the days, weeks, and months after the flood, helped to draw in crowds by promoting footage of the flood. "As usual, the management of the Jefferson put one over by securing the Dayton Flood Pictures and showing them FIRST," boasted an ad in the *Fort Wayne Journal-Gazette* on April 4. "Note: If it is WORTH showing, the JEFFERSON will have it FIRST."

You might think that the Fort Wayne public had seen plenty of water in person, but the management of the Jefferson certainly didn't think so, splashing the Dayton Flood Pictures at the top of an ad, which then told potential moviegoers about their other films that weekend, including *The Clown's Revenge*, a Danish film short (with sixty scenes, the ad promised) and *Bachelor Bill's Birthday Present*, a comedy starring Edwin August, who had a thriving film career during the silent era but, by the time of the talkies, would be reduced to playing extras in Hollywood films, some of them classics like *Mr. Smith Goes to Washington* and *The Magnificent Ambersons.*

"A big special feature program has been arranged for the auditorium tomorrow which contains six reels of pictures and thirty-six views of the Ohio floods all shown to these delightful strains of music rendered by Schmidt's orchestra," announced an article in the *Newark Advocate*, the paper of record for Newark, Ohio on April 12. The following day in the same town, at the Orpheum, guests would "have a rare treat in store for them when 2,500 feet of flood pictures will be shown. These are moving pictures of the different Ohio cities that suffered from the recent high waters. The films have been receiving the highest praises wherever shown, and every Newark resident should take advantage of these pictures being brought to this city." A three-reel feature would also be shown. Admission, only a dime.

It wasn't just Ohio and Indiana theatres trying to pull the public in with disaster voyeurism. Around the country, theatres were touting their flood pictures. In San Antonio, Texas's paper the *San Antonio Light*, an article promoting the Wigwam Theatre raved about the new flood footage that Pathé's Weekly, the first American newsreel, would be showing. "This week's Pathé will be unusually interesting because of the fact that pictures of the recent floods in Dayton and other Ohio towns will be shown as well as scenes taken in Omaha shortly after the tornado there."

In an age when television news didn't exist, nor radio, many people around the country who had family and friends in the flood zone naturally craved information about the disaster. It would have been a disservice not to promote the flood pictures, and yet one can smell the greed when the article continues, "When Pathé's Weekly shows pictures, they are good. It is obvious, then, that you will see the best flood pictures yet shown."

On March 30, when many cities were finally drying out but some were still losing citizens to the unforgiving waters, the International Bible House in Philadelphia put on an ad in the *Indianapolis Star*, the *Fort Wayne News*, and other cities affected by the flood, and plenty that weren't, in states as far away as Montana, explaining that "agents can make $10 to $20 selling $1 book on 'Horrible Disaster by Flood and

Tornado,' greatest opportunity for agents since 'Titanic'; enormous demand for authentic book; 350 pages, 50 illustrations. Representatives sent to scene of disaster for true account and photographs of appalling calamity. Big profits for agents who begin at once. Part of publishers profits contributed to Red Cross relief fund; purchasers thus help sufferers; highest commission, 50 percent of better; freight paid; credit given; extra inducements to general agents or crew managers; outfit free. Act quick; be first around and make $10 to $20 a day."

The International Bible House had competition. The J.S. Ziegler Company, in Chicago, had a similar advertisement, stating: "'TRAGIC STORY of America's Greatest Disaster,' flood, wind and fire; the biggest money-maker agents ever had; $15 daily if you start now; large $1 book 100 illustrations; outfit free." Anderson Supply, also in Chicago, had an ad running for a book called "Horrors of Ohio Flood." Agents would buy the book for 15 cents and sell it for $1. The American Educational League, another Chicago company, didn't mention the title of their book but promised that it was the best one out there. In Altoona, Pennsylvania, and other papers across the country, there were ads for *Our National Calamity—By Flood, Fire and Tornado*, by the author of "Titanic," of which millions of copies sold, the ad raved.

The author was Logan Howard-Smith, although the ads never said that. Howard-Smith, whose pen name was Logan Marshall, knew his name wasn't what sold. It was the tragedy. He was twenty-nine, a 1905 graduate of the University of Pennsylvania, and had already written the *Life of Theodore Roosevelt* in 1910 and the aforementioned *The Sinking of the Titanic and Great Sea Disasters* the year before. But what he did, at least with his book about the Great Flood of 1913, could hardly be called writing. Howard-Smith's book, *Our National Calamity—By Flood, Fire and Tornado*, which can today be purchased on Amazon.com, was little more than copy taken from dozens of newspapers, word for word, and slapped onto pages and then bound between covers. It was gripping reading, full of juicy stories and crack reporting, all right, but he himself had hardly written a word, except perhaps for the preface of the book and a scattered number of passages or segues.

But at least Howard-Smith, store owners like the Morris Brothers, and theatre owners were giving the public what they wanted. Many more were stealing and profiting from unsuspecting flood victims during the flood itself and in its immediate aftermath, essentially blackmailing them for goods and services. One of the most heinous con artists to profit off the flood was that of Ben W. Kinsey and his army of quack doctors.

Kinsey had graduated from Jenner Medical College, then a night school with a shaky reputation, in 1909, and after running a private practice for a year, he had become an assistant and pupil of Max J. "Phenomenal" Kraus, a notorious traveling "physician," a word that should only be loosely associated with him.

Kinsey started a company called United Doctors, a business that had a blueprint that was very similar to Kraus's solo operation, which lacked a fancy name. Kraus advertised himself heavily in newspapers—and so did United Doctors. Kraus would alert the community that he was coming to visit soon and would be available to treat the people for whatever ailed them. In 1910, he put out word that he was in Cincinnati, negotiating to rent space in Hamilton's largest auditorium, where he would discuss the latest forms of electric treatment in medicine. He promised that he would treat any of the members of the paying audience, who he picked out of the crowd, for free. It made for good press, and the customers who came after the first paying customer, he could gouge.

Kinsey took Kraus's model and did him one better. He started hiring other like-minded quacks and set up scattered offices around the Midwest and like his mentor, advertised frequently in the paper, alerting the community that the United Doctors was coming to town, and those who were sick should get in line.

The ads worked. For starters, they were often paid advertorials, written like newspaper articles but fully paid for by the advertiser, who was, in this case, United Doctors. United Doctors were quick to pay their bills, which may explain why newspapers were slow to investigate claims that they were defrauding the public.

The medical community—the real physicians—were horrified. One respected journal of the time, *The Railway Surgical Journal*, called United Doctors "a medical parasite." Meanwhile, the staff of the *Journal of the American Medical Association* believed emphatically that the people behind United Doctors were crooks. As they wrote in an article that appeared in their January-June 1913 issue, many of the doctors that Kinsey hired were of dubious character. For instance, one of them, George L. Dickerson, a physician from Indiana, had had his license revoked in part because he had loaned his medical diploma to his brother, who wasn't a doctor. Two other "doctors," a W. D. Rea and G. W. Bourne, had visited Lockhart, Texas in February of 1913 as part of a similar healing tour, and the American Medical Association, wanting to confirm their suspicions, sent a healthy man to be their patient.

Both Rea and Bourne said that their healthy patient had diabetes and wouldn't live another six months unless he received treatment from them, and it was about that moment that they mentioned the cost for their care would be $45, a princely sum back then. A prosecutor then came after the doctors, who agreed to scrub all of their engagements in Texas and leave the state.

An ad that appeared in the *Warsaw Union* in Warsaw, Indiana, in October of 1913, was typical of the time. It read in part:

"These Doctors are among America's leading stomach and nerve specialists, and are experts in the treatment of chronic diseases of the blood, liver, stomach, intestines, skin, nerves, heart, spleen, kidneys or bladder, rheumatism, sciatica, diabetes, bed-wetting, tape worm, leg ulcers, weak lungs, and those afflicted with long standing, deep seated chronic diseases, that have baffled the skill of other physicians, should not fail to call. Deafness has often been cured in sixty days."

By the time any deaf person realized that they hadn't been cured, these doctors were long gone.

They just asked that you bring a two-ounce bottle of your urine for chemical analysis and microscopic examination. And for the squeamish, there was nothing to worry about, either: the United Doctors, as their article-ads stated, "were among the first in America to earn the name of 'bloodless surgeons,' by doing away with the knife, with blood and with pain in the successful treatment of these dangerous diseases."

So it was no surprise to anyone, and a great relief to the unsuspecting and desperate masses, when the United Doctors began releasing advertorials that ran in papers like Newark, Ohio. "FLOOD SUFFERERS SHOWN SPECIAL FAVORS BY THE UNITED DOC-TORS," said the headline in the *Newark Advocate*.

The story stated, "In view of the awful calamity that has visited the state of Ohio in the recent horrible flood, which has caused an enormous loss of life and property and thrown countless hundreds of men and women out of employment, the United Doctors have decided to throw open their doors once more to those who may be suffering and unable to take treatment owing to the flood conditions and their results."

The article then went on to give the address of United Doctors and stated that people who showed up would receive "free consultation, advice and no charge for service whatever will be made. The only charge made will be sufficient to cover the medicine used in the treatment of the case. This is your last chance of Free Treatment and is made only because of the intense suffering caused by the flood."

And just in case anyone wondered if they were a good candidate for United Doctors, the article finished by saying, "The United Doctors treat among other ailments Chronic and Deep-Seated diseases of the Nerves, Blood, Heart, Liver, Kidneys, Bladder, Skin, Spine, including Rheumatism, Epilepsy, Gallstones, Goitre, Constipation, Dyspepsia, Neuralgia, Dropsy, Asthma, Catarrh, Deafness, Loss of Nerve Force, Weak Lungs and Diseases of Women and Diseases of Men."

In other words, everyone. Everyone with money for medicine, that is.

Lest one fault the newspapers for running these articles on the newspaper pages and next to flood articles, the editors often (but not always) put the initials "advt" afterward, standing for advertisement or advertorial. The editors at the *Newark Advocate* used the initials "s&m" at the article's conclusion. It may have been a sadomasochistic form of journalism, but it stood for sales and marketing, a point that most readers would miss or not understand.

United Doctors' offices would start closing within a few years, and the visits would stop, due to complaints from the public and lawmakers who started to catch on and began writing laws to stop fly-by-night medical operations; but during the flood of 1913, they ran rampant as lawmakers and other public officials were distracted with flood recovery. The incident in Newcastle, Pennsylvania, was not the only instance either of rescuers trying to profit during the flood. It is the most infamous example, given that police officers were involved, but they were hardly the only greedy rescuers.

Newspapers reported many examples of people charging for boat and carfare to get people from here or there. In Peru, Indiana, some boatmen charged several new mothers with their babies in arms five dollars to be taken from a building to dry land. In Dayton, according to one newspaper account, a husky young doctor had an argument with one man who demanded ten dollars—five per passenger—before he would bring two injured women in his car to the hospital.

The doctor didn't have ten dollars, and the man kept insisting. Finally, the physician picked up a piece of driftwood and clocked him senseless. Then the doctor put the unconscious jerk into the car with the women, drove to the hospital, and treated all of them.

There was at least one other surgeon in Dayton—a Dr. Ray B. Harris—who couldn't take the greed either and, in his words, "I personally thrashed two drivers who presumed to haggle."

In Columbus, a 35-year-old undertaker by the name of O. H. Osman was arrested by the police for taking possessions off dead bodies. Osman, who three years earlier had been a telephone operator at the Columbus State Hospital, an insane asylum, was now collecting bodies—and quite a bit more. Evidently thinking that most people were as dishonest as he was, Osman approached two Ohio National Guard soldiers, Clyde McCullough and an F. L. Killworth, asking them to "throw" all the bodies possible to him, saying that he would pay them if they did.

The two guardsmen arranged a meeting with Osman at the morgue, and when they arrived, the undertaker was in the middle of telling an underling to remove the clothing off an elderly woman's corpse and taking money out of the pockets. But instead of sealing a deal with Osman, McCullough and Killworth took the undertaker into custody.

This next tale appeared in one of the Dayton papers. It may be apocryphal, sort of a wish fulfillment story that made the rounds— but it may well be true, too. According to one news item, a Mr. Charles Thatcher, his wife Louise, and a neighbor were trapped on the floor of their house when a boatman offered to rescue them for a cost of $100 per passenger. Mr. Thatcher proposed the boatman accept $25 a person, for that's all he had, but the offer wasn't accepted, and they were left behind. Later, they heard a shot, presumably from another angry homeowner. A few minutes later, the Thatchers and their neighbor saw the boat float by, with the boatman slumped over, dead.

Chapter Fourteen

Children in Harm's Way

From the first rays of daylight, rescuers were back in their boats, hauling families out of second-story windows and off of roofs. Among those families were Harry Laban Blair, a 66-year-old Canadian-born house painter, and his wife, Hattie, their daughter, Francis, and their son-in-law Ralph Leffler, a horseshoer. Their happiness turned to sheer terror, however, when they realized George, all of five years old, had not climbed into the boat with them.

It sounds incredulous and the height of irresponsibility that a set of grandparents and parents wouldn't realize their grandson and son hadn't climbed in their boat, but to give them the benefit of the doubt, they had all been stuck in the same house, and then on top of the house, for two days, with only one pancake to eat among them. They were starving and clearly not thinking straight.

To top it off, there were other people on the roof and a hoard of boats coming and going, carrying people to safety. It was melee and quite possibly, on top of everything else, raining. But the chaos they came from was nothing compared to what it was like on the boat once everyone discovered George was missing. The family was in hysterics, especially when they were told that the current was too strong to go back for him.

It's just as well that they didn't risk their lives going back. The five-year-old had climbed into another rescue boat, just before the rest of his family had clambered into their own, and George was calmly waiting at the shoreline for everyone else to catch up with him. The experience only highlighted how marginal and disorganized rescue efforts were—noble and courageous, but it was clear that neither Fort Wayne or many other cities in the flood zone had any real plan in place to deal with flooding and bringing its citizens to safety in its wake. Later, communities would begin to address this.

The level of devastation inflicted by the flood was always a matter of perspective in every city, whether Fort Wayne, New Castle, or even Dayton. If you were marooned on your roof with no or little food, you tended to tell your friends that it was the worst flood ever. If your house was on dry, high ground, your life could go on in a relatively normal way—or you could use your resources to help your fellow neighbors. That was the tack the Peters family took in Fort Wayne.

Living above much of the city on the appropriately named Rockhill Street, Fred and Bessie Peters, a family with some wealth, opened their two-story, affluent home, which overlooked the St. Marys River, and allowed refugees to gather their wits and camp out. With the only working telephone in the area, the house became something of a social gathering place where neighbors could come and try to find out how family members and friends were faring.

"Men come in, in their wet clothing from the river, and are immediately given warm, dry clothing and hot coffee and sandwiches," the *Fort Wayne Journal Gazette* reported at the time. "Coffee is sent by Mrs. Peters to the workers. She has relieved a great number of people in the last few days and given a beautiful example as many of her friends as possible have tried to follow."

Mrs. Peters let all of her three children, Fred Jr., Stuart, and Jane Alice help as much as they could and feel important to the flood relief cause, which probably boosted their confidence since the Peters otherwise had a rocky, dysfunctional marriage. Fred Peters had been injured shortly before his marriage in a work-related accident that left him with only one good leg and, worse, periodic headaches that turned him into a tyrant. Which is why the following year, Bessie divorced her husband and transplanted herself and her children to California. And then many years later, her youngest, Jane Alice, just five years old during the flood, grew up to become the actress and comedienne famous for screwball comedies during the 1930s— Carole Lombard.

Lombard wasn't the only future celebrity caught up in the flood. Her future beau, movie star Clark Gable, was a twelve-year-old living in Cadiz, Ohio, at the time. According to Warren G. Harris' book *Clark Gable: A Biography*, the Gable family's house was threatened by rising waters: ". . . for a solid week the rains poured down and threatened to wash away their three year old home."

Somewhere in the Indianapolis area was a future gangster, nine-year-old John Dillinger.

Roy Rogers, the famous singing cowboy film actor and singer, was almost two years old and living in Portsmouth, Ohio, which was also hammered by the flood. According to Robert W. Phillips's book, *Roy Rogers: A Biography, Radio History, Television Career Chronicle*, Rogers's dad, Andy, took the family's houseboat through the streets of Portsmouth, serving as a rescue boat for anyone in need of help.

Vincente Minnelli, future husband of Judy Garland and father of Liza Minnelli, not to mention acclaimed movie director, was a ten-year-old who had recently moved to Delaware, Ohio. He had been visiting there for years, to spend the winter with his grandparents; but his parents, who were touring the country in a theatre troupe called the Mighty Dramatic Company, decided to plant their roots and open a costume shop and settle on Fountain Street in Delaware. While the family survived the flood, they had entertainment equipment from their traveling theatre days stored near the river that wouldn't make it.

Bob Hope was also ten years old and living in Cleveland, where the city was affected by the flood but nowhere near to the degree of the rest of the state.

Down the St. Marys River, south of the house where the future Carole Lombard lived, the water was eleven inches deep in the first floor of the Allen County Orphans' home. That in and of itself was not so terrible—it did not seem as if the water would ever reach the second floor—but the current was strong, and it was not a reach to fear that the orphanage might eventually collapse if the weight of the water kept increasing. Everyone felt that the children needed to be evacuated now. In another part of the city, the children at the Indiana School for Feeble Minded Youth, a name that would be changed to the much less stigmatized Fort Wayne State School twenty years later, were shepherded out of their home, where the waters had now reached the front yard. Everyone knew what had happened with the Allen County Orphans' home; nobody was going to take any chances with any other orphanage.

That morning, Miss Hammond went to the orphanage with Henry E. Branning, and they both stopped at the Gebhart farm. Miss Hammond waited at the front of the farm while Branning went looking for Charles Gebhart, a saloon owner. He found him behind his barn, feeding chickens. Branning asked Gebhart if he could man a rowboat and ferry the orphans to safer land. Gebhart didn't hesitate.

Gebhart secured a rowboat—probably his own, as he did live near the river—and they made their way to the orphanage, which was completely surrounded by water at this point. It wasn't very deep—the water was only eleven inches high on the first floor of the building—but it was moving quickly, and wading through it was foolhardy.

Gebhart rowed both Hammond and Branning to the orphanage, pulling the boat up to the fire escape, which seemed as if it would make a safe and easy platform for the children to leave from. Hammond and Gebhart remained in the boat while Branning went inside to arrange passage of the first of the children. The plan was to go to a farm that the county orphanage owned, just a fourth-mile to the west but on dry earth where the children would be safe. The first three passengers were Della Sturm, eight years old, and two seven-year-old girls, Opal Jacobs and Kittie Wise. The three girls huddled alongside Miss Hammond in the pouring rain. Next to board were three older girls. Mrs. Overmeyer had decided she would put three older girls as a counterpart to the younger children. If there was trouble, the older girls could help Miss Hammond. And so Esther Kramer, Ardah Woods and Alice Mannen, all fourteen-year-old girls, carefully made their way into the boat.

"I am going to take my friend with me," said Ardah, referring to her Bible tightly clasped in her hands. Everybody seemed to think this was a good idea. Particularly on a day like this.

Once they were in, right about 10 A.M., Gebhart began to paddle toward a farmhouse about one-quarter mile to the west.

Opal dug her hands as deep into her muff as she could, trying to stay warm and be responsible. It was Miss Hammond's, and Opal had been told to take good care of it during the trip.

In another boat that had been commandeered from good Samaritans, E. G. Moore and Branning helped two more girls into the boat and were about to add more passengers when something went terribly wrong. "My God," shouted Moore, "it's struck a post!"

It was, more accurately, a telegraph pole. Gebhart's boat hit it, sending everyone tumbling into the rushing river.

From the inside of the orphanage, the children who were watching— virtually all of them—broke into screams.

Gebhart saw Miss Hammond about twenty feet away, hugging the pole that the boat had hit. Underneath her arms were three girls, two of them under one arm, and one under the other. He didn't see the older girls.

The children in the orphanage saw them. So did Branning, Mrs. Overmeyer, Moore, and Mark Ormiston, a 42-year-old husband and father of two boys who was employed at a nearby brickyard, driving either a wagon or a truck. They watched the foamy, muddy yellow waves swallow the four older girls. One of them just seemed to vanish instantly. Two of the older girls, however, could be seen being dragged by the current toward the railroad tracks that normally carried the train from Fort Wayne to the town of Bluffton, Indiana. One of the four, Esther Kramer, could swim and managed to fight the waves for at least a few moments and then grab hold of a railroad track, to keep herself from being carried any farther. But a few seconds later, the water, moving too fast, jarred her free, and she was gone.

Fighting the river's onslaught, Gebhart swam to the telegraph pole, lunging for it and then wrapping an arm around Miss Hammond, whose grip on the post was loosening.

At the orphanage, Moore and Ormiston reversed course, helping their two girl passengers back out of the boat, so they could row toward Gebhart, Hammond; and the three little girls they were trying to save.

Twisted, Gebhart's back was pressed up against Miss Hammond's, one of his arms clinging to the telegraph pole, and the other to Miss Hammond.

Miss Hammond, meanwhile, held on to Della, Opal, and Kittie, telling the girls to keep their mouths shut and not to swallow the water. She shouted to Moore and Ormiston to hurry.

Moore and Ormiston rowed as hard as they could against the current, which kept smashing them back.

Miss Hammond felt Kittie Wise, who had had a death grip around her teacher's waist, slipping from under her arm to her back. Della, too, was struggling to keep her head above the waves.

Gebhart twisted his body around as far as humanly possible, so that he could barely make out little Kittie Wise, her arms hugging her teacher's waist. But Kittie was under the water and didn't appear to be moving.

Gebhart had no hands free to help Kittie. To let go with either hand would result in Miss Hammond, himself, and all the girls being released into the fast-moving waters. Sickened and panic-stricken, Gebhart realized he was watching Kittie drown a mere few feet from him.

He bent over, dunking his head under the water, using the one part of his body that was still available. He grabbed her clothing with his teeth. And he pulled.

But he couldn't pull hard enough, and after a moment, just as his strength and oxygen was giving out, Gebhart just knew: *She's dead.* And he opened his mouth, pitched his head back up, and, choking for air, turned to see Moore and Ormiston rowing toward them.

"Hurry," screamed Miss Hammond, "I can't hold on much longer!"

As Moore and Ormiston rowed toward them, Gebhart endeavored to pull Miss Hammond and the girls closer to the telegraph pole, maneuvering himself so that with one arm, he was embracing the post and the teacher. With his free arm, he began loosening Kittie Wise's grip, to free her from Miss Hammond.

"Don't let her go," begged Miss Hammond. "Take her in the boat, too."

"I can't do it," said Gebhart. "She's dead. We've got to let her go and save the living."

Then he pried Kittie's hands off and released her to the river, which eagerly accepted her.

At about that moment, Moore and Ormiston rowed up beside them, struggling to keep the boat in, and Gebhart held on to the boat and the post, steadying the craft enough so that both men could pull up the girls, one of whom, Della, was now also limp and lifeless.

Next, they hauled Miss Hammond into the boat. Gebhart was going to follow, but the boat lurched free from the post and one of the oars hit him in the chest. Gebhart, clinging to the boat, managed after a few moments to pull himself into it.

Ormiston and Moore rowed everyone back to the orphanage where Mrs. Overmeyer was sobbing. Miss Hammond held on to Della, trying to wake her. Opal clung to Miss Hammond's muff. She was still taking care of it, just like she had been told.

Inside the orphanage, puddles collecting at the survivors' feet, Della lay on a sofa, unmoving. When Dr. Frank Dinnen opened her eyes, the pupils were rolled back.

10:15 A.M., Dayton, Ohio

After enduring a night in total darkness, except for a two- or three-inch candle that was used sparingly, a man only known as Dr. Reeve, in a letter to his daughter, Lottie, in California, painted a grim picture of life in downtown Dayton.

"I am sitting at upper window, mother's room," wrote the 87-year-old Reeve, who could see the Callahan building from his home. "Outside a raging torrent pours down Wilkinson street, another mighty river down Third Street toward west. No human being in sight—no signs of life. Below, in our yard on piles of wreckage, a fine piano. Yesterday, I had got breakfast at the Arcade and brought some to mother. Danger whistles had sounded before I was up, I supposed for breaking of levee; but I banked on the great flood of '66, when this house stood high and dry with all around overflowed."

Reeve and his wife were stuck in their house with another couple, a Mr. and Mrs. Penfield, and he noted in his letter that he had recently seen a horse struggling in the current and pass by his home. He also had just come from his flooded first floor in an unsuccessful attempt to retrieve a lamp from the back office. The water had fallen four inches from the previous day, and so he took off his clothes and went down to the last step, "up to my arm pits in the cold water, but the room so full of floating furniture that I could not make my way to it."

As for food, things were bleak, but Reeve and his wife and the Penfields were in part being kept alive by their neighbors. "All we have is some crackers, nuts and a few apples. This morning, some young men on the roof of the next house gave us coffee."

Mrs. Penfield was able to reach over from their roof and grab the coffee from one of the men, stretching out to hand them a drink.

The black coffee, sans sugar and cream, was helpful to keep dehydration at bay, but, as Dr. Reeve lamented, they were otherwise in pretty poor shape: "We have no water, no light, no telephone connection, no cars, no papers—nothing."

Of course, the Reeves and Penfields were hardly alone, especially when it came to food, which was in serious lack of supply throughout Dayton. Daisy Wallace, a resident of Dayton, held down the fort with her two teenage boys and her live-in father; her husband, Clinton, was apparently stuck at work. Mrs. Wallace managed to keep her family alive on Tuesday and Wednesday, but the cupboards were bare. This was, naturally, an age before refrigerators existed, and although many families had iceboxes, people didn't tend to store more than a day's worth of food in them. When the flood struck, the only food item in the entire Wallace household was a grapefruit. They were stuck in their home without food or drink, other than their grapefruit, for forty-eight hours.

At the Bell Telephone Company, the twenty women and fourteen men trapped were getting hungrier by the moment. The day before, around 4 P.M., a cord was thrown from the building to the Y.M.C.A., and the staff there filled a basket with forty sandwiches inside, so that the telephone workers could then pull it slowly back to them. That had helped a lot, but it was, after all, one sandwich apiece, and six additional split thirty-four ways, and by Wednesday morning, the telephone workers were famished once again. But this time, the Y.M.C.A. workers signaled that they had no more food to spare, and they had three hundred people trapped in their building.

March 26, around 11 A.M., Fort Wayne, Indiana

Della was somehow revived. She was in shock, and Dr. Dinnen suspected she might be in the beginning stages of pneumonia, but for the moment she seemed to be in pretty fair shape. That evening, he would tell a local reporter, "Little Della is just chuck full of water."

Dr. Dinnen also examined Miss Hammond. He felt Miss Hammond was in a state of shock and should be taken to her house in the next boat to leave the orphanage.

Less than an hour after Gebhart and Hammond reached the orphanage, they made another attempt to ferry the children away. This time, Henry Masterson and Private Charles Reynolds, an Indiana National Guardsman, were at the oars. Gebhart and Hammond were passengers, along with four boys from the orphanage who were given the now-dubious honor of being selected for the voyage. Harold Boggs, fourteen, Clyde Feightner, eleven, Glenn Baird, ten, and Burtan Rhoades, ten, climbed into their vessel.

The thinking was that three men in the boat might be able to protect the children more easily.

It went fine, at first. But as the boat reached the Broadway Street bridge, the current sped up, and as the boat came near to a house, there was a rope strung up from it to another house, and while Masterson, Reynolds, Hammond, and the young boys successfully ducked their heads, missing the rope, Gebhart wasn't so lucky. It caught him, so that while the boat went forward, he didn't, and suddenly the boat capsized once again, with its passengers pitching into the water.

Masterson and Gebhart emerged from underneath the rushing water first, finding the water shallow enough that they could stand and pull the boys onto the porch of a store. Theresa Hammond had, as the boat toppled over, lunged for the rope and clung to it. Private Reynolds, however, missed grabbing it, and if he had a chance to stand, he could not find his footing, and the current whipped him away down the street.

George Young, a Fort Wayne resident, suddenly became part of the story. He was watching everything unfold from across the street and immediately made his way through the water, hanging on to the rope, heading toward Miss Hammond. Another man on the scene, Clyde Siples, set his sights on trying to save Private Reynolds. And if Reynolds's plight hadn't been so perilous, Siples might have laughed.

Reynolds, flailing and traveling fast down the water, grabbed hold of the first thing he could find: an outhouse.

He kept trying to straddle it like a boat, but it was, it was later described, like trying to step onto a rolling barrel. But he hung on to the outhouse, his weight and legs slowing the outhouse down. Siples was able to reach both in his boat, and Reynolds scrambled aboard.

They both rowed toward the Henche shop where George Young and Theresa Hammond were waiting with Gebhart, Masterson, and the four boys. The dripping-wet adults surveyed their surroundings and progress. Four boys were shivering and soaked, but no longer trapped at the orphanage, which was something positive. Still, four girls were dead, and fifty-four orphans were still marooned. Gebhart, Reynolds, and Masterson rowed back to the orphanage and conferred with Mrs. Overmeyer, Dr. Frank Dinnen, and the other officials, deciding that with two capsized-boat incidents behind them, for now, despite the rising water on the first floor, and the safety of the structure in doubt, the orphans and their guardians would stay put after all.

Morning and into the afternoon, Peru, Indiana

The Hagenbeck-Wallace Circus was furiously trying to adapt to the rushing water and save their animals. The cat trainers spent their morning putting in platforms that they built for the animals to stand on, over the water, which was rising six inches every hour.

The trainers left, hoping they had found a way to save their animals, but as the day went on, they didn't feel very good about their chances. Still, they had done what they felt they could do. They couldn't just let the animals loose on Peru. There were already some rogue elephants out there.

But the platforms weren't enough. Most of the lions, tigers, leopards, and panthers drowned in their cages, a tragic ending for animals that had once roamed the lands of Africa. But there were a few exceptions. Three lions named Sultan, Brutus, and Mitch somehow outlasted the flood on their platforms, and the polar bears probably enjoyed the chilly water—they certainly acted as if they did, trainers later noted, and Big George, a hippo that lived in a big tank in the corner of the elephant barn, managed to come out just fine. The trainer in charge of Big George told reporters that the hippopotamus had remained under water for twelve hours at a time—an impossibility, as thirty minutes is a hippo's biological capacity—which makes one wonder about this guy's experience in working with hippos. Expertise aside, however, at least Big George came through, especially when there was so much other carnage.

The Bengal tiger rammed his body against his cage repeatedly, creating a hole large enough for him to crawl through and escape certain death. It would be lovely to say that then the Bengal tiger rallied the surviving animals, cornered Captain Emil Schweyer, the trainer who had caught them in Africa and brought them to this flooded no man's (and animal's) land, and then given the man a piece of their minds. Or at least that the tiger escaped to the surrounding forests and lived a happy life feeding off deer and fox. But instead, after all of the Bengal tiger's hard work in smashing an opening in his cage, the animal lunged into the awesome force that was the river.

Not even a Bengal tiger could beat it.

Sam Bundy, meanwhile, was still saving lives all over town. On Wednesday morning, March 26, 1913, Bundy hadn't taken a rest since 1 A.M., March 25.

Bundy's physical prowess impressed the community. He seemed to have no fear of the water, and really, he didn't. But he respected it.

Bundy's method was to steer his boat closer to the river banks, where the current was slightly less wild. It meant he had to travel across more water than if he stuck it out in the middle, and it could take more time, but Bundy was getting results and avoiding the catastrophic boat capsizing that other, rasher rescuers were dealing with. At this point, locals were keeping track of how many people Bundy had saved in his boat. The number was closing in on a hundred.

12 *P.M., Zanesville, Ohio*

City officials, for some time now, had been watching their historic Y-shaped bridge, which crossed both the Licking and Muskingum rivers, knowing it was in its final hours. It was first built in 1814, 99 years earlier, although it had been rebuilt a couple of times due to damage from smaller floods since the 1850s. Realizing it was going to collapse completely and create further havoc downriver, city officials decided it would be better to control the collapse and effectively euthanize it. Dynamite was laid out, and the resulting explosion was, naturally, heard for miles. It probably saddened the officials to blow it up, but with no bridge floating downriver and crashing into homes, it was an act that may well have saved some lives.

12 *P.M., Fort Wayne, Indiana*

Assistant Fire Chief George Jasper heard the news about the failed rescue at the orphanage. Jasper was directing the rescue work in Lakeside, a neighborhood in the city, but, alarmed, he immediately ordered several of his firemen to take six boats to the Allen County Orphans' home to assist in transporting the orphans to dry land.

1 *P.M., Dayton, Ohio*

The lunch hour came and went at the Beckel House. "Will try to give a lunch at four o'clock," a staff member had announced shortly after breakfast, with the warning, "and that will be all we can give today." As the Beckel House survivors discussed their ongoing, seemingly never-ending situation, everyone heard an alarmingly loud noise, and as they ran to the window, they saw that a drug store about half a block away had collapsed, and slowly, much of it began to float away. Moments later, there was another crash, and everyone heard a man across the street on a roof shout that three buildings south of the Phillips Hotel had just gone down.

Judge Jones believes it was 1:30 P.M., when a man near him said in a worried, low voice: "What if a fire breaks out?"

Almost immediately, someone shouted, "Oh, merciful God, there it is!"

Not three hundred feet away from the Beckel House, a column of flames climbed into the air. The floating remains of the drug store were on fire, and it had crashed into St. Paul Evangelical Church about three hundred feet away, across the street. In the same block, to the east of the building that was now on fire within clear view of them, were three wholesale liquor stores. There was also a paint and supply store, a paint warehouse, a hardware store, *and* an ammunition shop. You couldn't find a more inviting place for a fire.

Everyone—guests, staff, and the refugees who came from the street the previous day—whispered to each other, possibly trying not to frighten everyone into a wild panic. Everyone was in agreement. The fire was going to spread from the church to the stores containing ample liquor, which would then turn into a fiery hell. This fiery hell would then take down the entire block and almost certainly leap across the oil-slicked, waterlogged street and take down the block of buildings that the Beckel House was in.

Everyone agreed. It was time to get as far away as possible from the fire, even if it meant that they would be tempting a watery fate.

Everyone started for the exit.

Everyone in the vicinity—not just the Beckel House guests, but the people in all of the buildings anywhere near the fire—started to move, some of them walking, many of them running, but all of them rushing from roof to roof, and when that wouldn't work, creating makeshift bridges. While the Beckel guests would head for the sturdy Callahan Building, many Dayton residents were making their way to the Beaver Building, a five-story concrete, fire-proof power plant that had been erected just four years earlier. By the time everyone had gathered there, the building housed three hundred men, women, and children, including fifteen babies.

Meanwhile, at the Beckel House, several people—probably the staff—collected Clarence Bennett, the dying owner, from his bed and carried him on a stretcher. A housekeeper, who had apparently been injured when the northeast corner of the hotel initially collapsed, had one broken arm in a sling, and she was going to somehow have to travel from building to building. There were possibly one or maybe two children among them as well, Jones would recall. Then everyone commenced what Jones called "a remarkable march of retreat. Some two or possibly three hundred persons clambered, climbed, and crawled from one end of the square on Third Street, from Jefferson to Main. Just how it was done, in every particular, probably no one can ever tell. We got out on the roof of the Beckel annex. We went up and down fire escapes. We cautiously crossed frail-looking skylights. We scaled fire-walls. We took ladders along, and from slippery roofs went to open windows, passed through buildings, and from windows to roofs again. We reached a ten-foot alley. A ladder was pushed across it to the next building, and we crawled over, one at a time."

Somehow, all made it across the ladder straddling the water-filled alley to safety, away from the encroaching inferno.

They reached the twelve-story Callahan Building, which was at the end of Main Street. They could go no further.

It was a tall, towering building, impervious—at least it seemed so—from collapsing in a flood, although everyone worried about that nonetheless. But the building, to the best of anyone's knowledge, wasn't fireproof, and just a few hundred feet behind the Beckel House group was what Jones described as a "roaring, leaping pillar of flame, devouring everything before it."

The choices seemed pretty obvious. Stay and burn, or jump into the icy, muddy water and eventually drown, or fight the current for as long as possible and then die from the cold and exhaustion. Nobody seemed willing to burn to death, but nobody felt like trying the water. Not just yet.

2:30 P.M., Fort Wayne, Indiana

The river water was out of control. There were two opposing currents in front of the orphanage, creating a whirlpool. The fire department had strung two ropes up from the bridge near the orphans' home, allowing the boats to connect themselves by a pulley and make the trip in relative safety. Only it was hardly safe. It ensured that the current could not carry the boat itself away, but capsizing was still a possibility. Only the strongest oarsmen were making the attempt to reach the orphanage.

The police were now involved. Earlier in the morning, Police Chief Abbott had issued an order that anyone using a boat to save chickens, household goods, or some otherwise meaningless item compared to human life should give up their vessel immediately if it was needed.

Well, it was needed now. Abbott ordered all available boats to the orphans' home. Only three boats would remain in three other neighborhoods—Lakeside, Spy Run, and Bloomingdale. The rest were at the bridge, where the boats were being tied together to form a giant raft. He would soon give his okay for a life-saving crew from Chicago to come in and help, but they wouldn't be here for hours, and in the meantime, he would try to do what he could. He currently was overseeing an operation in which all of the boats in the city were being tied together to form a giant raft bridge that apparently the children could use to cross from the orphanage to dry land. It wouldn't work—it thankfully never got to the stage where any child attempted to use it—and the chief probably knew it was a weird idea, but he was running out of other ideas, options, and time.

Columbus, Ohio, 2:47 P.M.

Governor Cox, who was plenty concerned about the entire state, and the city he lived in, received word that the entire downtown section of Dayton was now on fire and would probably be destroyed.

The papers were full of equally dire news for Dayton. A boatman rescuer told a reporter that over at the courthouse, he saw bodies floating like logs.

Cox was feeling more than desperate. He ended up putting out the statement, remarkable by today's standards since few, if any, politicians would likely suggest something that might put ordinary citizens in harm's way: "Farmers and everybody who by any possible means can get boats to Dayton ought to do it this afternoon even at the risk of their own lives. I appeal through the United Press to all the people along the rivers leading into Dayton to try to get boats here. I appeal especially to the people at Troy, where I understand, there is a boat club. The buildings on Third Street in Dayton are now afire and people now in them are dying."

Around 3 P.M., Dayton, Ohio

On Third Street in Dayton, the guests of the Beckel House were on the second floor of the Callahan Building and trying to come up with some way to avoid burning or drowning. Two of the men secured the tools, or makeshift tools, that enabled them to cut a cable in the elevator shaft. They tied one end to the building and the other to what Jones called a "rude kind of scow," a flat-bottomed boat, possibly created from the elevator, one would think. Wherever they found the scow, it worked well enough. The group sent the scow through a second-story window and into the water and managed to get it across the river to the old courthouse, where there was some high ground around and at least one person there, able to secure the elevator cable.

But the scow, which everyone envisioned being able to ferry each guest across, then capsized and floated away.

One man came up in a boat and helped further secure the cable, Jones would recall, but the man in the boat wouldn't stay and maybe couldn't. "His craft whirled away on the current," wrote Jones, adding, remarkably, given how many rescuers were out and about in Dayton: "That was the only boat we saw during the flood."

It wasn't for lack of trying, however. Fred Patterson, John H. Patterson's son, and a boat mate, Nelson Talbott, were trying their best to get to downtown, but the swiftly moving forces were too powerful and unpredictable.

"We penetrated almost to the center of the city," Fred told reporters. "Everywhere persons cried out to us to rescue them, but it was impossible, for we were barely able to keep afloat. Large sums of money were offered us to take persons from perilous positions. The windows of the Algonquin Hotel seemed filled with faces and the same conditions prevailed at most of the buildings we passed. We did not see any bodies."

Shortly afterward, Fred's father released a statement to the public, hoping someone with some influence would help them: "Our greatest need is a dozen motorboats and men to run them."

Help would be coming. Governor Cox issued a telegram to the editor of the *New York Times*, saying that his motive for contacting them was to spread the word that Dayton needed everyone's attention. "Please give great publicity to our appeal for help," wrote Cox. "My judgment is that there has never been such a tragedy in the history of our Republic."

Cox went on to mention that the next morning at daylight, fifty boats would go into the business district from South Park. The naval militia, with a hundred boats, was scheduled to leave Toledo at midnight. Yes, Cox was sending in the navy.

For now, though, Dayton residents, especially those downtown, were still on their own, which is how the Beckel House guests came to have an elevator cable stretched across the wild river street but no boat to cross it in. Three or maybe four of the strongest men in the group nevertheless grabbed on to the cable and struggled across it, each of them going across hand by hand, neck-deep in freezing cold water. Several times, they were almost ripped away from the cable but each man hung on until they arrived at the other side. Still, it soon became clear that virtually nobody else had the stamina and strength after two nightmarish days to try this method of escape. They were still stuck choosing between burning to a crisp or drowning in an icy current of filth.

3 P.M., Fort Wayne, Indiana

Chief Abbott tasked four Fort Wayne residents—Jack Miller, Bob Wartell, August Melsching, and Ed Hiatt—with taking three jugs of water to the orphanage. If that went well, they would return and take food to the children and adults overseeing them.

The police and fire chief sent a request to Winona Lake, Indiana, a popular recreational town forty miles northwest, which had a big lake and several boats. They asked for all the motor boats that they had so they could be shipped aboard a Pennsylvania train. Still, the chiefs realized that at the earliest, the motor boats wouldn't reach them until nightfall, which meant the rescue work would have to be done by lantern light. And possibly in the snow. As the four men ferried over water and food, a heavy blizzard hit Fort Wayne.

Somewhere in the afternoon, Chicago

The Chicago Association of Commerce wired $100,000 to the National Red Cross. It was just one of hundreds, if not thousands, of organizations sending money to the flood-relief cause.

Sometime in the afternoon, Peru, Indiana

Frank McNally and Icea Hesser, the seventeen-year-old he saved from drowning, were finally able to leave the tree that had been their home for the last twenty-four hours.

Climbing into the boat, the two must have asked their rescuers about Hesser's cousin, Delight. Nobody had seen her. Somehow it didn't matter to McNally that he brought approximately seventy-five people from danger and onto dry land. Long after he was warm and dry, McNally would keep thinking of Shields. The guilt was eating away at him. He would overcome his emotions, but not for a while. Weeks later, he would be put on a suicide watch.

But McNally wasn't the only one thinking of Shields. As word got around of her accident and other boats overturning, the local populace became terrified, causing some to make arguably irrational decisions. Indiana Senator Stephen Fleming, who was in charge of a relief train sent to Peru from beleaguered but in better shape Fort Wayne, observed at the time: "Many people are still in their homes in the inundated city, frightened at repeated capsizings of rescue boats working to and fro among the stricken homes, positively refuse to accept assistance and almost crazed by their fear, insist upon remaining in the houses, although many of them are standing in water in the second floors of their homes."

But perhaps they were right to be so paranoid. There had been a lot of capsizing, not just with McNally, but other men like John E. May, a farmer from nearby Stanford, Indiana. He rowed all of Monday night and by Tuesday morning had rescued 122 people from their homes. Then around ten in the morning, a passenger ended up capsizing the boat—a woman who was said to have had a bird cage wrapped in a shawl, which may have contributed to the accident. Both the woman and May drowned. He wouldn't be found for another two days.

Then there was Gilbert Kessler, the man visiting his cousin in Peru. He had been rescuing people, and while he mostly was successful at it, he had two women succumb to madness and jump out of his boat. On the first occasion, he was in a boat full of passengers, heading to the courthouse. The waves were rocking the boat pretty badly, and suddenly a woman stood up and wailed: "Oh, what is the use? We'll all be drowned anyway."

She then jumped into the water, the unbalancing of the boat sending Kessler and another oarsman into the water but apparently leaving the rest of the passengers inside. Kessler saw a "slender arm" in the water and tried to grab for it but couldn't, and then quickly turned his attention to climbing back aboard the boat. He was then able to row to the oarsman, who apparently had managed to grab on to a tree or driftwood, and save him.

It happened at least one more time, according to Kessler, who noted that most of his female passengers were as stoic as they came. But he brought with him a frantic woman who leaped into the water, figuring it was better off to die now than wait a little longer.

"The current swept around street corners with tremendous force, and only the most experienced oarsmen could propel the craft with any degree of success," said Kessler of the flood. Which is why it may have been, as uncomfortable and dangerous as it was, that some people stranded on their houses were better off remaining there.

Late afternoon, Dayton

By 4 P.M., the Beckel House crew was spread out over the Callahan Building, minus the four men who had managed to cross the river via the elevator cable. Judge Jones maneuvered himself between two rooms on the second floor of the Callahan Building, which had about twenty-five or thirty people in it as well as, improbably, a horse. How the horse got into the room, he never found out.

Everyone stood or sat about, grave, whispering, trying to figure out some strategy for survival. Jones watched a mother, sitting quietly, her features fixed in a serious-looking, desperate manner, clasping in her arms a boy who looked to be seven or eight years old. "The child clung to his mother and tried to be, and was, brave," wrote Jones. "Once in a while a tear trickled down his face, but the mother never wept."

Everyone could see the fire in the reflection of the river, but nobody was certain what it was doing or just how close it was to closing in on them. The only direction they received was what was shouted at them from some men on the roof of the Phillips Hotel, men who fortunately had some megaphones.

Megaphones were a device that Thomas Edison had invented in 1878, but these were makeshift megaphones that the Phillips guests had constructed out of cardboard and calendars.

It wasn't quite as good a system as seeing the fire for themselves, but it would do. The Beckel House guests learned that the Beckel House was still standing, although the fire was creeping closer to it, and by proxy, closer to where they were now. Anyone who offered up their opinion on the situation agreed that long before morning, everyone would be dead.

Chapter Fifteen

Jittery Nerves

4:30 P.M., Columbus, Ohio

James Thurber, the famed author and humorist, recalled years later, in a classic short story, "The Day the Dam Broke," that at least one neighborhood in Columbus was traumatized when everyone learned that a storage dam had broken and they were about to be engulfed by their own personal tsunami.

The West Side of Columbus was "under thirty feet of water," wrote Thurber, but he explained that on the East Side, the flood waters would have had to have climbed another ninety-five feet to devastate the homes. But understandably, with public schools closed, at least four bridges in the city washed out, no running water working in the city anywhere, and people drowning across the state and in surrounding states, everyone was nervous on the East Side as well.

Thurber included. Eighteen years old and in his senior year at East High, Thurber spent part of March 25 on High Street, a lengthy street that effectively cuts through the center of the city, dividing the east and west portions of the community. Thurber and a friend, Ed Morris, came out of a store and into the cold rain and saw a couple of police officers on horseback who were shouting to everyone that

240

the dam had broken and that everyone should go east and find higher ground.

In his essay, Thurber would write, "There are few alarms in the world more terrifying than, 'The dam has broken!'" Thurber didn't panic when he heard the policemen shout, but he didn't stick around to see if they might be wrong either. As detailed in the fine biography *James Thurber: His Life and Times* by Harrison Kinney, Thurber put a humorous spin on what happened next, but his account was absolutely factual—and when put in context with what newspapers reported at the time, the melee that broke out was simply incredible.

The first man to run looked to be a businessman, speculated Thurber. "It may be that he had simply remembered, all of a moment, an engagement to meet his wife, for which he was now frightfully late," wrote Thurber. "Whatever it was, he ran east on Broad Street (probably toward the Maramor Restaurant, a favorite place for a man to meet his wife). Somebody else began to run, perhaps a newsboy in high spirits. Another man, a portly gentleman of affairs, broke into a trot. Inside of ten minutes, everybody on High Street, from the Union Depot to the Courthouse, was running."

As Thurber described it, "Two thousand people were abruptly in full flight." They were shouting, too: "Go east! Go east! Go east!"

Among the throng were George Smallwood and his colleagues, nineteen-year-old Gus Kuehner and Bill McKeanan, *Columbus Dispatch* reporters who had just a short while earlier found their car, dangerously close to being swamped at the Town Street Bridge. They had just parked it on higher ground when they heard someone cry, "The dam has broken," and they, too, broke into a feverish run. Kuehner, thinking he was being helpful, quickly stopped to free some animals in a livery stable and, between two white horses, ran up the hill on Town Street.

It was pandemonium, according to Thurber, who reports that his aunt was in a theatre on High Street at the time, and that the panicked crowd stormed out into the street, the male patrons behaving the worst. "And east they went," wrote Thurber, "pushing and shoving and clawing, knocking women and children down, emerging finally into the street, torn and sprawling."

Indeed, Thurber was in the midst of a full-fledged panic, one that actually engulfed both the east and the west side. Thurber treated the incident with his usual whimsy but at the time, it was quite serious; and looking back, oncoming floodwaters aside, it's amazing that nobody was killed in this particular mad rush to get out of the way of the oncoming water. People ran downstairs, jumped and climbed out of windows, sprinted through alleys, and pushed others out of their path, as a throng of terrified people did everything they could to escape what was obviously a tidal wave chasing them. Policemen darted into stores, screaming at customers and shopkeepers, "Flee for your lives, the dam has burst!"

They fled.

Children on roller skates, delivery wagons and heavy trucks, automobiles, women pushing baby buggies, peanut vendors with push carts, and even one man on horseback—they all raced down High Street and to Third Street, heading away from the river.

Telephone operators, hearing the news, started calling people on the East Side who hadn't heard the news, warning them to get ready to run for their lives. Mothers, fathers, and children panicked, preparing their house for an onslaught. Word got out to newspapers in nearby cities. The *Lima Times Democrat* put out a bulletin, getting the time of day wrong: "With a great roar, the levee at the foot of Broad Street let go shortly before 11 o'clock today, sending a deluge of water that swelled the Scioto River covering a great area."

Some rescue workers left their posts, heading toward High Street to help with the onslaught of this new flood.

Early versions of what would become the ambulance siren had only recently come on the market, and some drivers were having fun hooking up "automobile sirens" to their cars. But in this instance, drivers turned on their sirens and sped down the street at top speed, trying to get out of harm's way.

One woman left her house and then screamed that she had left her cat on the second floor. "I won't go without it," she shouted and turned to run back in the house. The journalist who took down this scene in an account of the panic admitted, "The reporter was in a hurry himself and didn't stop to see whether she saved her pet or not."

Mothers led sobbing children through the sidewalks and streets, hurrying and hoping to outrun death.

One policeman tried dragging a woman, described by one paper as a "little foreign woman," out of her home on Scioto Street. "But I have a—" she started and then was cut off by the officer screaming at her to run.

"I will not go without my baby," she shouted back and, good for her, raced back for her infant.

Another parent wasn't quite as responsible. One man, carrying a baby wrapped in pink, stopped another man—who turned out to be a reporter for the *Ohio State Journal*—and said, "Either I must drop this baby, or I will drop myself." He then gave his baby to the reporter and fled. The reporter, bewildered, held on to the baby and also continued running.

Another mother, trying to drag her two children down the street, was heard shouting, "Come, or I'll break your arms."

Elizabeth Lewis, a resident of West Second Avenue, gathered all the cash, as well as some gold, that she had in the world—worth between $115 and $180, she would later estimate. She put it all in a black-bordered handkerchief and then joined some friends in the race to get the heck out of Dodge. Then, in the confusion, she dropped the precious cargo and presumably never saw it again.

Someone with the National Guard released fifty horses, allowing them to race for their lives, running east on Town Street toward High Street, where they almost ran down several people who were also fleeing for their lives.

An elderly woman, accompanied by a police officer, tried to run, but she couldn't, and so the police officer, terrified for his own life, left her behind.

Another woman slipped in the mud, and while two men stopped to carry her, they were so winded that they were forced to drag her down the street toward safety.

A soldier—probably someone from the National Guard—ran down the street with a screaming child.

In the midst of this madness, the teenaged Thurber ran, and at one point he was quite certain he was near death when an older man shouted, "It's got us." Fortunately, Thurber soon learned that the sound the man had heard was the wooshing sound of roller skates, worn by a kid who was also trying to get out of the way of the oncoming wall of water.

But as Thurber fans who have read his short story already know, the dam hadn't broken at all. It was a false alarm.

It ignited, however, a city-wide panic so full-blown that a crowd gathered around the statehouse, clogging the entrances. Several men started climbing up the building, attempting to scale the dome. A bugle blew, and whistles shrieked, as a mob of people crossed the Rich Street bridge, running to the East Side, where the West Side people assumed it was safe. Many men and women collapsed at the other side, but then police officers urged them to keep running. One woman was seen on the side of the road, wringing her hands and praying.

Meanwhile, "all the time," wrote Thurber, "the sun shone quietly, and there was nowhere any sign of oncoming waters. A visitor in an airplane, looking down on the straggling, agitated masses of people below, would have been hard put to it to divine a reason for the phenomenon."

Thurber called it the Afternoon of the Great Run, and news of the mob racing for their lives was syndicated to newspapers across the nation. On the east side of the country and the west, both the *Washington Post* and the *Los Angeles Times* ran the Associated Press story that described the rumor gone out of control: "The scene that followed was one of wild panic in all parts of the city. Patrolmen, soldiers and citizens in automobiles, tooting horns, ringing gongs and calling through megaphones a warning to everyone to seek safety in the higher parts of the east side sent thousands in flight, while many, stunned by the supposed impending disaster, collapsed from fear or gave way to hysteria."

"A panic was caused at Columbus, Ohio, Wednesday afternoon, when patrol wagons dashed through High Street, warning people to flee for their lives," said a bulletin in the *Statesville Landmark* in Statesville, North Carolina. "The police had received a report that the storage dam, which furnishes the city its supply, had broken and was sweeping down upon the city billions of gallons of water. In the downtown district and throughout the city, the wildest excitement ensued until it was found the report was not true."

It was more than an hour before the report was officially denied, the Associated Press observed, and stated that the police blamed a military man for getting the rumor going.

But the news of the Afternoon of the Great Run wouldn't break in Columbus's *Dispatch* for another year, Smallwood told Kinney, explaining, "There was silent agreement among us on the paper that the panic run was best forgotten. It wouldn't have done much for Columbus."

It's amusing and understandable that Smallwood remembered it that way, but actually all three Columbus newspapers did report the panic. "Never before in the history of Columbus was there such a scene of panic, even consternation," observed the *Ohio State Journal*. The *Columbus-Citizen Journal* echoed the same sentiment: "It was an experience without parallel in the history of the city." *The Columbus Evening Dispatch* described it as a "frenzy of excitement," and while Smallwood may, at the time, have wanted to forget about the wild rumor, his own paper observed that everyone knew about the incident: "By word of mouth and by telephone the word was thrown back and forth until the entire city became aware of it."

Thurber wasn't the only one to find gallows humor in the flood. In a disaster in which children drowned, older people found themselves paralyzed, and there was near incomprehensible levels of suffering, the flood could bring in the funny.

One letter-writer told his family out East that from his perch in Logansport, Indiana, he witnessed a woman who was helped onto a rescue boat, and then several minutes later, after they pulled away, she started screaming, "My baby, I forgot my baby!" The men quickly managed to get the boat back to the window, allowing the frantic woman to scurry back into her home. A few minutes later, she emerged, carrying . . . a cat.

Rescuer John Stanley, also in Logansport, Indiana, would later tell the story of another animal lover whose priorities were either misplaced or very telling: "I rowed up to a house, and a big, heavy woman got three children in the boat and got in herself, carrying a large bull dog. After she was all settled, she asked anxiously, 'Do you think there is still room for my husband?'"

And then there was this gem in a Fort Wayne newspaper on March 29: one woman went to the police department and asked if a boat could take her to her house, at the far end of a suburb, so she could get a dress she needed for a party.

A rescuer in Indianapolis, Dan Balls, bumped his boat into half a dozen porches, tore some of the skin off his hands, wrestling with the oars, and poured several buckets of water out of his frail rowboat, making his way to a woman who kept shouting to him.

Once he arrived, preparing for her to board, she said she didn't want to leave her house: she just wanted to know what time it was.

Balls presumably gave her the time, or an estimate, and perhaps the woman started to rethink her decision to stay. "Where will you be in an hour from now?" she asked.

"At the bottom of the river, if I keep on the way I've been going," Balls growled, paddling away.

Another rescuer in Indianapolis, making his way down Mechanic Street, saw an elderly man leaning from a second-story window of a house and waving frantically, as though he only had minutes to spare before the flood or perhaps a fire consumed him. The oarsmen rowed to him immediately, only to discover he had no desire to leave. But perhaps the men could give him a package of tobacco?

And maybe something was in the water at Logansport, Indiana, because another story there that surfaced later was that of four young men trapped in the second story of a house on the now-appropriately named Canal Street, just one block from the Wabash River. They all wrote letters and stuffed them into one bottle. After the flood, it was found, and the local media had a grand time reporting on their messages.

"I am in the second story of a building and can't get out," wrote an Albert A. Anderson, a resident of Logansport. "Would like some nice little girl to help me, if you can do anything for me."

Another man who gave his name as G. W. Lindersmith wrote, "We are in the flood and can't get out. Whoever finds this, please answer for a sweetheart."

The third writer was even more direct: "I will love the girl that gets this and will answer it. Will marry her. Bye-bye with love, Mr. Harvey Hasket, Logansport, Ind."

And the fourth writer said, "Whoever may be the lucky one and deem this worthy, answer, answer, answer. Elmer Hershberger, Logansport, Ind., No. 318 Canal Street."

You almost have to admire the men, facing possible death by drowning and using the experience as possible leverage for finding dates.

5:20 P.M., Columbus, Ohio

Shortly after the panic in the city, three police officers stood next to their car at the edge of the Mound Street Bridge. They debated whether they should cross it—it didn't exactly look safe, but it seemed as if it would hold for a while. The officers wanted to get to the workhouse, or at least as close to it as they could, to check on things, and so they decided to chance it. Another police officer and a watchman at the city morgue decided not to.

The officer and watchman had the better instincts.

The three men piled into the car and crossed the bridge. Fifteen seconds later, they heard several snaps, and everyone turned around as the Mound Street Bridge began to lean and sway. Then a beam cracked, and there were more snaps. Then the iron bridge crumbled, its remains sinking into the water. From the moment of the first snap to the moment the bridge disappeared under the water, only thirty seconds had passed.

Around the same time, rescuers were doing their best to remove Anna Greene, an African-American woman who was forty-one years old and, according to the rescuers who lifted her, weighed over five hundred pounds. Her husband, George, presumably had no trouble leaving the home, nor did their two lodgers, Melvin Holty, thirty, and Simpson Galloway, twenty-six, a janitor and a street laborer respectively. George was a hod carrier, which was someone who helped bricklayers lay bricks. It was a demanding job, collecting bricks from the delivery pallet, wetting them down, and generally making sure the bricklayers could continue constantly working.

They had one child, who had died young. Perhaps it was grief, or just bad biology, that led Anna Greene to such a weight problem. In any event, she was carried out of a second-story window, set into a boat, and taken to the railroad station. She was placed on a flatcar and taken to a railroad station and from there to Memorial Hall, the name of the building that was once a memorial to Civil War veterans and had been reconverted into the library. It was serving as something of a rescue and relief center and happened to be two blocks from James Thurber's home.

Evening, Fort Wayne, Indiana

A. F. Melsching, Ned Miatt, and J. Miller, three young men who worked at the Fort Wayne Electric Works, volunteered to cross over to the orphanage and remain in the building with the women and children until a rescue could be put into action. There were two men already there, Albert Nieman and Ellsworth Grant, but the thinking was that the kids couldn't have enough adults watching over them.

Sometime in the evening, Indianapolis

Mischa Elman, the violinist, and Rudolph Ganz, the Swiss pianist, played an informal concert with their accompanist, a Mr. Kahn, in a concert hall on the ninth floor of the Claypool Hotel for an audience of weary travelers and stranded refugees from the flood. It was, recalled Elman later, "like playing in a hospital ward."

Evening, Dayton, Ohio

It had been a long day for everyone. Ben Hecht, the Chicago newspaper correspondent who we last encountered at a telegraph station in the early morning, had spent the day in a canoe, interviewing rescuers and gathering whatever information he could for a story he intended to file that evening for the next morning's paper. But at some point at the day's conclusion, Hecht, understandably exhausted, nonetheless did the unthinkable: he fell asleep in his canoe. Even if he had managed to pull up to shore—he never said either way in his biography, although it's implied that he was still in the water—it was, of course, a stupid thing to let happen.

Fortunately for Hecht, some rescuers came across the young reporter, out cold in his canoe that was slowly drifting away, saving his nemesis Chris Hagerty from having to write his obituary.

Meanwhile, about three miles away from his father's company, NCR, and at the bottom of what was known as Huffman Hill, now a historic district, Fred Patterson and a couple of other rescuers found themselves on the roof of a house, trying to save a family from burning to death. The water was high enough that the family could no longer get through the windows. How did Patterson even know there was a family in there? He probably heard gunshots, a common strategy—firing bullets into the air—for attracting attention.

With no way to bring them out through the windows, and no time to spare with the fire—which possibly started from a nearby gas pipe bursting—that was creeping up towards them, Patterson and his men cut a hole in the roof.

Fred and his fellow rescuers got the family into the boat; but as they were rowing away, they overturned and went into the river. It was a close enough call that Patterson and others in the boat were reported dead by a newspaper in Xenia, but he managed to reach shore, as did his fellow rescuers. The family, weakened from days stuck on their roof without food and water, did not.

By now, Fred Patterson had seen enough tragedy for a lifetime. He was particularly disturbed when he saw a Catholic priest named Father Rire in a boat with a mother and daughter. The boat overturned, and while someone in a house reached out and grabbed the priest, his passengers—the mother and daughter—drowned. On another occasion, Fred Patterson was in a boat, shouting at a man in a tree, encouraging him to hang on until he could get underneath him so he could fall into his craft. The man did his best, but lost his grip from the branch, plunged into the raging current, and quickly was sucked underneath the water. Right in front of him and yet too far away, all Fred could do was watch.

In downtown Dayton, the one area Fred Patterson and other rescuers couldn't successfully penetrate, the Leonhard Manufacturing Company, which made and sold harnesses, saddles, and trunks, was fighting a losing battle against the floodwaters. There were workers inside the Leonhard building as well as men on top of the roof, crossing from an adjacent building, obviously believing that they were moving from a weak building to a stronger one. They were wrong.

Police officers and other government workers—stranded in the city building across the street—watched aghast as the Leonhard building collapsed.

Forty men were killed.

Evening, Illinois and Missouri

Two states to the west of Ohio, concerned residents read the paper and wondered how safe their own communities were. The *Alton Evening Telegraph*, the paper of record for Alton, Illinois, which hugs the Mississippi River, ran a story on their front page, stating that "as the result of the heavy rains throughout the country, all of the creeks and small streams are swollen many times their ordinary size. Reports reaching Alton show that the rains are continuing and there is no telling what the next few days may bring."

It continued to say that wheatfields were swamped, particularly those in Missouri Point, the nickname for the area just north of St. Louis. Then the *Alton Evening Telegraph* ended its report with a parting observation that summed up the feelings of many Americans in many states that day. "With the Missouri and Mississippi rising on both sides of Missouri Point, the people are beginning to do some worrying, and some wish they had built more levees than they have done, and talked less about it."

Evening, Columbus, Ohio

Governor Cox would later recall that around this time, he left his office and went out into the town "to get some food," which probably meant going into a rescue center, since there would have been scant options to procure food otherwise.

He had been working the phone lines and sending telegrams all day. Zanesville, Marietta, Tiffin, and Delaware, among other places, were asking for him to send troops and food like he had done for Dayton. Columbus was suffering too, of course. As the flooding continued, the rain continued, although it had slowed down with about an inch falling for the day, occasionally interchanging with snow. But at least Cox could see progress being slowly made in Columbus. Dayton, in particular, from his vantage point, appeared doomed. Cox would say about that evening: "Nature never before seemed so pitiless."

THURSDAY,
MARCH 27, 1913

Chapter Sixteen

Another Long Night

The Great Flood of 1913 wasn't choosy. Whether you were rich, poor, old, young, Caucasian, African-American, a recent immigrant, a citizen whose ancestors came here on the Mayflower—the water didn't discriminate.

People were another matter. In 1913, racism was as bad as you might imagine. Schools were typically segregated. Hotels. Restaurants. Public parks. Amusement parks. Life, meanwhile, was separate but hardly equal, which was the law of the land since the Supreme Court favored segregation in the case of *Plessy v. Ferguson* in 1896. For instance, Dr. George Edmund Haynes, a well-respected social worker of the time, conducted a survey that he did in 1913 of Negro urban life and reported that "playgrounds in Negro neighborhoods are so rare as to excite curiosity."

On March 22, 1913, in the *Washington Post*, the headline of one news item coming from Decatur, Alabama offers a glimpse of where black people ranked in a society mostly run by whites. The news item's headline read WHITE BOY KILLED OUTRIGHT, and then in the paragraph-length article, the boy's name and age were mentioned, followed by "and a number of negroes are reported killed by the cyclone which struck this section last night."

And if anything, life for African-Americans was getting worse. When President Woodrow Wilson came into power, along with the Democratic party in Congress, Southern politicians began introducing bills to segregate the federal civil service, the military, and public transportation in Washington, D.C. That didn't happen, but Wilson gave in, allowing several of his Cabinet members to segregate several executive departments. Not long after, the dining facilities and restrooms throughout the federal government were racially segregated. It was a quiet permission slip to the rest of the country that if you want to segregate, go right ahead.

As noted, the floodwaters of 1913 were more than happy to take anyone, regardless of their color, but historically blacks usually had the worst of it, something that has had implications even today. The least expensive, least well-built homes, often not much more than shacks, were often near the river, where land was cheap because of flooding and devastation after a hard rain. If a flood came in, blacks living in impoverished homes along the river usually didn't have a telephone to call for help, or a car that they could quickly crank up and speed away in. Making matters even worse for any black resident in a flood, many African-Americans in 1913 didn't have the means to pay for swimming lessons; and even those who could were often refused entry into public pools and public swimming beaches. So when a flood came, simply due to their social status many blacks were at a disadvantage compared to their white counterparts.

But the flood of 1913—at least looking through a lens from a century away—seems to have brought out the best in humanity. Maybe it's because much of the flood was in the Northern states where the melting pot, a phrase that became popular after the 1908 play *The Melting Pot*, was a bit warmer, so to speak; but whatever the reason, there are a number of accounts that survive of whites saving blacks, of blacks saving whites, and of whites and blacks teaming up to save housebound flood victims, welcome stories when there were absolutely other tales of ugliness, racial and otherwise, around the country.

Little is known about Bill Sloan, a baseball player in the Negro League, as they called it back then, but he is said to have saved 317 people in Dayton. Precious few, tantalizing stories make the imagination reel. He was said to have rescued the Caleb family of five persons from a raft which they had been clinging to for forty-eight hours. He worked at least some of the time with two other men, presumably white since the papers didn't identify them as colored, Frank Thoro and George Crandall. Sloan is said to have worked for sixty-eight hours before surrendering to exhaustion and sleep. The boat Sloan and his comrades used was a steel-bottom boat. Sloan is said to have stolen it at gunpoint, but, so the story goes, from a selfish factory owner who wasn't using it and had refused to allow it to be used by the rescuers.

According to some accounts, another Dayton resident, a Robert Burnham, was rowing a skiff when it struck a tree and his passengers, a black woman and her two babies, fell into the current. One has to appreciate his effort, but it was a sad ending. Both infants drowned; and while Burnham pulled the mother to shore alive, she died en route to a hospital.

Mayor David M. Green, of Urbana, Ohio, rushed into flood waters and managed to pull Charles Dickinson, a black man, out of the water.

Arthur L. McGuire, a forty-year-old police officer, won a bronze medal and $1,000 from the Carnegie Hero Fund for saving a black family from drowning in the River des Peres in St. Louis on March 25, 1913.

Robert Kenney, a 45-year-old African-American from Troy, Ohio, died on March 25, 1913, trying to save four white men from drowning in the floodwaters. The Carnegie Hero Fund gave his father a silver medal and five hundred dollars in cash as a reward for his son's bravery.

In Columbus, at the penitentiary on Spring Street, four trusted prisoners and the warden were on the front porch, watching the river go by when they saw a flat-bottomed boat capsize. An African-American woman was on it and pitched into the water.

"Go on and get her, boys," the warden shouted. Granted, he didn't jump in himself, but the four prisoners rushed in and were able to grab hold of her and pull her out. They took her into the prison, gave her dry clothes, and led her through to the rear entrance, which led to dry streets, and sent her on her way.

Another Columbus resident who was black, James Washington, who worked for the city's cleaning department, was credited with saving the lives of eighteen white men, although since most of them were "Italians," according to the local press and given some of the scorn Italian-Americans received in those days, maybe it wasn't quite as important and impressive as if he had saved mostly Anglo-Saxons.

In Rushville, Indiana, Carrie Meadows, her granddaughter, and a man of the last name Williams, all African-American, were in a home that had no attic or second-story window. When they found themselves trapped, and the water rushed in, they placed the kitchen table on the stove, and for a while Meadows and her granddaughter were able to safely sit on that while Williams stood on the oven. Eventually, the water reached Williams's waist, while he held the stove steady.

By the time the (white) rescuers broke through the roof, cutting a hole for grandmother, granddaughter, and man to climb out of, the river water was just sixteen inches away from the ceiling.

March 27, Dayton, midnight

The rescue work was finally stopped at midnight with rescuers reasoning that it was too dangerous to continue in the dark. Bonfires had been lit up along the water's edge, which had given rescuers some light to work with; but many people trapped in homes and buildings saw them and simply thought that even more of the city was on fire.

There were many fires, far too many to count. On one part of Third Street, far from the fires that threatened the Beckel House and downtown, there was even a fire near the old bicycle shop where the Wright Brothers worked for many years. The Wright Brothers had a bicycle shop in a few locations, but their last one, at 1127 West Third Street, they had worked at from 1897 until 1908, a time when they were, of course, working on building and experimenting with their airplane, which took off for the first time in 1903. In the shop were blueprints and plenty of papers having to do with the construction of airplanes and early flight navigation. Fortunately for history's sake, the fire narrowly missed the shop.

The bonfires along the river were necessary, to be sure, but they had another negative as well. The extra light in the darkness also reminded would-be rescuers and the public how helpless they were to save their fellow residents. People could be seen clinging to buildings, far off in the distance, clearly freezing, hungry, and frightened. Occasionally, a person, unable to continue, would slip from their perch and fall into the still-rushing murky yellow water.

March 27, throughout Ohio, after midnight

Almost everywhere on Governor Cox's map of Ohio continued to have its share of crises. Cleveland, at the top of the state, was seeing lumberyards and trains destroyed by the Cuyahoga River. Two days earlier, in fact, in the village of Brighton, near Cleveland, a train had crashed through a bridge battered and weakened from flooding, going into the Fitchville River. The engineer, fireman, and brakeman all died. In Akron, another city up north, they were dynamiting locks on the Ohio and Erie Canal so that the floodwater could drain into the Cuyahoga instead of homes and factories. The flood ended canal travel for good, which was already an endangered species in Ohio.

The reservoir in Lewiston, a town in northwestern Ohio, looked poised to burst, and Governor Cox spent a good deal of the night making calls and doing whatever he could to make sure enough resources were being put in place to keep the dam from bursting. When he couldn't find the head of public works, a fellow by the name of John I. Miller, and then learned the guy had the nerve to be asleep in his hotel room, Cox went apoplectic. The next morning, he sacked Miller and replaced him with James R. Marker, the state highway commissioner.

"That poor fellow fell down lamentably," Cox said that day of Miller, who in fairness, may have been working hard since things started falling apart two days earlier and had decided he needed to sleep sometime. Cox may have come to that conclusion himself. By June, he had reappointed Miller to his post.*

At the bottom of the state, Marietta was cut off from civilization, and Cox had no idea how anyone there was faring. In Portsmouth, another city at the bottom of the state along the Ohio River, Cox was

---

* It's always fun when you come across in your research how much someone's salary was back in 1913. Miller's job paid $4,000 a year. The average salary in 1913 was $585 a year, and $1 in 1913 would be like having $22 today.

hearing that the good news was that the five-year-old flood wall had been constructed so that if the river rose to sixty-two feet, the city would be protected. What he didn't realize was that within the next twenty-four hours, the Ohio River would climb to sixty-eight feet.

The middle of the night, New Castle, Pennsylvania

It was quiet, and cold, and dark. And many people were still trapped on their roofs.

March 27, 1 A.M., Peru, Indiana

Sam Bundy had been at it for forty-eight hours. He was exhausted, but there was always another desperate family or individual to save, and at night the screams seemed louder. Bundy had his routine down pat, each time he picked someone up. He would tell the people to keep still and not get excited, to sit down right away and not to worry.

Then he would steer the boat into the current, through alleys, over small buildings—yes, over small buildings; the water was *that* deep—and he would pass under the tops of trees, all the while gradually working his way closer and closer to the shore, where the current wasn't putting up as much of a fight and he could get his passengers to dry land.

Occasionally, the wealthier families of Peru insisted Bundy receive some payment for his work. The Miami Indian never asked anyone for money, but he found himself unable to say no when a man named Warren Stites gave him a check for $50, when a Delbert Daniels handed him a $75 check, when a J. D. Emehiser gave him $50, and when a Cyrus Crider handed him a check for $75. Bundy wasn't a rich man. When he was eighteen and still living with his parents, he was a farm laborer. In the 1910 census records, the pathetic handwriting indicates that he was working at either an automobile dealer or a garage. By 1915, he appears to have been a farm laborer, and in 1920 he was a lineman for a railroad. Bundy had a past of having little money, and his future was going to be much of the same. There was no way he was going to refuse when it was offered as thanks.

But he had honor, too. There was also no way he was ever going to ask any flood refugee for payment. He was in his boat to help people.

There's no other explanation why anyone would risk their life repeatedly for forty-eight hours.

2 A.M., Fort Wayne

Captain Wallace and his boat, and five crewmen, arrived in Fort Wayne straight from Chicago. They had some orphans to save.

2:30 A.M., Fort Wayne

The newly falling snow, which would stop three inches later, and the rivers, continued to rise throughout the night, and did nothing for morale.

Henry Michaels, a resident of Fort Wayne, was sitting in a chair, holding a newspaper and staring out the window, a position he started in the evening and continued all night. He would tell a reporter the next day, "I wanted to stay for the novelty of it, but I got all the novelty I wanted last night. There wasn't a sound all night except the swish of the water. It was just like sleeping in a grave. It got pretty cold, too, this morning. While I didn't want to be taken out yesterday, I was mighty eager to be taken out this morning."

3 A.M., Fort Wayne, Indiana

Captain Wallace and his boat, and five crewmen, arrived at the orphanage to find everyone, even the youngest children, wide awake. There were fifty-eight children and about a dozen adults, mostly the orphanage staff, like teachers and the cook, in two rooms on the second floor. Everything was going well, though, and the building still appeared safe enough. Because it was so dangerous to be on a boat in the dark, Wallace decided the rescue could wait until morning. Upon learning that, some of the youngest girls took a nap. Seven-year-old Opal Jacobs, one of the girls who almost drowned, slept in Mrs. Overmeyer's lap.

3 A.M., Dayton

Louis Gintsy, a mail carrier, was stuck in a flooded house on Wayne Street, and he and his family were frantically eyeing a fire, which was burning up houses and approaching their own. He laid out the facts to his wife. They could face down the fire or the flood, but one way or another, they were going to battle one of the elements, and their odds of survival weren't good.

"It's an even break," Louis said.

"I'd rather die in the flood than in the fire," said his wife. Besides, going with the water at least gave them a fighting chance.

Louis agreed. Their minds made up, the mail carrier stepped into the swiftly moving water. It was as high as his hips. He went back and picked up one of their four children. The plan was to carry each child to safe ground and then come back for his wife if all went according to plan. It was a plan fraught with danger—they could all be swept away to their deaths, but they couldn't wait any longer, not even until daylight.

Louis carried his first child into the water. He and his family soon found themselves very pleased with their decision. They all had a colorful story to tell about escaping the flood, and two hours later, very much alive and on safe ground, they watched their house dissolve into flames.

Nearby, a man named Shelly Burns had been stuck in a stable for the last two days and now was confronted with the same question the Gintsy family had to wrestle with. There was a fire at the rear of the building he was in, and he had to ask himself: Did he prefer burning to death, or possibly drowning?

"I'll take a chance on the flood," said Burns, and then he jumped out of the window, plunging into the water.

Only things didn't go as planned, and he didn't have any of the luck the Gintsy family possessed. On his way down into the water, Burns got his arm stuck on some wooden debris. Getting stuck may have saved his life, for he didn't drown and was rescued when the sun came up and oarsmen were out braving the waters again.

But Burns likely wondered more than once if he would have been better off remaining where he was, especially since the stable did not end up burning. He remained stuck for several hours, hanging from the stable by one arm, his arm in complete agony and half his body submerged in icy water, and left wondering if the fire would catch up to him anyway, or if the water would rise first and drown him.

3:15 A.M., Fort Wayne

A fire broke out at a wealthy home, starting with the greenhouse and then moving to the actual house. A brilliant blaze could be seen everywhere. Everyone assumed the worst. The Allen County Orphans' Home must have caught fire.

Throughout the night, Dayton, Ohio

Judge Jones stood on the windowsill, not because he particularly wanted to look outside, but because his fellow refugees decided that he and another fellow had the best shouting voices. Jones and the other man took turns shouting across the waterway to the Phillips Hotel, where there were the men with megaphones who were keeping the Beckel House guests apprised of how the fire was doing. At another window, the one person who was close to death, whether the fire came or not, Clarence Bennett, owner of the Beckel House, was well enough that he stood up for a long time most of the night, staring out the window and listening to the voices coming from the Phillips Hotel.

"Oh, Callahan people," they would shout, "the fire has worked one door nearer. What do you say?"

Jones would then shout a question in response, and then hear something like:

"No, the bank is not burning yet."

While there was a bank inside the Callahan building, there was another one a block away, across the street from the Beckel House. The guests from the Beckel House calculated that if the Fourth National Bank went up in flames, then it would probably jump across the street and strike the Beckel House. That meant the entire block would go up in flames, including the Callahan building. But the Fourth National Bank was said to be fireproof, and so everyone kept hoping for the best.

If it did burn, and the flames came, everyone had decided that they would divide into parties of three—two men to each woman. The consensus was that if anyone could and should be saved, it would be the mother in the group, and her child. The problem that nobody dared say out loud was that nobody could figure out how anyone, no matter how committed and serious, would possibly be able to do a thing to keep the mother and her son from burning up or drowning with everyone else. But having the plan made everyone feel better.

Nobody could see anyone. Even Jones, at the window, didn't have any moonlight; it was snowing and raining. Everyone was shivering, although, as Jones put it, "Little was thought of cold, hunger or thirst. We were waiting, waiting, waiting, to know whether it was to be life or death."

The men with the megaphones kept up their news bulletins well after midnight. "The Beckel does not seem to have caught yet," they continued to shout. And then: "Oh, Callahan. Another store has caught but the bank is safe yet."

And then: "The wind seems to be rising and blowing this way."

Helpful to know, but the last thing they wanted to hear.

But at one in the morning, Jones suddenly heard: "Oh, Callahan; fire seems to be going down. Think the bank will stand. We believe your danger is almost over."

Everyone in the two rooms—and arguably anyone on other floors throughout the Callahan building who heard the message—breathed a collective sigh of relief. Many people murmured, "Thank God."

Jones felt a wave of hope wash over him. The last twelve hours in particular had been a nightmare. He wondered, *is it possible the worst is over?*

Not quite. As if in answer to his question, an explosion rocked the building. There was light now—blood-red and green fire lit up the night air. Burning embers and sparks tumbled from the sky, and smoke drifted past everyone. The air was hot now. Jones wrote later, "I could only think of the Day of the Last Judgment."

The fire had jumped across Third Street, harrowingly close to the Fourth National Bank but attacking the Lowe Brothers Paint Store Company instead. Paint was highly combustible, and the building exploded into oblivion.

It was time, several people shouted.

The judge spoke up sharply, trying to sound reasonable, hopeful, and confident, three characteristics he was not actually feeling. He told people that they had lasted this long, that going into the water was certain death, while waiting a little longer might keep everyone alive. Perhaps because of his years of training, speaking with authority from the bench, everyone remained. It was quite likely the longest night of everyone's lives; but by morning, thanks to Jones's calm and reasoned demeanor, everyone would be alive. The fire missed all of them.

Chapter Seventeen

Light at the End

6 A.M., Fort Wayne, Allen County Orphanage

The children who were sleeping were roused awake and given their breakfast. It was just another morning, if they could ignore the grownups standing around, the boats outside moored to the front porch, the horrific flashbacks of the drownings from the day before, and the sense of foreboding that filled the entire room.

Early morning, Dayton, Ohio

Ben Hecht woke up with a start. He was on a bed—well, a cot, really, and wearing a peculiar nightgown, peculiar because it wasn't his own. Baffled at first, Hecht gradually recognized where he was: the National Cash Register plant and surrounded by Red Cross staff and bedridden patients.

He had fallen asleep in his canoe, been "rescued," and then brought here.

Hecht shouted for his clothes. A nurse came up to him and told him he couldn't leave until he had been examined by a doctor. Hecht protested—he was fine, he had just fallen asleep, he needed to go so he could file a story for the first edition of the *Chicago Daily Journal*.

The nurse wouldn't be dissuaded. Hecht stood his ground, "yelling in my skimpy refugee's nightgown, as unlike a journalist as could be imagined."

Suddenly, Hecht was joined by his old pal, Christian Dane Hagerty. He had been collecting information about the flood's refugees.

"Tell them, will you," begged Hecht, looking imploringly at Hagerty. "Tell them I'm a newspaperman and not a goddamn refugee."

Hagerty looked him over and smiled, as if he was considering telling the nurse otherwise. But then to Hecht's utter relief, Hagerty offered his confirmation: "He's a newspaperman."

Morning in Dayton and Columbus

Governor Cox dreaded the thought of calling John Bell. Not that he didn't want to talk to him, but he knew the telephone operator was famished, weary, and wet, and, judging from the skies in Columbus, he couldn't imagine what Bell and Dayton were going through now.

Still, he asked Columbus operator Thomas Green to put him through.

"Good morning, Governor," John Bell said, happy as a clam. "The sun is shining in Dayton."

Snow would fall on the city later in the day, and Bell became less buoyant as the day wore on, but both men would later agree that it was a turning point. There had been hours of doubt, but now they knew that the flood couldn't last forever.

Approximately 7 A.M., Fort Wayne

Seven-year-old Opal Jacobs, who remembered vividly the terror of her last boat ride, refused to board. Some of the men forced the screaming girl on the boat, who was then held and comforted by a woman from the First Presbyterian Church.

Four boats took all of the children, all at once, with the remaining adults in a fifth boat. Just as the last boat left, as if on cue, one of the porches of the home, the one connected to the fire escape, broke free from the house and floated a short distance into a grove of trees. That was the closest thing to anything going wrong on this boat ride. The sun was peeking through the clouds and the rain had finally stopped falling.

March 27, morning, from approximately 8 to 10 A.M., Peru, Indiana

Sam Bundy was finding it increasingly challenging to steer his boat. After fifty-five hours of rowing down streets and plucking people out of houses and trees without even a nap, his body was finally begging for him to call it quits. But when Jake Marsh offered him two hundred dollars to rescue his wife and daughter and several other family members, trapped in at least two different places in the city, Bundy found himself torn.

The money would help out on the home front, and if he refused, and if these people didn't survive the flood because he hadn't gone after them, it would gnaw at him for the rest of his days.

It may not have been the smartest course of action in his exhausted state, but he said he would go.

Bundy only needed to travel three blocks in downtown Peru, but nobody else would take their boat for good reason. Those three blocks contained a raging current that still had not abated. When Phillip Landgrave, a local school official, watched Bundy board, he couldn't help somberly thinking, *Good-bye, Sam*. But to his and everyone's relief and surprise, around 10 A.M., Bundy returned with the mother and daughter, two hours after he set out.

Landgrave explained Bundy's success to a reporter: "He did not do like the others, but he took his own time and did not become excited. He used his own sure method and came back with the folks he went after."

But Bundy was depleted, and he knew if he tried another trip to pick up the rest of the family members, he wouldn't return. Bundy tracked down an extremely competent rescuer, Irwin Baldwin, and offered him the $200 instead, the whole enchilada, if he would make the second trip. Baldwin agreed and, to Bundy's relief, returned safely with the rest of Jake Marsh's family.

Bundy decided he was finished with rescue work. He had gone at it for fifty-seven hours straight. "I am glad that I came, even though it might be some time before I fully recover," Bundy told a reporter. "I saw some harrowing scenes but no one can say that I faltered when duty called me. I'm going back home now to sleep—to dream of the flood." Then he added, sincerely: "I hope not."

Morning, March 27, New Castle, Pennsylvania

The city woke up to learn that civilization as they knew it was regressing. The west side of the city was hit the hardest, but people in all directions were without gas or water, and without much food. The grocery stores were mobbed, and by noon they were cleaned out.

Meanwhile, in the midst of the handful of crooked officers on the New Castle police force were men like Thomas Thomas. Aside from having a memorable name, Thomas was, by all accounts, an ethical, likeable man, not to mention a husband and father of three. He had only been on the force for about a year and a half, appointed by the mayor after working at the city's tin mill. He had been in the flooded streets of New Castle since Tuesday, leading and rowing people to safety. If the reports are true, Thomas Thomas hadn't taken a break since then.

For the last forty-eight hours, he had been rowing families to safety. Affected by the gratitude of those he helped and the cries of people whom he hadn't reached yet, Thomas apparently couldn't stand the thought of stopping. Even when it began to snow, he continued rowing.

Thomas was pushing himself too hard. He didn't realize it, but if he didn't stop and take a long break soon, his luck was going to run out.

Morning, Fort Wayne, Indiana

Judge J. Frank Mungovan turned loose ten drunks who had over-celebrated the fact that they worked a couple of hours helping to secure the Lakeside dike and at other danger points. He turned them free, the papers reported, because the jail was in such an unsanitary condition as a result of the failure of the water supply that he didn't want to send any more men to it.

Thursday morning, Indianapolis

Mischa Elman, the violinist, and Rudolph Ganz, the Swiss pianist, heard that the first train out of Indianapolis would be leaving that morning. Many of the guests decided to stay put, fearing that their train would crash through a bridge like so many had already done, or become embedded in a riverbank somewhere, but Elman and Ganz reasoned that with people already getting sick in

Indianapolis, and the potential for disease spreading in the flooded city, wherever they went probably wouldn't be much worse than staying where they were.

They took the first train. Elman was struck by the fact that there were no porters, which was eerie and inconvenient. He had to lug his Stradivarius and Amati with him.

It would take ten hours to make the two-hour trip to Goshen, Indiana, and as Elman told the *New York Times*, "We saw many dead bodies floating in the swollen river. Terrible! We also saw submerged houses, many, very many, poking their roofs out of the yellow swirling water that ran like a mill race, and other houses that leaned like drunkards up against bridges. We all felt shaky, of course, whenever our train passed over a bridge. At Goshen we caught a train for Toledo, where we had the good luck to make a close connection with the Lake Shore Limited. We were without food all day, except for a hot dog at one little way station. There was a man there who kept cutting open rolls as fast as he could and slapping in a piece of sausage. Those tasted good."

But Elman found a lot of beauty and wonder in being in less than ideal circumstances with so many fellow travelers, saying, "It was a wonderful experience, and I would not have missed it for anything— but I would not care to go through it again," and then he added, "Yes, I intend to compose a piece describing my feelings—and also my cold feet."

Mid-morning, Fort Wayne, Ohio

Another day, another crisis.

The headline on a late morning edition of the *Fort Wayne Daily News* gave everyone a start. It blared: DAM AT ST. MARY'S RESERVOIR BREAKS.

With the second headline, right underneath: THE FLOOD WILL REACH FORT WAYNE IN FROM FOUR TO SIX HOURS SAYS WEATHERMAN PALMER.

So the dam at St. Mary's was broken. Just what the city needed. The paper didn't say how much water was behind it, but every resident over the age of six years in Fort Wayne knew that just twenty-five miles south of the city was the largest artificial body in the world, which had been completed in 1845 as a feeder for the Great Miami and Erie

Canal that went from Lake Erie to the Ohio River. In fact, it held over 13,000 acres of water, 2 billion cubic feet of liquid, and the way everyone saw it, a wall of water would hit St. Mary's first, and then go into Rockford and Willshire, both villages in Ohio. From there, it would take out Pleasant Mills, Indiana, Decatur, and then aim for destroying Fort Wayne.

The alarm had been sounded by someone manning an oil-pumping station near the dam, and he had said on the telephone, "Can tell no more. Must run for life."

Morning, Dayton, Ohio

Dayton residents heard the news. St. Mary's dam had broken. Men dashed through the streets, shouting, "Flee for your lives," and, "The reservoir has broken."

The paper in nearby Xavier described the situation thusly: "Without waiting for confirmation, the now thoroughly frightened people are leaving the city like rats from a sinking ship. People are frantic. Children are separated from their parents, women are throwing their babies away in their terrible fright. The streets on the east side are black with hundreds and thousands of fleeing people. They have only one thought and that is to flee."

One has to think and hope the reporter was mistaken and a little melodramatic himself—babies being thrown away?

But, sure enough, similar to what had happened the day before in Columbus, there was absolutely no foundation for the alarm. And once again, there was an understandable panic in the streets. Of course, it may seem as if there weren't any dry streets to panic in, but there were plenty of neighborhoods in Dayton, particularly in the northwest and southeast parts of the city, away from the rivers, that were relatively untouched by the flood. Hundreds of individuals and families in Dayton gathered their kids and important papers and hopped into their horse-and-buggies and automobiles, clogging the streets that were drivable and made haste to the National Cash Register headquarters, pushing themselves past guards, storming offices, and threatening to overwhelm the already-overcrowded facility.

The mob didn't settle down until Patterson stepped forward and spoke, explaining that if the dam had broken, it was sixty-five miles away, and that the water wouldn't make their situation much more grave than it already was. In fact, some professor later calculated that even if the dam and its 17,000 acres of water had become free, and assuming there was no water on the ground across the several million acres that it would have spread over, the area would have been one foot deep. Not nothing when you own a half-sunken two-story row house, but not a tsunami either.

The Thoma family were among the people in the crowd at NCR. Norma Thoma's father Albin, an optometrist, wasn't sure how much more fearing for his life he could take. He just wanted to get back to his home in Piqua, although he couldn't have been sure he would have been much better off.

His house was far enough away from any waterways, as far as he knew, but Piqua had serious flooding as well. Years later, on September 12, 1983, Gene Rees, an 89-year-old farmer, told the Shelby County Historical Society of how he had visited Piqua with his uncle, where they saw a house leave its moorings. On top of the roof were a man, a woman, and a little girl. Rees and his uncle were horrified—and completely helpless to do anything but watch. The parents and girl were all crying for help—until it hit a bridge and they plunged into the water and disappeared.

Sometime in the afternoon, Columbus

Even while some people were still trapped in their homes, including 250 very hungry and cold people at the Sun Manufacturing Company, there was a morbid, grim sign that the flood would eventually end: two trucks, full of dead bodies, rolled out of the west side of the city.

Relief trains, meanwhile, with food and clothing were coming in, and fifty armed deputies patrolled the city, all with orders to shoot any looters.

2 P.M., Fort Wayne

It was determined that the St. Mary's River had gone down three inches since 5:30 A.M. With the rain slowing down to a trickle, the end of the flood finally seemed to be in sight.

Throughout the day, Oil City, Pennsylvania

While waterways were going down in the region where the flood first began, Oil Creek was rising at three inches an hour. The river gauge measured twenty feet, instead of the usual foot or two, or even zero, since often the creek bed was dry. The entire business district was under water. The city's newspapers and industrial plants had also shut down since their power rooms were flooded. But what was really unnerving to the residents was that about four thousand barrels of oil had washed away from the Carmania Refinery plant.

People were afraid that this would be a repeat of June 5, 1892, when something similar had happened: miles of the river had caught on fire and dozens of people had died.

When people heard about the oil barrels, succumbing to humanity's voyeuristic instinct, they ran to the river to look at the barrels rather than getting as far away from it as possible. The railroads were ordered to make sure their locomotives extinguished their fires, and a government order went out saying that nobody was allowed to light a fire. Not even a match.

Throughout the day, Adams County, Pennsylvania, March 27

Adams County, scene of the infamous 1889 Johnstown Flood, saw their streams two inches higher than they had ever been since that fateful day. Every cellar in the city was full of water, footbridges were destroyed, and travel was virtually impossible. Still, the bigger bridges held, and there were no deaths. Which was something of a minor miracle, or simply better geography than some of the other flood-prone cities. In the days and years after the Johnstown Flood, there was no legislation, in the city, county or state level, that attempted to protect its residents from future floods. Although it was considered a manmade disaster—the dam, for starters, was poorly maintained—the courts saw it as an act of God. The survivors not only received no money for their damages, they had no assurance something like this couldn't one day happen again.

Afternoon, Dayton, Ohio

"Don't send us money. We can't use it," said J. C. Hale of the National Cash Register company, who was in charge of the relief and wanted food, clothing, and actual life-saving goods. That sentiment would change later, but for the moment there was a cash shortage in Dayton, rendering the checks useless at the city's banks. That may have inspired Governor Cox to give the state a ten-day banking holiday, knowing full well that people weren't going to be able to pay their bills on time.

Meanwhile, that afternoon, NCR's founder, John Patterson, sent a message out that went on the news wire across the country. It was an urgent yet calm missive, furnishing directives on exactly what the city was going through and what it needed. And it's easy to see why later, after the disaster would pass, the citizens would come to the conclusion that they needed something that a few scattered communities across the country had begun employing: a city manager.

Patterson's message read:

"Situation here desperate. All people except on outskirts imprisoned by water. They have had no food, no drinking water, no light, no heat for two days. We have had no house to house communication by telephone for two days. Dayton water works stopped two days ago. Fire raging for 24 hours in center of city and now spreading. Beckel Hotel burned."

(He was wrong about that last part.)

"Weather suddenly turned cold with strong wind and snow; water current too strong for rowboats and rafts," continued Patterson's message. "Need help. Can reach us today from nearby cities. Help should be in form of motor boats and people to run them. We need good rowboats. We need troops for protection and help. Fire engines, motor trucks, and automobiles are needed, also provisions, clothing, and medical supplies. Our factory is safe, it has its own power, heat, electricity, and water plant. We and private houses are caring for many people, but they are only a small part of the sufferers.

"We cannot reach central, northeastern, northern, or western parts of the city. Consequently, cannot answer any of the telegrams of inquiry about safety of the people that are coming in. Railroads reaching Dayton are practically all out of use."

Patterson sounded like the mayor of the city, and indeed his factory was becoming more like a city within a city every day. If Fred Ward, reporter for the *Columbus Citizen*, was right, NCR even had turned its basement into a jail, where guards were keeping robbers and vandals. Patterson's company not only embraced the idea of reporters visiting NCR, Patterson set up a separate living quarters for them, on the upper floors of the building, which were now stocked with beds. It made sense, even if Patterson hadn't understood the value of favorable publicity—he did—because the hotels weren't exactly welcoming new customers, unless the new customers had a canoe handy, and the reporters had to stay somewhere. But Patterson not only gave journalists lodging, he had their muddy clothes cleaned and pressed overnight, and the reporters were welcome to use other amenities the company provided, like the dining room, the barber shop, and shoe-shining services. Even more helpful, Patterson managed to get a Western Union wire for the reporters to use at NCR, and for the next three months, newspaper men—sometimes as many as seventy-five—gathered at Patterson's company to collect news.

City Hall couldn't have done it better. As Carlos F. Hurd, staff reporter for the *St. Louis Post Dispatch*, observed, "To me, as I walked through the eleven floors of its administration building, it seemed that its work could not be more effective if it had been built for the express purpose it is now serving."

But why shouldn't Patterson act like the city's mayor? Dayton's actual mayor, Edward Phillips, had hardly been seen or heard from since the flood started, and while it wasn't first and foremost on people's minds in the beginning, as they struggled simply to survive, it was a question that was coming up more and more: Where was the mayor, anyway?

The mayor was marooned at his house with his family. He was stuck at home for about seventy hours, only escaping late in the afternoon on Thursday, March 27, after rescuers took Phillips and his family away. As he told a reporter, "The water caught us early Tuesday morning. During Tuesday, the water was fourteen feet deep around the house, and that night, I chopped a hole through the ceiling of a second-floor room, and we spent the night in a little attic. The big west side fire was just two blocks from us, and when the wind began to carry burning embers in our direction, it looked serious. I watched the roof nearly all night."

Phillips probably had no choice but to wait out the flood, but it didn't help his political career. By the following year, he was out as mayor; and as if to add insult to injury, Dayton would change its system of government, reverting to a then-relatively new way of running a city, in which a five-member commission—which includes the mayor, functioning as the commission's chairman—chooses a city manager to run the show. Phillips's most enduring legacy may not be as a businessman, but that today most cities employ a city manager.

Not surprisingly, given how many communities were in the flood's way, Mayor Phillips wasn't the only politician who didn't exactly receive praise for how he handled the flood. Governor Ralston of Indiana was roundly thrashed in the editorial pages of the *Indianapolis News*.

As it observed in the days after the flood, "The people in West Indianapolis leaped into action to aid flood victims within an hour the night of the flood. The Governor, however, was still struggling more than a day and a half later about the issue of possibly losing control over the distribution of the relief supplies the flood victims needed so desperately. He was worried that some glitch might spring up concerning the method of distribution and then criticism might fall on him. He followed the safest course. He equivocated."

3 P.M., New Castle, Pennsylvania

The bridges kept collapsing. The Black Bridge, a wooden bridge, had been the first to fall into the Shenango River, followed by the Grant Street Bridge on Wednesday afternoon, and now the Pennsylvania Railroad bridge. As was a common practice during heavy rains, railroad cars—in this case, coal cars—were loaded up on the edges of a bridge, to keep it weighted down, and so everyone believed the bridge would survive. But the waters proved too strong, and in another three hours the bridge at Gardner Avenue would fall too.

Around this time, Thomas Thomas was joined by an alderman, John H. Gross. Thomas, on continuous duty since Tuesday, was exhausted and must have welcomed having a partner to help him help others. Still, Thomas should have found a warm bed instead and left the rescuing to others after more than forty-eight hours at the helm. But then one wonders if he knew about some of the graft among his fellow officers who were not as pure of heart as he. Maybe he felt that he simply couldn't leave the rescuing to men like William Kerr, who were busy blackmailing stranded families.

Gross was going to help Thomas with his latest rescue. Thomas had brought back a mother of six children. Her kids and the father were back at the house, and Thomas was going to go back for them, or some of them, anyway, since it would be impossible to fit nine people, including the rescuers, in a single boat.

But they never made it. Thomas and Gross's boat overturned. Fortunately, they were in the vicinity of two Shenango Mill employees, John Henderson and Abe Rhoner. They had found themselves trapped at their place of employment, a tin mill, the same that Thomas had worked at before becoming an officer, and they ended up constructing a wooden boat out of factory scraps to use for rescues. It was a rudimentary boat, to say the least. They had no oars; just wooden boards for paddling. By the time Thomas and Gross fell into the drink, Henderson and Rhoner had saved at least twenty-five women, taking them from the windows of two-story homes.

Both men heard Thomas and Gross scream and immediately hopped into their skiff and started rowing toward them. They found Thomas and Gross, their necks just above the churning water, hanging on to a fence, in the middle of a pile of garbage and driftwood, all piling up from the current.

Rohner held the boat to the fence, and Henderson went into the water and took their rope and tied it to the front of the porch. At least whatever happened next, they wouldn't lose their boat.

Neither Gross or Thomas could talk, they were so cold. Their fingers were so cramped that they couldn't hold a rope. Henderson and Rohner were at first at a loss—the men couldn't use the rope to make their way to the boat—but they ultimately helped Thomas onto the roof of the porch. Then they aided Gross, who, when he tried to stand, fell back down.

Both men seemed delirious from the shock and the cold, and after searching the house for a place to light a fire and coming up empty, it was clear that Henderson and Rohner couldn't just leave them there, nor could they take them anywhere far either.

Fortunately, a woman in an upstairs window, three houses away, shouted that she had a fire going in her room and they could bring the men there. Henderson and Rohner did, taking each man one at a time on the skiff, making their way as carefully as possible to the woman's house. Once the officers were with the woman, whose name we may never know, Henderson and Rohner then rowed back to the tin mill on an errand for coal. They brought it back for the woman's fire, so they could keep it going. Gross, and especially Thomas, were fine with where they were. They didn't want to go anywhere. Thomas recognized his limits. He was officially off the job.

Henderson and Rohner then bid the three farewell and boarded their skiff. It isn't clear if Henderson and Rohner were asked to go to the police station and report the whereabouts of Thomas and Gross, or if they simply took the initiative. Either way, it would have been better if they had simply rowed back to the factory. Henderson and Rohner rowed their skiff to dry land and then headed to the police station, carrying their skiff with them in case it was needed, and probably fearing that someone might take it in a city where boats were now very valuable. They came to the Gardner Avenue Bridge, which looked unsteady but crossable.

After making it across, Henderson and Rohner found an officer, Lew Thomas, and informed him of the whereabouts of Thomas Thomas and John Gross. The two men made it clear that they were safe and warm and should remain in the house until the water had settled down.

Then they left, returning to the Gardner Avenue Bridge around 6 P.M. Henderson and Rohner once again mulled over whether they should cross the bridge once again, and then the decision was made for them. It collapsed.

Feeling very lucky and shaken, they found another bridge belonging to a railroad and traveled as far as they could until they put their skiff back into the water, rowing to the tin factory they were now calling home. They felt very good about how they had spent their afternoon and that everyone knew Thomas and Gross were safe and sound. They had no idea that what they had actually done was inspire people to form a rescue party.

But that is what happened. Two police officers went after Thomas and Gross, a national guardsman named Fred Moore and another man of very questionable moral character, the one who had been taking money before saving flood victims: William Kerr.

Evening, March 27, Portsmouth, Ohio

As the *Portsmouth Times* would observe fifty years later, everyone in this river city, with the Ohio River to the south of them and the Scioto

River to their west, was pretty apathetic when it came to devising escape plans in case their homes were suddenly underwater. The residents were well aware that they could be flooded out and had faced down many floods, but that was exactly why nobody worried. The city had a 62-foot flood wall, and one local official had recently theorized that maybe someday there would be a fifty-foot flood at the maximum. He apparently forgot or was unaware of the 1884 flood that had reached 66.3 feet on February 12.

Still, for those who remembered that flood, that was one for the record books. It seemed inconceivable that the river would ever get that high again.

And while the rest of the state was worried about its bridges, Portsmouth had its brand new $75,000 steel bridge crossing the Scioto River, and they were confident that it could survive anything mother nature threw at it.

But during the evening and night of March 27, the Ohio River rose to 67.9 feet. Some people reported seeing a tidal wave, fifteen feet high, going down the Ohio River and smashing into the Kentucky shore. The river soon poured over the flood wall, into downtown Portsmouth, and for anyone thinking of escaping across that steel bridge—no such luck. Perhaps to the concrete industry's collective smug satisfaction, the Scioto River knocked Portsmouth's pride and joy into oblivion.

And yet, while the flood wall was nowhere near high enough to save Portsmouth from flooding, it was high enough to save the community from being blotted off the map—and high enough to save lives. There was a stampede of horse-and-buggies, galloping up into the hills, and a swarm of people, grownups and children, racing down the streets and sidewalks, carrying kerosene lanterns and lamps, all running for higher ground. Those who didn't feel they could make it that far knew the drill, running for their second floor or the roof. Horses left alone were drowned in their stalls. Buildings, many of which were boarded up by shopkeepers hoping to save their plate glass, were overturned. Everything that wasn't nailed down became part of a muddy sea of debris. The waters were as high as nine feet in downtown Portsmouth, and an estimated 4,500 houses were flooded. By the time it was all over, the mayor estimated that there was half a million dollars in damages.

But thanks in much part to the flood wall, which bought everyone more time and kept much of the river out of the community and from swamping the city even more than it did, not one man, woman, or child in Portsmouth was killed.

Sometime during the evening, Alto Pass, Illinois

While the rivers, creeks, and streams weren't flooding elsewhere as dramatically as they had been in Indiana and Ohio, the water was still picking off its victims in other states. It was around this time, in Alto Pass, Illinois, that George and Ella Van Cavaness, farmers and parents of five children, discovered that their two-year-old was missing and found their child's body floating in Hudgeon's Creek.

7:30 P.M., New Castle, Pennsylvania

William Kerr and Fred Moore reached the house where Alderman Gross and Officer Thomas Thomas were. By the time they reached the home, there wasn't a ray of light left in the sky. Thomas and Gross were roused awake and taken to the boat. It was never said, but one imagines the kind and hospitable woman who sheltered them was left behind.

That Kerr wasn't the most honest person in the world doesn't, of course, mean that he meant any harm toward Thomas. They may have been best friends. He might have been subconsciously trying to make amends for his sleazy behavior in the last couple of days. He may have been ordered by a superior to go after Thomas. But the fact remains that Thomas would have been better off sleeping through the night. He was so weak that he couldn't sit up in the boat.

Gross felt ill as well, but he managed to at least sit while Kerr and Moore rowed in the choppy water. There was no light, save a search-light that someone was operating, which moved up and down the muddy creek. They were heading toward a railroad bridge, the same one that, several hours earlier, Thomas and Gross's original rescuers, Henderson and Rohner, had crossed on their return trip for the police station. Near the bridge was a slew of submerged railroad cars, and the current was sweeping everything it could underneath, including the boat that Kerr and Moore were rowing.

It capsized, and everyone pitched into the river. Knowing Thomas's condition, Gross lunged for his friend and managed to place him on the roof of a boxcar, just barely over the rushing water. Gross grabbed on to something—but he would never remember what—a branch from a tree? Part of the boxcar? Gross hung on and looked back at Thomas, horrified by what he saw.

In front of his eyes, the current knocked Thomas's limp body off the boxcar, and he was swiftly pulled under the water.

Gross had a quick thought that he would be joining him soon. Then everything went black.

FRIDAY,
MARCH 28, 1913

Chapter Eighteen

Water Retreating

Friday, March 28, 1913
Midnight, Columbus

Ernest Bicknell's train pulled into Columbus. After five days of being on a train, first heading to Omaha and then back toward Dayton, the Red Cross's national director was at last getting closer to his destination.

Morning, Hagerstown, Maryland

The Potomac climbed its banks and hit the streets. The residents were bracing for it and most of them, well acquainted with what was happening in the states to the west of them, were ready. As the local paper put it, using their city's nickname: "Harrystown soon knew what it was to be—Omahahawed and Daytonized. This morning early, the people in Liberty Street were awakened by the lapping of gentle waves at their door steps. They hastily arose, as did people on Jefferson and Valentine, all those streets being in the midst of the flooded district and found their cellars abrim with yellow wavelets and their gardens flooded and no escape except by waiting."

But Hagerstown was quite lucky compared to Omaha, Fort Wayne, and Dayton. While there were thousands of acres submerged and a lot of damage, there were no deaths in the city from the flood, and after about noon, when the Potomac River reached a high of eighteen feet, the water levels began to slowly recede.

Hagerstown wasn't the only community in Maryland affected by the flood. Cumberland, sixty-seven miles to the west, had considerable damage to its farm lands thanks to Evitts Creek, rising to higher levels than anyone could remember. The Hampshire Southern Railroad, which ran forty miles from Romney to Petersburg, was expected to close for several days due to a bridge being knocked into oblivion. Another railroad based out of Maryland, the Baltimore and Ohio, had to close all of its tracks after a mudslide near Connellsville, Pennsylvania.

And while almost everyone in Maryland came through the flood unscathed, one man did not: John Hoke of Emmitsburg. Exactly what happened will never be known, but it's safe to say he wouldn't have been a casualty of the flood if, the evening before, he hadn't been drinking.

The night of March 27, Hoke, the head carpenter at Mt. St. Mary's College in Emmitsburg, had to cross Tom's Creek at Hartman's Bridge to reach his house. He probably would have made it, had he not stopped after work for a drink or two . . . or maybe five.

A friend of his walked with him through the town most of the way, but then Hoke must have felt that he was sober enough to get home on his own.

The friend never saw Hoke again.

The next day, Hoke didn't turn up for work, and his wife was frantic. If she was able to call their older daughter living in Hagerstown, or John's brother or sister, they, too, were panicked. All day, everyone wondered. Where was John Hoke?

Late in the day, a little boy in the town provided the answer. He revealed to presumably his parents that earlier that morning, he saw a man in waist-deep water, clinging to a bush and shouting for help. Probably frightened by what he saw, the little boy said nothing to anyone all day. Or maybe he was on the fast track to becoming a future demented serial killer.

Once people learned that Hoke had been alive in the morning, they started hazarding the guess that the inebriated carpenter had decided not to go home but to sleep near the creek. When he woke up, he was surrounded by water and, either frightened or still hung over, wasn't able to get out of his predicament before the current swept him away.

Morning in New Castle, Pennsylvania and surrounding areas

The worst may have been over for Dayton, but other communities were still in a pitched battle against their rivers and creeks. Residents in Cairo, Illinois were preparing for trouble with the Mississippi River, and down south along the Mississippi in Memphis, Tennessee, the city was warning everyone to prepare for a flood. This was, of course, the big difference between the start of the flood and the end. People had enough warning to get out of harm's way.

Yet not everyone could. Samuel Whitlatch, rowing a boat on Main Street in Parkersburg, West Virginia, capsized and drowned. Parkersburg in general was having its share of problems on this day: the county jail was flooding, and the prisoners, hopefully none of them too dangerous, were being released.

In New Castle, everyone woke up to read in the morning papers that their state still appeared to be falling apart. People in the lowlands of Pittsburgh were fleeing for higher ground as the Allegheny River climbed and at least one man probably died. The streets of Bridgewater, Pennsylvania were five feet underwater. The Beaver River was climbing five inches every hour, and there was now a chasm where the Sharon Bridge, which connected New Brighton and Fallston, used to be. But what must have sent everyone reeling was the news that a beloved police officer, husband, and father of three had drowned. Thomas Thomas and a five-year-old boy who had fallen into Neshannock Creek were New Castle's only casualties. That there hadn't been more was arguably due to Thomas Thomas's efforts, who essentially gave his own life for the cause.

As for the alderman, John H. Gross, he woke up in his own bed, a physician at his side. The doctor had been there all night, tending to him. Gross soon learned that Fred Moore had been taken to the Shenango Valley Hospital and would live. He learned that William Kerr had a bad gash on his head and was suffering from a severe cold. And then doctors confirmed what he already knew, that Thomas Thomas was no more.

His body would be retrieved in a few hours, at noon, lodged underneath a beam under Box Car Number 7140. A grim congregation of seven police officials was on hand to assist with pulling out the body, including Lew Thomas, the man who had initially learned that Thomas and Gross were recuperating in a home and had passed the news on to the mayor, who apparently was the well-meaning one who had initiated organizing the ill-fated rescue party.

Throughout the day, Omaha, Nebraska

In every age and era, there is always someone out there who is happy to exploit a tragedy. Police officers and bystanders started noticing that several attractive young women and teenage girls, who were homeless and penniless in the wake of the tornado, were being approached by some well-dressed men who were offering the ladies some well-paid jobs in Chicago and St. Louis.

Their motives were purely humanitarian, the men said.

F. E. Eilleck, one of the men working at the relief station, didn't think this was the case. The working theory soon became that these were men who were part of the white slave trade. Police intervened, as far as anyone knew; these shady-looking men left the city—without any young women in tow.

Rescuers were still finding citizens in dire need of help. *The Cedar Rapids Evening Gazette* tells the story of one unidentified mother who left her house after the tornado. It was apparently not too badly damaged, but the wind had come close enough and terrified her, and the woman was afraid her house might catch on fire. Leaving behind her ill, bed-ridden husband, she ran outside with her baby and sat all of Sunday night in a creek, covering herself and her baby with a wet blanket, hoping to protect herself from fire. Of course, this made matters worse. By the time she was found, apparently several days later, the baby was barely breathing. A doctor was called in, and one can only hope that everything worked out for this family.

Noon, Parkersburg, West Virginia

More than half of Parkersburg's business district was underwater, as were a large number of houses, and the Ohio River was still rising—and widening. The Ohio River is often a quarter-mile to a mile wide, depending on the area of the river; during this flood, the Ohio River, in some places, was as wide as twelve miles.

The gas, electric, and water plants would be shutting down in a matter of minutes, and streetcars would sputter to a stop.

The newspaper plants were all flooded out as well, save for the *Parkersburg Sentinel*, which was too close for comfort to the river and had its first floor flooded, but the printers were evidently able to bring some equipment upstairs. The editors and reporters were brought to the building in boats, coming through the front door. Then they took the stairs up to the second floor, where they worked on putting out a newspaper with as many updates on the flood in their town as possible. It was slow going with the printing of the paper—they were only managing to produce two papers a minute—which meant they had to raise their prices—but they got the paper out to their newsboys, who sold their papers from boats.

Afternoon, Columbus, Ohio

After a lengthy conference in the statehouse, Ernest Bicknell and Governor Cox left for Dayton.

"There will be harmony between the state and the Red Cross," a weary Bicknell told reporters. "That is positive. All relief channels must be brought together."

Throughout the day, northwestern New York

In Rochester, and throughout the western part of the state, the water was higher than it had been since 1865. The Genesee River flooded Plymouth Avenue and Front Street in Rochester, capped off by a three-inch snowfall. In Lyons, the Clyde River climbed eleven feet, forcing families out of their homes into the freezing wind. In Troy, there were fires and many families fleeing their houses. The villages of Marcellus, Camillus, and Marietta were described in the papers as "threatened with being wiped out."

Throughout the day, Dayton, Ohio

The water came to Dayton fast and furious. It left it the same way.

It seemed like it would never end, but once the water began evaporating and draining, it was a relatively speedy exit. Jennie Parsons, a resident of New York, who became stuck with her family at a relative's house, told the story of waiting out the flood to *McClure's Magazine* and recalled that Friday morning, she could see the iron fence surrounding the house, and by noon, the lawns were showing. Soon after, neighbors were dropping by, mucking through the mud to come visit.

"Hello, up there," was the most common refrain Parsons remembered hearing. "Everybody all right?"

Parsons added that "the funniest thing was that everybody had forgotten what day of the week it was. It seemed months. And you could hear people saying, 'What day is it, anyhow?' We had to get a calendar to find out."

About 11:30 A.M., right around the time the Beckel House guests were freed, the owner of the hotel, Clarence E. Bennett, still dying, still in the Callahan Building, breathed his last. He was free of his pain, and so were his guests, who fanned out across the city, perhaps in a daze, but also, at least some of them, in a hurry.

At least two of the actors from the comedy *Officer 666* wasted no time trying to communicate with the outside world. Lorenza Wellen, an actress with the play, sent a telegram to her theatrical managers reading: "Am stranded. Love from company 'Officer 666.'" But that's all she wrote, and so while the managers were glad she was alive, they were still just about as perplexed and anxious as they had been before.

Another actor in the play, Jeffrey French, bought a ticket for the first train out of Dayton that he could get, but the ordeal evidently had been too much for him. While he was at the station, running for his train, he collapsed and died.

Everyone was in a state of assessing what they had been through. "It was the worst experience, more so than the one I had in the Galveston storm," declared a Dayton resident who gave his name to the papers as B. Traynor. He added that "in the Galveston disaster, I lost everything I had," emphasizing that the infamous 1900 hurricane was no picnic.

This flood was one for the ages.

Evening, Dayton

Charles Adams waded through several yards with Grandpa Adams, and they returned to their house to see what they were in for.

It was as wretched as they feared, but at least the house was still standing. What was left of the furniture on the first floor was piled in corners. Viola's piano, which Charles and his father and neighbors had so carefully placed on the table, had fallen over backward, "where it lay in a hopeless ruin," wrote Charles several years later. "We waded through to the dining room where we saw one thing at least, inviting, compared to the mud and grime surrounding it. Over in one corner of the room we found the dinner table right side up and the top of it practically as clean and white as when we left it early Tuesday morning, save for the lapping of the water up around the edges. The cracker jar and a dish of salted peanuts on the table were perfectly clean."

It was a similar surreal sight that Orville Wright and his sister Katharine would find at their home, and at the homes of undoubtedly numerous Dayton residents. Charles came to the same conclusion that Orville had.

"The only way we could account for this freak was that the table had risen with the water, missed the lighting fixtures and had floated to the top near the ceiling, coming down again with the water, right side up. The high-water mark was just three inches from the ceiling, which was enough to allow the dishes to float clear without forcing the top surface of the table under water."

But otherwise, the floor covering was mud, the walls were filthy, and Charles and his father were staring at a veritable domestic disaster. There was nothing to do but start cleaning.

SATURDAY,
MARCH 29, 1913

Chapter Nineteen

Cleaning Up

Saturday, March 29, 1913

The weathermen didn't predict the flood, but if the public had only asked a psychic for a weather forecast—then everyone living near a river or creek could have moved their belongings inland and so much of this could have been averted.

Nobody actually suggested that, but the implication was there when Mme. De Thebes, the famous French seer, granted an interview with the press that appeared in papers. "I am in hiding because I do not want to be interviewed," said De Thebes, who then continued with her interview: "I fear to tell the world what I see, that America is just at the beginning of these awful catastrophes which nature is going to heap upon her this year. I am ill myself with horror at the awful things I foresee. Let those in America who survive this present disaster protect themselves against further cyclones and inundations, for I cannot see any calm returning to America before April 21. September is to be the most dangerous for America, and everybody there ought to be ready to flee from floods, fire, or cyclones any moment. In that month most of the horrors, however, will develop from winds."

September 1913 came and went without any major problems.

Then Mme. De Thebes, still clearly in hiding and not wanting to be interviewed, capped this off by saying, "I truly wish, tell the dear Americans I could be mistaken and that my vision might be wrong, but I know my hope is vain. I have told you what I have seen in the past regarding America, and from that you may tell that what I see in the future will prove true. These catastrophes are the will of God. His destiny is at work, and you in America are helpless—practically so. You can only safeguard yourselves, wait, and endure."

She continued, clearly hating the attention and therefore saying very little: "It was three months ago that I predicted how wind, water, and fire would assail the United States in March, and I have kept repeating it ever since to all the Americans I have talked to—telling them the disasters were on the way. The Americans would not take heed—they always hoped that I might be wrong about my prophecy, but you see I was not. I understand their attitude, for I, too, also hope always that I may be mistaken. I have spent a terrible three months awaiting this present disaster."

"Is there no way, you think, for us to avoid further troubles?" asked the correspondent, William G. Shepherd, no doubt knowing he had a fun subject and loving every minute of this interview.

"Alas, no," she said. "The finger of God is at work in America. It is an occult force. I do not know why it is there, I do not know why it is there, or how it came. None can tell, but all the terrible, hidden influences that generate holocausts are at work in the skies above America, and I cannot see the end. From 1910, America should have taken precautions, putting herself on the defense until 1918, for she is in the grip of terrestrial evolution, and each of these years, the enemies—fire, wind, and water—will assail her. A large portion of her territory will slip into the sea within the next few generations, and I foresee that event will be much more terrible than the present one."

She was, of course, just one person in a long list of people who have either made a living off of making predictions or found fame predicting doom for a country or the nation, a list that includes Jeane Dixon, who in 1956 predicted in a *Parade Magazine* article that in 1960, a Democrat would win the election and be assassinated or die in office; and Harold Camping, an 89-year-old California evangelical broadcaster who twice in 2011 predicted the end of the world, fortunately to no avail.

While Mme. De Thebes may sound like a con artist or a kook to most modern readers, the Parisian seer frightened plenty of people, and this was an age in which the occult was, if not taken seriously by the mainstream media, at least reported on fairly regularly. On March 20, just a few days before the flooding, an elderly woman named Mary Finke walked into a New York City police station and informed a lieutenant that President Woodrow Wilson would be assassinated on March 25. How did she know?

"The spirits told me that President McKinley was to be assassinated," she said in broken English. "I was told about the *Titanic* disaster and last summer they told me the Black Handlers were going to get after Governor Wilson." Mrs. Finke was referring to gangsters who specialized in extortion.

When the supposedly fatal day of March 25 arrived, Woodrow Wilson was dealing with the floods throughout the bulk of his nation, trying to get a tariff bill passed through Congress, and playing host at a short reception to about five hundred Canadian high school teachers from Toronto. It was an annual affair for these teachers, a visit to Washington, and Wilson wanted to be accommodating to our neighbor to the north. It was, despite the flood, a simpler time.

But Wilson got through the day unscathed, and in Fort Wayne, the weather forecaster, Walter S. Palmer, felt that Madame De Thebes's predictions wouldn't amount to anything. Palmer informed the *Fort Wayne News* that numerous calls had come in to the bureau, regarding another interview the press-shy predictor had given, indicating that another flood would be coming on April 15.

"There's nothing to it," Palmer told the paper's readers. "There is not a thing in our indications to show that there is the slightest likelihood of the flood being repeated on the 15th."

That said, given that Palmer and the other weather forecasters across the country hadn't predicted the first flood, his assertion may have not reassured too many residents.

It was understandable that people wanted to think that some being or reason, whether the occult or God or fate, was responsible for the flood. It seemed too improbable that this could just happen. That all those lives were lost, just like that. In any case, for those who believed in a mystical power, there was no shortage of stories claiming that the floods had been seen before they had actually come. One of the strangest tales was reported in the *Bakersfield Californian* on March 28, 1913. One Mrs. S.C. Lennox, a resident of East Bakersfield, claimed to have received a letter from her cousin, an Elsie Smith, from Peru, Indiana.

Smith, like Lennox, claimed to be a clairvoyant. In Smith's letter, Lennox claimed, it said, "I can see you crying as you read this letter. Don't cry over me and my troubles."

As Mrs. Lennox was reading the letter, a telegram was delivered from relatives of hers in Ohio, saying that her cousin, Elsie, was missing. The next night, Mrs. Lennox saw her cousin's name listed as having been one of the drowning victims of the flood.

A cynic might wonder if Elsie Smith wasn't quite the clairvoyant that she made herself out to be, given that she didn't see her own fate at the hands of the flood. But then again, maybe she did. The newspaper report of her death turned out to be wrong, and Elsie Smith was alive and well and unharmed by the flood. Her husband, Elbert, a railroad worker, however, was not so lucky, meeting his end on March 27, 1913, along with a colleague, Adam Betts. The two men were trying to get home from Hammond, Indiana, along with another railroad man, Frank Holland, when they were caught up in the flood. Somehow Holland managed to cling to a tree, where his friends didn't; when Holland finally unwound his arm, it was so stiff that rescuers feared it might break.

Still, as odd as the Elsie Smith story was, it has nothing on the story reported in Xenia's *Daily Gazette* on May 9, a tale that if it wasn't so sad, might make a good campfire story. According to the *Daily Gazette*, a Mrs. Stella Mercer told her brother, Omar Toy, that he should look for his wife's body at a farm owned by a family named Dresbach. If the report is true—a big if—Mr. Toy, who lost his baby son to the flood and then his wife after spending a harrowing night in a tree, went to the farm a mile south of Columbus and located a spot that seemed like the one his sister had described to him. It was a pile of mud, about four feet high.

Then he began to dig.

Just a foot into the mud pile, Toy discovered a human hand, only it didn't belong to his wife but to a six-year-old girl, Dorothy Busick.

Columbus, March 29

Many rescuers were now being turned away by trapped homeowners, unbelievable as that might sound at first. Some people rightfully felt that the worst of the flooding was over at this point, and they wanted to stay and protect their property.

There was some reason for the homeowners to be concerned and want to stick around. Authorities and the business community were always worried about looters, although many poor and ethnic residents were arguably just as concerned that they would be seen as looters. One African-American was shot in Columbus because he had seven gold rings on a hand, and while, yes, he may have been looting, he could have just as easily rescued his family's jewelry and stuck them on his hand, or maybe he simply liked to wear rings. You didn't want to be black and searching for food in an abandoned home or business and then have anyone white and carrying a gun discover you.

While surely many people throughout history who were shot for looting were actually, indeed, looting, they at least deserved a trial; but in 1913, you could generally forget about seeing a judge and a jury of your peers. Orders to the militia and police were usually of the "shoot to kill" variety, and indeed, this happened on this day in Columbus. Edward McKinley, a white man, one paper noted, as if so people could express surprise that it wasn't a "colored" person robbing homes, was apparently ransacking a house, or just had, and had a sack of valuables with him when a squad of soldiers, designated to hunt down looters, fired upon him.

Rumors were still flying around in regard to the flood, deaths, and now looters. In the *Cincinnati Enquirer*, on April 3, 1913, there would be an article about how seventeen men had been shot the night before on the steps of the Callahan Bank Building in Dayton. According to the Brigadier-General George H. Wood, the man in charge of the Ohio National Guard, it wasn't true, none of it, and that day he wired the *Enquirer*'s managing editor, who printed a retraction the next day. Wood was always emphatic that no looters in Dayton were shot. The city had seen enough death.

The homeowners in Columbus who refused a boat ride to dry land were correct. The worst of the water was over, and yet, emotionally, the worst was also to come: locating and identifying bodies.

Corpses were laid out at a firehouse, and in some cases entire families were set out, waiting to be identified, and rescuers were morphing
from rescuers into search-and-recovery mode. A temporary morgue
was also set up at Green Lawn Cemetery, where so many people, dead
and alive, soon found themselves. Mrs. Edna Keller Burkhart's body
was found near Green Lawn Cemetery in Columbus, almost buried
in a pile of mud about ten, maybe twelve, feet high. She would have
been completely missed, except for some of her hair sticking out,
which someone spotted. Three days later, the corpse belonging to
a Mrs. Lloyd Lynch would also be found at Green Lawn Cemetery,
underneath a mud-covered wagon.

The body of 28-year-old Cleveland A. Turney was found in a tree,
taken down, and laid out at the temporary morgue at Green Lawn
Cemetery, awaiting identification, where he would then receive either
a funeral or a hasty burial in a potter's field, depending on his family's
resources. It was then that a young boy noticed some slight movement
in Turney's body. He shouted for the doctor, who quickly administered
restoratives, which were probably smelling salts. Turney was revived,
taken to a friend's home, and shared his story.

Turney had been with his wife, Junia, when he was separated from
her in the flood. Turney hung to some driftwood until he slammed into
a tree on Green Lawn Avenue. He managed to climb up to branches
where he found a harness, and, necessity being the mother of inven-
tion, he tied himself to the tree. Then he allowed himself to pass out
until he woke up at the temporary morgue. Turney no doubt regaled
friends and family with his tale of the flood until his actual death in
1963, when he was seventy-eight. His wife, who survived the flood,
passed away in the same year, several months earlier.

March 29, Dayton

Mildred Grothjan recalled in a letter to the *Dayton Journal Herald*, "To
walk down Main Street was a sad experience. Most of the big plate
glass windows had been broken, and they were boarded up. Newsaldt's
at Fourth and Main offered rewards for the recovery of jewelry and
silver that had washed out of their store through broken windows.
The owner of a shoe store on Main near Fifth had the remains of his
stock on tables outside his store, with a sign that read: 'Big sale of

muddy tans'—a bit of humor in an otherwise grim scene. Rike's had moved from Fourth Street up to Second and had just had a big spring opening a few days before.

"What a different sight their beautiful store was now. The streets were piled high with merchandise that had been shoveled out of the stores, and everywhere was the sickening smell of disinfectant that had been sprayed over everything. The mud—and later the dust—was ankle-deep. That, and the odor of disinfectant lasted all summer."

Carlos F. Hurd, the *St. Louis Post-Dispatch* reporter of *Titanic* fame, wrote that the property damage could easily be compared with the destruction in Galveston and San Francisco and then added: "The very streets have literally been torn away and big slabs of asphalt from other streets are lying all over the brick pavement of Main Street, which is a line of deserted business houses, with windows gone and interiors wide open. Walking on the mud-piled sidewalks is forbidden and in many places would be hardly possible."

After the flood, the advantage of having those holes that had been cut in the floor proved two-fold, at least those with underground rooms. People would scrub the floors and push everything, the water and some of the mud through the hole so that it would fall into the dirt cellar.

The city was already quickly putting itself back together. Western Union set up a telegraph office in, of all places, the Beckel House. Its first floor was full of mud, but the stories above it were fine. The fire hadn't touched the place after all. It wasn't long before telegrams were pouring in from people inquiring about friends and family.

Ben Hecht was still in Dayton, collecting anecdotes and quotes and then telegraphing his stories to his editors at the *Chicago Journal*.

"Three-fourths of the city is high and dry," he wrote after stating that he didn't think the death toll would be too high. "The streets are streaming with people. The weather is bright and warm. The skies seem to be smiling, and the people are taking heart. The apparently impossible tasks of rebuilding the city, of finding homes for the sorrowing refugees, starting again to live as they did before the flood, occupied Dayton today.

"The martial law declared two days ago has been raised for this afternoon to permit refugees to seek their homes. Creeping and splashing through the mud are countless people on their way home. Home often means a half house, torn and scattered across the entire street. But it is home, anyway, and the men grabbed spades to shovel out the mud while women try to cook their meal. Sometimes it isn't a half house; only a mud hole greets the refugees."

Then Hecht described how a man named Howard Lowrey found a mud hole on lower River Street. "He stood knee deep in the water watching people pass. A woman carrying a child came trudging along. She was his wife, and it didn't matter that the home was swept away. The family reunited, laughed and cried and started off arm in arm for a refugee home. There are thousands of similar scenes. They would fill a volume that would bring tears and smiles and tell a story such as the world has never heard."

Hecht described other surreal scenes: "Some of the steel structures have been twisted out of shape, others are overthrown and scattered along the squares. Mud lies two feet thick on the floors. In the teller's cage of the First National Bank building, a horse was found. Another animal was discovered on the second floor of a department store."

Hecht doesn't mention whether the two horses were alive. It seems likely that the first wasn't, assuming the teller's cage was on the second floor, but that the horse in the department store came out all right. In any event, there were dead animals alongside the dead people throughout the city and all were being removed as fast as possible to prevent the spread of disease. Two wagonloads of dead dogs were removed from Main Street on this day, and forty-five horses that had drowned in a bunch were taken out at one time.

"It is not true that cats have nine lives," declared a story in the *Oelwein Daily Register*, the paper read by the people of Fayette County, Iowa. "There are thousands of dead cats in Dayton."

Everyone knew they were losing their city, their neighborhoods, their homes during the flood, but now that the water had receded, people were starting to realize just what had been lost purely on an economic scale. Daniel Rheim, a Fort Wayne saloon owner and resident of Bloomingdale, Indiana, was illustrative of what the flood had done to people's net worth. The previous fall he had purchased a piano for $550. About a week after the flood, he paid a junk dealer $10 to haul it away.

Orville Wright returned to his house, where he and his brother had lived since 1871, the year of Orville's birth. The house at 7 Hawthorn Street was still standing, but it was in wretched shape. Orville was stunned to find, though, amidst the wreckage, on a table, a bowl of moldy oranges. The bowl of oranges—a favorite snack of his—had been on the table when he and Katharine left. Similar to what had happened at the Adams residence, the table rose in the water, and the bowl of oranges remained on it, and then when the water levels dropped, so did the table and the oranges.

Mr. Wright and American history was, overall, pretty lucky. A fire broke out in a building near the old bicycle shop where he and Wilbur had worked for many years, drafting blueprints and constructing parts for their flying machine. In the shop were those blueprints as well as diaries and photographic negatives of the brothers' early experiments. Fortunately, the fire missed the shop.

But the shop had certainly been through the wringer. The Wright brothers' famous 1903 Flyer, the airplane that started it all, had been dismantled shortly after its first flights and then put in crates in a shed behind the store. The crates storing the Flyer were completely submerged—for eleven days. You might think that would have completely done in the famous biplane, but when Orville eventually opened the mud-covered crates, he discovered that the mud had actually preserved the contents. The 1903 Flyer wasn't destroyed and it—or parts of it, anyway—since 1948 has been proudly exhibited in the Smithsonian.

There were other casualties of history as well. Lyles Station, Indiana, was a tiny community that began in the 1840s as a settlement for freed slaves, getting its name from Joshua Lyles, a freed Tennessee slave who donated six acres of ground to the community to start a railroad station. It was named Lyles Station in 1886 and by the time 1913 rolled around, it was a community of eight hundred residents with fifty-five homes, a post office, the railroad station, an elementary school, two churches, two general stores, and a lumber mill. The Patoka and Wabash Rivers pretty much ended progress at Lyles Station, however, and today, other than a few scattered homes, a church, a grain elevator, and the school, there's very little left of Lyles Station.

Libraries throughout the region were decimated. The city of Zanesville, Ohio, lost 5,000 books. In Piqua, the library lost 8,500 books when the water filled the entire first floor. In Hamilton, 13,000 books were destroyed. But the damage was worst in Dayton's library, which lost 45,000 books, not to mention desks, chairs, bookcases, and filing cabinets. The November 1913 issue of *The Library Journal* described the destruction at the Dayton library this way:

"Floors were covered several inches deep with black, slimy, sticky mud into which books were imbedded as a thick carpet. Furniture was overturned, wooden book shelves warped and fallen and heavy card catalog cabinets lifted and carried far out of place or overturned face down in the slime, a typewriter on its face in the mud, the office and catalog room closed by the swollen walnut doors. The mud was too wet and heavy for immediate removal, so the building was opened for drying and the following hours spent in seeking workmen, shovels, wheelbarrows, and rubber boots."

Since the library staff was mostly women, and they felt they could use some male testosterone to help with lifting, "three or four sturdy Germans" were found at a nearby automobile factory, according to *The Library Journal*, and added to the staff.

But then occasionally, people would shake their heads in wonder and amusement at what wasn't destroyed. In Dayton, the Newcom Tavern and Log Cabin somehow escaped ruin. It was the city's oldest standing structure.

It had been built in 1796 and moved and turned into a museum one hundred years later—the move paid for by long-time Dayton benefactor John H. Patterson—and while it had been swamped by the flood, along with just about every other house in the city, unlike so many of its modern counterparts, it stood. It's still standing today.

There were also telephone lines to restore. As a 1913 issue of the trade publication *Telephony* explained, "Gangs of cable men in mud-holes with water waist deep and with pumps working over their heads to keep the water down, labored night and day endeavoring to adjust the indescribable condition in which they found their work."

Most of the wires, *Telephony* added, were too wet and muddy and had to be replaced.

Outside the Beckel House, fire engines were pumping water from basements of what were considered the most important buildings for the city, like the Bell Telephone Exchange and the Algonquin Hotel.

Of course, what was bad for the flood-battered cities was good for
other cities, and all of the work being done in Dayton and throughout
the region demanded professional help. A 1913 issue of *Electrical
World* reported that as far as Duluth, Minnesota, linemen and electri-
cians were told that "every man who can climb a telegraph pole and
twist a wire is wanted at Dayton and other flooded cities in Ohio
and Indiana."

Not that it was a boon for the economy, since millions of dollars
were lost in almost every industry imaginable and unimaginable.
In fact, it's tempting to call the effect the flood had on the economy
a wash. For instance, you wouldn't think of the ice cream industry
during a flood, but a 1913 issue of *Ice Cream Trade Journal* reported
seventy-five factories making ice cream as being damaged. "There will
be little ice cream sold before July, and then the sales will be from 50
to 80 percent under those of last year," predicted the journal.

Mayor Phillips called an afternoon meeting of the council. His purpose was to issue emergency bonds to provide money to the salvage
corps to remove the dead horses and clear away mud, and then to provide food and relieve the National Cash Register Company and other
sources from the tremendous expense that they were going through,
caring for everyone; money would also go to help people who were
rendered helpless by the flood or unemployed thanks to the flood, and
finally, to help strengthen the police system.

Over in the mayor's office, Mayor Phillips didn't feel he deserved
everyone's wrath and blame and tried defending himself. "Had
council granted my request for a bond issue to dredge the Miami
River on January 6, 1913, I am firmly convinced that many persons
would have escaped," the mayor told reporters. "I do not mean that I
think dredging the canal would have averted the flood, but that if the
obstructions had been removed from the bed of the river, I am convinced that the inundation of West Dayton would have been delayed
until many people could have been warned of the situation and given
time to make their escape."

So either Mayor Phillips was pressured to do what he did next, or
perhaps he came up with the idea on his own, understanding, after
being trapped in his house during Dayton's darkest moments, that
his career in politics was over. He issued a statement praising John

H. Patterson and then called on all citizens to recognize the head of the National Cash Register Company as "mayor of Dayton during the emergency period."

It was quite a turnaround for Patterson, a businessman who had broken anti-trust laws and was still technically awaiting a sentencing that was expected to put him in jail for a year, and for Mayor Phillips who, before the flood, seems to have been well regarded and on his way to a promising political career. Now, Phillips was a footnote in his own city, and Patterson was a beloved hero who could do no wrong. In fact, it came out that day—although it probably wasn't exactly kept a secret—that Patterson was paying for the coffins and burials of the victims. Small wonder that people in Dayton were circulating a petition, asking the president to pardon Patterson.

"I don't want a pardon," Patterson told a reporter around this time. "All I want is a fair trial in a higher court. I am not guilty of anything. If I am, I want to go to jail just the same as any other man." Two days later, Patterson would wire President Wilson: "I am guilty of no crime. I want no pardon. I want only justice and some federal action that will make Dayton safe from recurrence of such a catastrophe as we have just had."

Small wonder Dayton loved Patterson, who ultimately was interested in business and not politics. He made it known that he wanted someone to take over and be in charge of the flood relief situation, and he soon found just the man: Edward T. Devine, president of the New York school of philanthropy and a leading social worker in the nation. He volunteered his services to the Red Cross, which sent him to Dayton. Devine had been in charge of the relief work after the 1906 San Francisco earthquake.

"The situation in Dayton is worse than that which followed the Frisco earthquake," said Devine, who was referring to not only the vast destruction in the city but lumping it in with the entire state of Ohio and beyond.

Mabel T. Boardman and Ernest Bicknell of the Red Cross seconded that. In a letter written in late March that Ms. Boardman sent to a prominent New Yorker, she noted, "Mr. Bicknell told me he thought it was the biggest and most difficult field the Red Cross had yet had to deal with. At San Francisco the work was concentrated and here it is spread out, so that we will have not only the jealousy of individuals but that of communities to contend with. Furthermore, I think the responsibility of a really serious disaster over a large territory comes more upon the Red Cross than it ever has before. Of course, this is as it should be, and I hope and believe we can meet it, but it will take time."

But what really concerned the Red Cross and those involved with relief was the concern of disease breaking out. "The serious feature of this situation is the danger of pestilence arising from unsanitary conditions due to the flooding," said Devine at the time; and indeed, two children in northern Dayton, according to a Dr. R.A. Dunn, who was interviewed after a trip there, had already died of diphtheria.

The dead bodies, at least the ones that could be recovered, were quickly being buried after being identified.

It was the most depressing of all the tasks. One woman's body was found in the west side of Dayton, her face disfigured, apparently from a fire, and in her arms was a six-month-old baby. Another woman was found lying across a picket fence, with her face so lacerated that authorities weren't very hopeful about her being identified. She was in her night clothing, suggesting that the flood had caught her asleep.

When all was said and done, the official death toll for Dayton was open for discussion. The Ohio Bureau of Statistics listed eighty-two names of people who died in Dayton, while cautioning, "it is impossible to say how many persons lost their lives directly and indirectly as a result of the flood of March, 1913." Historian Trudy E. Bell puts the figure at ninety-eight. Other sources place Dayton's deaths at closer to three hundred, but they may be considering nearby cities and neighborhoods. Whatever the number was, it was too many.

Away from Dayton

And people on March 29 were still going to their watery graves.

The papers reported a Miss Anna Smith, leaving Cincinnati and trying to cross the Ohio River and reach Newport, Kentucky, in a skiff with three men. For anyone who has seen the Ohio River on a good day, one can imagine that it wouldn't be easy to cross it in a skiff, not the most sturdy of boats to ford wild and unpredictable water. To have done it when the Ohio River was miles wide and at a time when thousands of miles of water was rushing into it seems like madness.

The craft capsized, and while the three men somehow made it to shore, Miss Smith did not.

Ohio River communities were, as everyone expected, still being swallowed up by the second wave of the flood, although Cincinnati was one city unexpectedly not devastated by the flood.

Cincinnati was considered on the verge of flooding when the water reached fifty feet. The highest anyone had ever seen it was 71.1 feet on February 14, 1884, and by April 1, it was 69.8—perilously high but not a record. The Ohio River expanded into downtown, flooding the Palace of the Fans (later Crosley Field), the baseball stadium; streets like Main and Walnut became rivers. Fifteen thousand people were left homeless.

But it caught few people by surprise by the time the flood came to these parts of the state, and for the most part, Cincinnati residents were helping neighboring towns, rather than needing help themselves. It also helped that the city is built on a series of hills—one of its nicknames is the City of Seven Hills—so many homes were far from the flooding, and the hills provided easy access for residents who needed to find somewhere to wait out the flood.

Newport and Covington, Kentucky, across the Ohio River from Cincinnati, were also quite submerged, with twelve thousand residents needing to find a place to stay. In nearby Lawrenceburg, only forty houses—out of five thousand—weren't underwater.

The flood ravaged Wheeling, West Virginia, picking off ten people there and making twenty thousand people at least temporarily part of the homeless class. Wheeling's Wheeling Island, the most populous island in the Ohio River, had some houses completely submerged— not even an attic window above the water—and many came off their moorings and went floating down the river. Half of Moundsville, West Virginia, and Bridgeport, and Bellaire, Ohio, were underwater. One of the saddest tales has to be that of William Sullivan in Huntington, West Virginia. He helped his wife and children into a boat, and then rescuers took them from the second story of his house. The waters kept rising and when he became convinced that they would not be able to return for him, he ended his own life by drinking poison.

Farther away, the James River in Virginia was out of its banks. The Delaware River in New Jersey was higher than it had been in years, sending many families to the second floors, and even as far north as

Vermont, the Connecticut River was overflowing. In Massachusetts, the residents were on standby, in case the rising river threatened any mills and factories.

Rochester, New York

The rain had been six to eight inches above normal in northern and central New York throughout all of March, but the rainfall that came on March 27 and March 28 dumped 4.4 inches of rainfall over the entire Genesee River basin and was still making plenty of trouble on March 29. The entire Mohawk and upper Hudson River basins were also flooded. Albany, Troy, and Buffalo were all cities enduring flooding and seeing their bridges smashed and their streets littered with hundreds of dead cattle.

Nobody was predicting doom for Rochester, but the end result of the flooding was that the Genesee River was rushing into the streets like it hadn't since forty-eight years before, in 1865, and merchants were moving their goods upstairs as fast as possible. Front Street caved in, highways were damaged, bridges went down, and there was one fatality. Police officers heard shouts, and when they ran to see what was the matter, they found a boy clinging to an overturned canoe rushing down Clarissa Street.

The boy and the canoe sailed through the city as dozens of people gathered along the riverbanks and threw ropes, hung out tree branches, and did whatever they could to save him. Just before he reached the Court Street dam, the boy stopped screaming. He disappeared under the big waves, and the canoe was swept over the dam.

Hornell, New York

Maybe people were becoming used to the flooding and assuming the worst was over, and so that's how seven-year-old Earl Rosier came to be allowed to play outside with his brother. They wound up on an unfinished abutment of the Erie Railroad Bridge, and after the boy stumbled and plunged into the river, it's safe to assume the parents spent the rest of their days wondering how and why it happened.

Fort Wayne, Indiana

A similar situation happened on the same day to a four-year-old boy, William Singer, who walked off a sidewalk and into some fast-moving water and was quickly whisked away. His mother waded in after him but was almost drowned herself until a neighbor pulled her back to shore.

A railroad man found the four-year-old floating in the water. He was still alive—barely. Two agonizing hours later, after a doctor and the Fort Wayne police chief labored over young William, using a new resuscitating device called a pulmotor, that pumps oxygen into the lungs, they had to call the boy's time of death.

It may be impossible to ever really know how many people died in the Great Flood of 1913, because there were surely some people who were never found and weren't registered as an official casualty. In his memoir, *Journey Through My Years*, Ohio governor James M. Cox says as much, stating that for Ohio alone, "the number of known dead was 361, but undoubtedly many more bodies were never recovered. Much sickness and many deaths followed the flood. Thirty-two persons were admitted to the Dayton State Hospital, the city's asylum, their commitment papers expressly stating that their insanity was a direct consequence of the flood."

Meanwhile, as Cox implied, when annual totals were tallied for publications like *Annual Report*, put out by the Ohio Bureau of Vital Statistics, people who died during the flood for reasons other than drowning were not counted in the totals, people like John and Katherine Stotler, seventy and sixty-five respectively. They were victims of the flood as much as anyone but weren't counted in the final death total, presumably because they didn't drown. On March 26, in Columbus, marooned in their cottage with the Scioto and Olentangy rivers overtaking their home, the husband and wife decided to commit suicide instead of letting the river kill them. You pick your poison, of course, but newspaper accounts say that they slit their throats, which all in all, doesn't necessarily seem like a better way to go than drowning, terrifying a death as it is. Their fear, hopelessness, and helplessness must have been beyond overwhelming to take such drastic measures.

Delia McNerny, a 69-year-old widow, also living in Columbus, died in her house on March 27, with the water still surrounding her home and in the first floor of her house. She caught pneumonia and passed away with two of her daughters, Susie and Annie, looking after her as best they could.

On March 29, Charles Potter, his wife and six children were all rescued from their house, which was still surrounded by water, and as they were spirited off to safety in a wagon on a muddy road, it overturned. Everyone died, but because they technically weren't victims of the flood, they weren't counted as such; but had the flood never occurred, it seems likely that the family would have lived to see 1914 and many years beyond that.

On March 30, also in Columbus, James T. Aughenbaugh, a blacksmith who had been rescued from a flooded house, died at 12:30 P.M., from, it was said, shock and mostly the toll his body had taken waiting to be rescued in a flooding home without heat and food.

The *Evening Independent*, the paper for Massillon, Ohio, reported that August Peters, a 68-year-old German-American, contracted pneumonia on March 26, when he had spent most of that Wednesday watching rescuers take stranded neighbors from their homes. Presumably Peters's house wasn't thought to be in any danger, but Peters was probably without heat, and chances are the first floor of his home was flooded, and he was breathing in a lot of damp air.

The *Logansport Pharo*, the newspaper of record for Logansport, Indiana, reported that on the afternoon of April 2 the baby of one Joseph Ofazio caught pneumonia and died, and probably never would have if it weren't for the conditions created by flood. The Ofazios's house had been penetrated by the flood, and after the water receded, they returned to the home before the walls and flooring were completely dry. Soon after, their baby was sick. Joseph Ofazio frantically took the baby to the town doctor, who gave the baby some medicine and warned the father to take the baby home to rest as soon as he could. Ofazio surely tried, but before he reached his house, his child died in his arms.

At some point in early April, James Robinson, fifty-five, was a flood casualty, but it also seems unlikely that he was counted in the overall death toll. He lived alone in his houseboat, five miles outside of Evansville, Indiana, and was sick; and while his daughter and her husband took care of him, they lived in a separate houseboat within view of his vessel. After the flood, their houseboat was in no shape to cross the Ohio River, and the tiny boats that they had had all been unmoored and carried away. Robinson's daughter tried to flag down passing boats, most of them distributing supplies along the river, hoping someone would check on her father, who she had initially seen but then he had disappeared inside the boat and hadn't been seen for days. He was finally found inside his houseboat, not a crumb of food to be found in any of the rooms. He had starved to death.

The morning of April 25, 1913, Elizabeth Crowe, a fifty-year-old African-American, died. *The Indianapolis Star* reported that "a nervous shock as a result of flood experiences is believed to have been responsible."

Henry Brand, forty-two years old and a blacksmith in Hamilton, Ohio, had been washed out of his home during the flood, but he seemed fine. And perhaps he was fine. But a few weeks after the water receded, the evening of April 28, Brand's nose began bleeding. It wouldn't stop. By 3:15 in the morning, he was dead. Speculation was that a latent head injury in the flood had done him in, but nobody could be sure.

Mrs. Lucy Chalsont didn't die in the flood either, but she was a casualty nonetheless. The forty-year-old who lived in the river town of Marietta, Ohio, lost virtually everything she had in the flood, reported the Associated Press, which noted in a June 21, 1913 article that the night before, she had waded into the Muskingum River and drowned herself.

Hamilton, Ohio, Saturday

Eventually the numbers relating to material damage would start coming in, too. In Hamilton alone, 5,600 houses were flooded, and another 335 completely destroyed. Even after the water evaporated, there was still the matter of getting people fed and clothed and keeping a roof over everyone's heads. In Hamilton, two bankers were given the disheartening assignment of recovering bodies and managing a morgue. It wasn't a straight-forward task. Many of the Hamilton residents had been carried miles away from where they lived.

Underneath the bankers was a team of undertakers from Cincinnati. Bodies were hauled to the lawn of the Butler County Courthouse and eventually taken inside the courthouse assembly room. A local newspaperman later described the sight as "appalling. . . . Scores of dead bodies lay about the room on temporary slabs, awaiting the attention of the embalmers, while as soon as this was done, they were placed in plain caskets."

The following day, there would be a funeral for forty-nine victims, the number of people who had been identified. There were thirty-four more victims still to be recognized, and there was another reason the city had to wait until March 30. Its cemetery had been under water.

It was hardly the calming funeral that the community needed. Mourners were well aware that nearby at the courthouse, the remains of two unidentified women and a four-month-old baby were out on the lawn in caskets, there for the public to view and identify.

Then during the ceremony, an automobile brought the body of another flood victim, causing an anxious ripple in the crowd, which seemed both darkly amused and terrified. The reverend had just uttered the words: "The grim reaper has been in our midst."

EPILOGUE:
THE DAYS AFTER THE FLOOD

Chapter Twenty

Remember the Promises in the Attic

Denver, March 30

Sarah Bernhardt, the 67-year-old legendary French stage actress known around the world, gave a benefit performance for the flood sufferers in Ohio and Indiana with John Drew, Jr., an American stage actor known for his Shakespeare performances. He was also the uncle of the famed actors John, Ethel, and Lionel Barrymore and thus the great-great uncle of future film actress Drew Barrymore. Together, they raised $5,000, which would be added to a $41,000 fund already raised by Colorado residents.

Everyone seemed to want to send either money or some sort of show of support. In Sacramento, California, at Folson Penitentiary, E. C. McCarty, a forger, drew up a resolution that prisoners there felt bad about the flood sufferers, and the resolution was somehow passed on to the media and published in papers on this day. The convicts said they wanted the public to know how they felt "to show the outside world that the prisoners are not heartless nor heedless of the suffering of others."

March 31, Garfield, Indiana

Farmers organized a bear hunt to try to bring down what was believed to be one of the escaped circus animals from the Wallace circus in Peru—after he appeared on the farm of one George Enoch. Unfortunately for the farmers at least, the bear managed to escape a hail of bullets.

April 1, Louisville, Kentucky

A large warehouse owned by the Rugby Distillery Company in the western part of the city, weakened by floodwaters, collapsed late in the night, and so into the river went five thousand barrels of whiskey valued at a quarter of a million dollars. Several employees hastily constructed a dam and saved a number of barrels. Presumably, at least a few Kentucky men went looking for these rogue barrels and saved some for themselves.

April 1, Fort Wayne

A full week after the flood began for most people, a poorly dressed and tired-looking man came to the house of one Mrs. Josephine Pfadt, asking for food and explaining that he was a refugee from the flood. She permitted him to come into the house and prepared him a meal. She then left her home for a few minutes to go to the home of a neighbor and when she returned, she learned that he had tried to embrace her little girl. The police were called in but failed to find any trace of him. It's an interesting story, if only to recognize that even in the good old days, there were some really bad people, and for the language that newspapers used when covering a troubled topic such as pedophile (the headline: ALLEGED INSULTER SOUGHT).

April 2, Bird's Point, Missouri

Forty-eight soldiers from the Missouri National Guard became stuck on a 200-foot-wide and 400-foot-long stretch of an earthen levee after the Mississippi River destroyed most of it. The soldiers had boats, but they were all swept away except for a two-man skiff. The two officers in charge boarded the skiff to make a four-mile trip—against the current—to Cairo, Illinois, where they knew they could get help.

For the remaining soldiers, it was a long rest of the day—and night.

"We could feel the dirt crumbling away beneath our feet," one of the men told a reporter later, "and we were kept on the move nearly all of the time. The section of levee on which we were marooned was under water as deep as three feet in many places, and time after time, we dragged some of the men away from the water as the earth crumbled away. We made it a point to stand as near the up-stream edge of our island as possible, so if caught in a cave-in, we would not be washed away by the current."

The Chicago naval reserves immediately went after the soldiers, rescuing them the next morning. Incredibly, all forty-eight men survived the night.

April 2, Missouri and Hickman, Kentucky

For George Shaver, a Missouri farmer, it was tragedy plain and simple, the flood still reaping victims even after the waters receded in Dayton. He and his two young children saw their house destroyed and his wife and their mother killed by falling timbers in their home. Shavers then put his wife's body in his boat, and with his two young children, who were clinging to her body, somehow steered them through the Mississippi River to Hickman, Kentucky, which Shaver deemed a much safer place to be. And it was. Soon after, they buried her in a little cemetery on a hillside.

April 2, New Madrid, Missouri

A resident, William Smith, and his wife, were reported to have attempted to cross the Mississippi River from New Madrid. They didn't make it.

April 2, Washington, D.C. and Catlettsburg, Kentucky

Senator Ollie James of Kentucky appeared at both the Red Cross and War Department to appeal for aid for the three thousand residents of Catlettsburg, Kentucky, who had to flee their homes. He said that conditions were worse there than Dayton or Columbus, now that the levees had broken and everything had been swept away. That hopefully got their attention.

April 2, 7 P.M., Paducah, Kentucky

The river had risen a foot and a half throughout the day and by evening the floors of every wholesale house and many retail stores were flooded. The forecast assumed the river would rise another four feet, flooding almost the rest of Paducah, except for five blocks that seemed high enough to be out of danger. But people weren't so sure. Paducah was on high ground, in general, but the community had never built any levees. Flooding was completely new to this generation. There hadn't been a serious flood since 1884.

Still, as bad as things were in Paducah, it was much worse in nearby Cairo, Illinois, which is why Paducah, a southern Kentucky town, was quickly becoming a rescue center. Situated on the Ohio River just a stone's throw away from Illinois and adjacent to Missouri and Tennessee, Paducah had enough resources that the U.S. military ordered a lieutenant and two non-commissioned officers to take every power boat they could find and three barges and make haste for Cairo.

The military's instincts were apparently spot-on. The remaining canoes, rafts, and the like were enough to save everyone in town, except for one inebriated man who fell out of a boat and into the current. There's a good lesson here for everyone. Floods and drinking heavily do not mix.

April 2, Dayton, Ohio

Despite the waters finally disappearing, the city was still taking stock of what was ahead of them, and authorities were doing everything, from trying to reunite families, to ensuring looting didn't become a problem, to avoiding an epidemic breaking out. People were on edge. C. J. Becker, a prominent real estate agent, had been using his car to help ferry people in and out of the city, and overall was just being a good citizen when a friend of his joked and asked, "How much are you getting for wearing out your tires and machine?"

"Thirty-five dollars a day," Becker said good-naturedly. He should have added: "Don't I wish."

A little later, Becker was stopped by a soldier who took him to a Major Hubler of the Ohio National Guard. The major wanted Becker to explain why he was running a sightseeing service, charging people thirty-five dollars a day to take them to see the hardest-hit areas of the flood.

It took several hours and signatures of people who knew Becker, before the real estate agent could convince the military that he was joking and wasn't some sort of sleazebag making a buck off the flood.

The city gradually was coming to life, however. Historian Judith Sealander, who wrote the book *Grand Plans: Business Progressivism and Social Change in Ohio's Miami Valley* tells of how in the aftermath of the flood, Dayton sent out committee volunteers and soldiers to conduct house-to-house inspections, an operation that reached every home and business in the city, with the goal of taking anyone with a communicable disease to a hospital.

"Groceries, bakeries, restaurants and schools were only allowed to reopen after passing a rigorous inspection and disinfection," writes Sealander, who then refers to a project Patterson created once it was apparent that his factory couldn't keep flood victims there forever. "The tent city refugee camp built on donated NCR property included electric lights, sewer lines, showers and flush toilets. Ten cleaning stations dotted around the flooded regions of the city offered home-owners free lime, chloride of lime, and cresol, along with instructions explaining how to use these chemicals to whitewash basements and disinfect floors, walls, and furniture."

April 4, Dayton, Ohio

A ten-hour downpour in Dayton did nothing to create a new flood, but it also did nothing for people's nerves, nor did it help alleviate the problem of further damage to people's homes, businesses, and health in the already-waterlogged city.

April 5, throughout the nation

Naturally, and not for the first time, the national conversation started toward the idea of flood prevention. Ex-president Theodore Roosevelt, who discussed flood prevention in his book *Progressive Principles*, released just the year before when he unsuccessfully tried to wrest the nomination from President Taft, got the ball rolling, writing an article that appeared in an early April 1913 issue of *The Outlook*: "The Ohio Floods: Can Such Calamities be Prevented?"

After citing the San Francisco earthquake of 1906 and the Great Baltimore fire of 1904, Roosevelt noted that the country was excellent when it came to spending money to help flood victims, but not so excellent at spending money on flood prevention. He brought up the flood of the previous year, noting, ""During the spring and summer of 1912, hundreds of farms along the Mississippi River, from Cairo to the Gulf, were flooded because of the inadequacy of a levee system, unsupplemented by source-stream control, to keep great floods within the channel of the river. More than one hundred thousand persons were driven from their homes, and some were drowned. Homes, buildings, agricultural implements, corn, forage, crops, cattle, horses, and hogs were destroyed in large numbers, and the wild animal life taken by the floods cannot be computed. Health problems of dangerous importance were created, and the injury to business and commerce aggregated hundreds of millions of dollars."

Then Roosevelt went in for the kill: "In order that the suffering by human beings might be reduced, the Federal Government promptly appropriated $6 million for the purchase of food and for the repair of broken levees. But not one cent was appropriated for the solution of the monster economic problem involved, or for the correction of the fundamental evil that has been created through changes wrought by man in the watershed of the Nation's greatest drainage system."

Technology might help matters, at least one expert posited. The head of the physics department at the University of Iowa, Dr. G. W. Stewart, challenged the nation to think about building more wireless stations and in a sense forecasting radio. Just as the *Titanic* had demonstrated how wireless communication could be invaluable in bringing help and sending out warnings during an emergency, the Great Flood of 1913 certainly offered another example of how much it was needed.

"Suppose Omaha and Council Bluffs had been cut off from the outside world and a great fire had started Easter night," speculated Stewart to the press, thinking how Morse code could be adopted for the modern world. "A wireless message, 'C.Q.D.,' flashed to Sioux City or Lincoln would have started special trains carrying fire engines to the stricken cities hours before they otherwise would have started. If Dayton and other cities in the flood region had been equipped with wireless, the great loss of life might have been averted."

Editorials in newspapers across the country obviously had made their opinions known as well. Some used the flood to remind critics of coastal cities that we're all in this together ("No section of the country can claim immunity from storms or from danger of storm damage," noted the *Galveston News*). The editors at the *San Francisco Call* probably just wanted to point out that they were grateful for their own weather but ultimately seemed to suggest the rest of the nation come out to the Sunshine State ("In California of the kindly skies on the same day, fleeting sunshine or warm, gentle rains for coast, valley and foothill; in the higher mountains more snow to guarantee full streams and crops for the summer to come").

Some papers championed self-reliance. The *Chicago Inter Ocean* pointed out that Omaha had refused outside financial aid, and that "St. Louis took care of her tornado losses alone," and that "San Francisco disposed with outside help at the first possible moment. So did Chicago in 1871. So do all American towns when 'trouble' comes to them."

Other papers urged that this was the time for everyone to come and help each other, like the *Detroit Free Press*, which put out an editorial right after the tornado and before the floods: "The President speaks for the nation when he asks the stricken city of Omaha, 'Can we help in any way?' The disaster that has overtaken our fellow citizens is one that might come to any of our cities. What is in the power of Americans at this time will be gladly given."

The *Middletown Daily Times Press*, of Middletown, New York, saw the problem as one that was much of our own making. "Just as the recent tornado losses have been at least aggravated by the tendency to erect unsubstantial buildings, so the awful floods of the Ohio Valley may be largely traced to the work of man," declared an editorial. "Wherever the balance of forces is upset, Nature sooner or later takes revenge."

The *Middletown Daily Times Press* then made its larger point: "The ruthless sacrifice of forest growth, turning vast acres of soil sponge into hard runways, is a familiar cause of flood damage. But even if the losses at Dayton and other cities were not due to any large extent to this reason, other consequences of man's acts do increase hazard. Men build factories and railroad tracks and bridges and dams along a stream, tending to restrict the natural outlet of the water. Their mills let loose debris and silt that fill up the river beds. A still greater factor is the erosion from the cultivated fields, which is far greater than that from the original uncultivated soil."

April 6, Equality, Illinois

The Gallatin Coal and Coke Company's two mines were completely flooded. Anyone around the mine fervently hoping that it might not be ruined had their ambitions dashed with the first explosion, sending water shooting two hundred feet, for the next three minutes, sending coal, cars, mine props, and timber spraying into the air.

Silence followed, but for only a few more minutes, until another explosion that finished off a building, the engine house, and the tipples, the part of the mine where the coal cars were tipped and emptied of their coal.

Anyone who thought, "Well, at least the east mine may still be okay," also had their hopes stripped away. An explosion soon took down that mine as well.

April 7, Frankfort, Indiana

Bodies were still turning up. Roy Rothenberger, who was one of the first victims of the flood, was finally discovered on the creek bottom near where his boat was overturned. Searchers were still looking for his brother, Roscoe.

April 10, Wilson, Arkansas

The flood was still showing its formidable power further and further away from its original epicenter. At a levee near Wilson, about a hundred African-American laborers were doing their best to keep the dam from bursting. They couldn't; and in one Associated Press article, there was a catty aside, typical of the times, of course, that suggested that it was all the fault of the men:

"The levee near Wilson, Ark., went out late this evening said to be due to the desertion of about 100 negro laborers today."

If desertion means running for your life, so you aren't drowned as a dam comes crashing down on you, then, sure, guilty as charged. Residents in the area may have felt the men deserted their post, or perhaps the anonymous reporter simply felt he was reporting exactly what had happened and not attempting any snark since he does, in fact, observe in the next sentence that the laborers "kept up the fight to the last minute."

The men were all able to reach land high enough to escape the rushing waters, but the cabins they lived in were not so lucky. The men watched their homes and all the trees in the valley disappear into the swirl.

April 11, New Castle, Pennsylvania

For weeks, there had been murmurs of police officers demanding money before ferrying flood victims to dry land. On a Friday afternoon, in Mayor Walter Tyler's office, a hearing was held to determine just what had happened. Many witnesses were brought in, as was the coroner. There had been murmurs, a whisper campaign if you will, that perhaps Thomas Thomas was the police officer taking money from rescue victims. He had, after all, been out there a lot, saving lives.

But the coroner threw cold water on the idea when he reported the money found in Thomas's pockets after his body was retrieved. He had $2.01 on him. Several witnesses fingered William Kerr as one of the men who had taken money, but it apparently wasn't enough evidence for the mayor. Or maybe Mayor Walter Tyler gave Kerr the benefit of the doubt since he had tried to save Thomas Thomas's life.

Kerr hung on to his job, but two other police officers were sacked, and a fireman was suspended.

April 14, New Orleans, Louisiana

A bloated corpse was discovered in the Mississippi River at a plantation. The body was five feet and six inches tall and the man estimated to be thirty-five years old, and while nobody knew who he was, they believed he was a flood victim and that they could identify where he was from. Inside was a card from where the man apparently got his dry cleaning, well over eight hundred miles away. It read: Williams and Brown, cleaners. Walnut Street. Cincinnati.

April 16, Dayton

While NCR initially told the rest of the country to send food and clothes and not money, they had now changed their message. The papers were now quoting John Patterson who said that money "is urgently required for putting our city in a condition to prevent the outbreak of serious disease and to rehabilitate the thousands, many of whom lost their homes entirely and all of whom lost their household and personal effects."

April 21, Mayersville, Mississippi

Just north of the town, there was a break in yet another levee, and soon four very populated counties, Sharkey, Isaquena, Washington, and Warren, full of cotton farms and farmers and work-hands, were inundated. Before the day was up, another fifteen thousand people were rendered homeless.

April 28, Louisiana

As the flood made its way toward New Orleans and the Gulf of Mexico, some 222 miles upriver many residents were stuck on roofs and second floors, and the property damage was high. A dike gave way, and the Mississippi River came pouring out, swamping the Tensas and Concord parishes, forming a lake nine hundred square miles and driving two hundred thousand people out of their homes. It was twenty feet deep in some places, and the force of the water literally knocked some railroad trains off their tracks.

April 29, Louisiana

Odds are, when a 900-square-mile lake forms out of nowhere, thousands of people are going to die, but incredibly, twenty-four hours later, officials in communities like Vidalia and Ferriday were stunned and pleased that the death toll was so far light. Two people—African-American, but that's all that's known—died in the flooding. Plenty of people were at risk of drowning or catching a disease or starving, however, which is why a relief camp had been set up, and every available steamer had been called for duty to take flood victims to the doctors, nurses, and American Red Cross officials waiting for them in Natchez, Mississippi. Meanwhile, other communities down the river were eyeing the Mississippi and other rivers warily. In Clayton, Louisiana, located on the Tensas River, the water was already in the city, ten feet deep and rising.

April 30, Natchez, Mississippi

Rescue parties saved many people on this day, but they couldn't save two mothers and nine young children on the roof, all of them screaming and begging for someone to come and get them. Two oarsmen in boats nearby wanted to desperately, but their boats were full of passengers already, and to bring anyone else on board would threaten to tip them over and risk everyone's lives.

All they could do was row away and watch and hope that they could return or send more boats.

But it was not to be. The inside of the house was full of water, and the force was just too great. Suddenly, the incomprehensible happened. While the oarsmen and their terrified passengers looked on, the home toppled over, and the screaming mothers and crying children all plunged into the river and to their deaths.

May 1, Poydras, Louisiana

Approximately sixteen miles south of New Orleans, the levee began to cave away a few minutes after five in the morning. Something had to be done quickly, or risk losing the community. The solution staggers the imagination.

Within twenty minutes, a farmer and about twelve African-American men arrived to find about two inches of water spilling over the levee.

Sandbags—two thousand of them—were on their way, but within minutes it wouldn't matter. The water was coming.

One newspaper article described the black men as willing, and the *Atlanta Constitution-Journal* called them "heroic," but given that they had come with their white boss, and no white men stepped up to do what these men were about to do, you have to assume the worst, that these men were either forced or told that their jobs depended on stopping the water. But it's also easy to assume the best, that these men simply did what they knew had to be done and that nobody else was brave enough to try, in order to save their families, friends, and townspeople.

In any case, two twelve-inch wooden boards were laid on the dirt levee, right where the water was dribbling over, and then the twelve men climbed onto them, effectively becoming part of the levee. They were "human sandbags," as the papers put it, and the twelve men were at risk that any of them might be, at any moment, sucked into the river

323

to meet a grisly end. Their bodies packed tightly into the part of the levee that was breaking away, the men kept the water in the Mississippi River where it belonged. Meanwhile, about a hundred black and white men filled sacks and carried them to the twelve human sandbags, so they could fortify the weakest part of the levee. The idea was that once it was secure, they could begin leaving their posts and replacing themselves with actual sandbags. It took an hour, but eventually all of the men were able to leave safely, and two thousand bags of dirt were in place. The levee held.

May 2, Clayton, Louisiana

The steamer *Concordia*, 156 feet long and 850 tons, was making its way down the Tenas River and taking flood refugees to safety when irony reared its tragic head. The captain lost control and the vessel's right bow was slammed into the north pier of the iron railroad's drawbridge, just two feet above the river. Captain Sam Pennywitt, an experienced river pilot, was evidently trying to go around the drawbridge when he lost control and crashed into it.

Two men on the deck, 73-year-old Ambrose Denton Geoghegan, a veteran riverboat captain along for the ride, and William Grimes, in his mid-thirties and the chief clerk of the steamer, were instantly thrown off the boat and never seen alive again. A black man whose name has been lost to history was also on the deck, as was a planter named Maurice Block. Both made a valiant leap from the steamer's deck to the drawbridge. The African-American landed in the water between the bridge and the boat, which was hurled back into the bridge by the current. The extremely unfortunate man was then crushed to death as a piece of flying timber from the steamer flew into the air, hitting Block, breaking his arm and injuring a shoulder.

As the boat began to sink, there was a mass exodus as crew and passengers leapt for the bridge, and others, tossed off the boat and into the water by the waves, attempted to swim to shore. Incredibly, when it was all over and after the steamer was carried away by the current and eventually sank, 107 survivors remained to tell the tale. But twenty-two people, twenty of them African-Americans, and most of them women and children, did not. They were among the last, and may have been the last, victims of the Great Flood of 1913, a misnomer if there ever was one. The Great Flood of 1913 was heartbreaking, horrifying, and horrible. It was unfair, often tragic, dangerous, and deadly. It was anything but great.

May, 1913, Dayton

Almost a year after the passing of his brother Wilbur, on a Thursday afternoon on May 1, Orville Wright flew in an airplane for the first time. It wasn't simply any typical flight, either. He was piloting a new hydroplane, seven miles north of Dayton on the Great Miami River. Wright told reporters that he hoped the machine would be useful in future floods, such as the one that had driven him out of his home.

Indeed, there seemed to be promise. Wright's plane, piloted by Orville and an assistant, William Jacobs, took off on the waters of the Miami River and then soared in the sky, gracefully curving around the edge of Dayton, and returned, skimming above the water until it came to a safe landing. He had already flown it about four hundred feet above the river, with hundreds of curious spectators watching below, but this was a more ambitious flight.

Orville Wright wasn't the only one soaring. It was a lift to the beleaguered city of Dayton, which was naturally still cleaning up and rebuilding. Wright flew approximately a hundred flights throughout May, June, and July.

Things were happening on the ground, too, though. The next day, on May 2, the Dayton's Flood Prevention Committee formed. Poor Mayor Phillips was nowhere to be found; John H. Patterson was designated the Flood Prevention Committee Chairman, and he appointed local business leaders to join the organization and share in the heavy lifting. The idea that Patterson might spend a year in jail, very real just a couple months before, seemed more improbable than ever.

In the aftermath of the flood, water-weary government officials and their constituents across the nation, even in states that hadn't been affected, demanded change.

In Pennsylvania, the state legislature passed an act allowing a dam in the northeastern quadrant of the state to be built, and creating a sixteen-mile lake, protecting towns from the Shenango and Beaver rivers. Indiana christened a flood protection commission, and throughout the state, new laws were passed, and dams and levees were built and rebuilt. Legislation involving flood control that had been stalled in states like Texas and California suddenly passed as the nation read about the ongoing difficulties in the Midwest.

But no community moved as fast to prepare for another flood as Dayton. The flood prevention committee quickly offered a job to Arthur Ernest Morgan, who was recognized as a brilliant water control engineer. He was hired by Dayton to prepare a flood plan to fight the flood plains, once and for all.

Morgan was born in 1878 in Cincinnati, grew up in Minnesota, lived in Washington, D.C., and was now based out of Tennessee. Morgan was an ambitious go-getter that stemmed from growing up in Minnesota as a sickly kid. As a teenager, he vowed to become healthier. He got a job outside and started pushing himself harder than most able-bodied people ever do. He slept in a tent in northern Minnesota when it was 30 below, and after his high school graduation, he traveled thirty miles down the Mississippi River on a three-foot wide log with just a buck fifty in his pocket.

Then he began making his way to Colorado, doing odd jobs like picking fruit and mining coal. According to his biographer Mark Bernstein, who wrote the book, *American Biography: Arthur Ernest Morgan*, Morgan bought fifty 30-cent editions of authors like Emerson and Kipling and attempted to sell these works he so loved to miners.

Morgan ultimately lived in Colorado for a time and completed his college education at the University of Colorado. After he finished, though, not having money or a job, he returned home and ended up joining forces with his father's surveying firm. They named it Morgan & Morgan, instead of Morgan & Son, at Arthur's insistence, feeling he was his own man, and after what he had been through, he had arguably earned that. He soon married and started a family.

It was during this period that Arthur Ernest Morgan realized he had an aptitude and personal affinity for water control and decided to become a water control engineer. There weren't many water control engineers in the country, as there were not many competitors, he liked his odds of getting work somewhere and continuing his very basic training in the field. Minnesota didn't have any statewide standards for drainage control, and so in 1904, Morgan, twenty-six years old, volunteered to create them for the state engineering society. Morgan threw himself into the task, and the following year, the society embraced his ideas, which were then written into state law. The governor then offered Morgan the job of state engineer.

Morgan actually declined, having set his eyes on a job opening as an engineer on a federal level, working for the Department of Agriculture's Office of Drainage Investigation. His biographer posits that Morgan also may have wanted to move away from Minnesota. His wife, Urania, died four months after the birth of their son, Ernest, and he may have wanted some distance from the tragedy. Understandable, but as his son was left in the care of relatives after his mother's death, he was also distancing himself from his young son, Ernest, Jr. Still, it was a different time, and a father's role in rearing children was not given the same gravitas it is today.

Morgan developed a reputation for being a supremely ethical and dedicated water control engineer, and by 1910, he left Washington and went to Memphis, starting the Morgan Engineering Company. He also married again. He was just shy of thirty-six years of age when Dayton found him.

Of course, hiring Morgan—and his staff of engineers—to canvass the land and draw up plans and build a flood control system would cost money, a lot of it, and so the city of Dayton devoted the weekend of May 24 and 25 to the sole goal of raising two million dollars to hire them. This was no small feat, considering that the city had lost an estimated $128 million in property. The neighboring city of Xenia's newspaper reported that "men and women, led by five bands, paraded the streets and stood in lines before subscription booths." Everyone from business owners to home owners, some who reportedly took out a second mortgage, pledged or gave money to the fund. Every church in the city on Sunday morning collected money for the rebuilding cause.

"Flags and banners floated from every house and store, and when the whistles announced the completion of the fund, the streets were thronged with thousands who sang religious hymns and danced and shouted in a great thanksgiving service," reported Xenia's *Daily Gazette*. The banners and the words on everyone's lips were the slogan of the flood prevention committee: Remember the promises you made in the attic.

In other words, the slogan was saying, in its own way, remember how you hoped, prayed and vowed this would never happen to you, to your city, again? Dayton as a whole was determined to make good on its promise.

But by the end of the weekend, the committee still hadn't raised enough, and late that afternoon (or perhaps in the evening, according to Bicknell's recollection), John H. Patterson wound up running a meeting in the large assembly hall in his factory, a meeting that every important businessman in Dayton was urged to attend.

Ernest Bicknell—finally in Dayton—later wrote about the meeting, saying that the big hall was full, and that the men in the meeting were "filled with uncertainty, not to say apprehension. They had been very hard hit by the flood and had given liberally to relief."

All weekend, in fact. "But they literally dared not stay away from the meeting. They could not afford to disregard the moral pressure of their neighbors and their powerful business associates," wrote Bicknell. "Mr. Patterson took charge of the meeting and ran it virtually single-handed. I was fortunate to be present that evening and witnessed a demonstration of moral and mental power which made an ineffaceable picture in my memory. As the hour of eight o'clock struck, Mr. Patterson rose and looked searchingly over the faces of the audience. Apparently satisfied that the people expected were present, he walked to the entrance of the hall, closed the double doors, locked them and without a word put the key into his pocket. Then returning to the front of the room, he began to speak. He spoke of the pride which those present had taken in the beauty and prosperity of Dayton and of the tragedy which had now laid her in ruins and had taken the lives of many of her people. With deep feeling but with infinite skill he brought that doubting and apprehensive crowd of hard-headed men into a malleable and sympathetic mood. Then he spoke briefly, touching on the plans under consideration that would forever prevent a repetition of the calamity."

According to Bicknell, Patterson said: "Before we can go forward with these plans, we must have at our absolute command $2,000,000."

It isn't clear how much the city had already raised that day, but they were well short of two million. "An audible groan rose from that crowd," recalled Bicknell. "Murmurs of dissent were heard. Men turned to each other and shook their heads muttering. Mr. Patterson paid no attention to these signs of protest but went right on with his appeal. Then, doubtless by prearrangement, he turned to a leading citizen, called him familiarly by his Christian name and asked him what he would give. This man made a fervent little speech and named an amount that made the others gasp by its generosity. This started the business in the right direction."

Everyone began pledging, including Patterson's son, Frederick, who upped his donation by $12,000, but still when it was past nine o'clock, the city was short a quarter of a million dollars. Patterson, whose company already had given a quarter of a million dollars, announced that NCR would double that amount and give half a million instead, and although Bicknell, who wrote about the event twenty-one years after the fact, remembered it as a somber occasion, contemporary accounts note that the crowd went wild. Men ripped off their coats and waved them around the air. The bands present began playing, "America (My Country, 'Tis of Thee)." Grown men were openly weeping. The total pledged, from NCR and from 22,000 individuals, was now a healthy $2.125 million. Morgan could now begin.

The summer and fall of 1913

Arthur E. Morgan hopped in and out of Dayton and surrounding cities like Piqua, Troy, Hamilton and Middletown, meeting with engineers, speaking at chamber of commerce events and going to gatherings like the Dayton Flood Preventing Conference in November. But what became more than patently obvious in all of this planning and winning hearts and minds was that laws would have to be passed to get this flood control system up and running. Morgan envisioned a conservancy with a board of governors that could have the power to condemn lands, issue bonds, and exercise police powers, all under court review. The conservancy act that he wanted and ultimately got would be able to regulate, widen, and deepen stream channels, reclaim wet and overflowed land wherever possible, and improve drainage.

1914

It took the help of Governor James Cox (who needed no convincing) and a Dayton attorney, John McMahon, who wrote the language for what would become the Conservancy Act, allowing the creation of conservancy districts in the state of Ohio. From here on out, the district's electors, like the mayor and councilmen, could tax their district and create an organization that would have the authority to plot out, develop, and even operate the water supply.

The conservancy districts, if officials set them up, would be allowed to do whatever they needed to do, to ensure that the waterways in their own district wouldn't flood, and that the water would remain clean for drinking, bathing, and swimming, and that the rivers, creeks, and streams in general would remain free and clear of garbage. As one U.S. government engineer would tell a crowd of Ohioans after the flood, the flood didn't occur in the rivers as God made them, but in rivers obstructed by debris, by buildings in the channel, and by bridge piers. Conservancies, it was hoped, would prevent that.

The Ohio General Assembly passed the Conservancy Act in February of 1914.

1915

John H. Patterson didn't want a pardon, and thus, he didn't get it. It took a while, but in 1915, the U.S. Court of Appeals reversed the lower court and sent Patterson's case back for a new trial. Eventually, the matter was dropped entirely.

It was also this year that the Miami Conservancy District was formed, devoted to protecting the Miami Valley, where Dayton lives and portions of nine Ohio counties, from flooding. Morgan, however, was just getting started. Ultimately, he was spearheading a plan that required twenty-one draglines (a piece of heavy equipment used in engineering), twenty-nine trains, and two hundred dump cars, sixty-three automobiles, many miles of railroad track, over a hundred pumps, over a hundred transformers and, was the largest public works project of its time, employing two thousand people.

There were five camp villages with 230 major buildings, 200 sheds and various buildings. Bunkhouses were put up with running water, and each camp had a mess hall and a store. Each camp village existed to build an earthen dam, dams made up of impervious clay and silt, sand, gravel, and boulders, all which would protect Dayton, Hamilton, Middletown, Piqua, Troy, and a slew of communities in the area that had all been besieged by the 1913 flood. These weren't any ordinary dams Morgan's crew ultimately made. For instance, the dam near Englewood, Ohio, is said to have enough dirt to fill the Great Pyramid of Giza. It can hold 6,350 acres of water. The area in the Miami Valley that was flooded took up 3,285 acres. There would have to be a flood twice the size of the Great Flood of 1913 for Morgan's work to be diminished.

When the rivers through the Miami Valley flow normally, the water passes through the dams without any trouble, and behind the dams is no water whatsoever. If the Englewood dam were to reach its maximum capacity, it would take twenty-three days for the water to drain and evaporate.

But when there are heavy rains, and the water starts to overflow its banks, the extra water travels through special conduits in the dams and collects in a space called the retarding basin, which is upstream of the dam. If it sounds confusing, it is the stuff engineers live for, and Morgan was clearly in his element. He would oversee the dams until they were all finished in 1922.

1920

Mrs. Ida Overmeyer gave her resignation to the orphanage after a quarter of a century of service and would live out her final years in St. Louis with her son, his wife, and their two daughters. Around this time, Theresa Hammond was married according to her niece, Sara Houk. Miss Hammond ended up marrying Dr. James Francis Dinnen, who everyone called Frank. He was the doctor who had cared for the orphans that fateful week more than eight years before.

He was married when he and Miss Hammond met, and the romance came well after the flood and his divorce, as far as the family knows, and that may be true. The doctor continued caring for the orphans and Miss Hammond remained teaching there for years to come, and so it may be that it took some time before love blossomed.

Because Dr. Dinnen was married in the Catholic Church, and he didn't want to scandalize his ex-wife, he and Theresa married in secret, in a civil ceremony, and eventually moved to Cleveland. They both lived into their seventies and passed away during the 1950s.

Charles Gebhart, Hammond's boatmate during the terrible tragedy at the orphanage, was accused several days after the incident of being drunk when he was rowing. At the time, he was a saloon owner—he also had been a gardener for many years—and the charge that he was inebriated during the rescues could have stuck, except that he had about thirty people, including Miss Hammond, sign a petition stating emphatically that he hadn't touched a drop that day. Gebhart claimed he hadn't had a drink for at least three months.

Gebhart himself, however, seems to have lived otherwise a fairly sedate and normal life free of tragedy and disasters. He gave up his saloon about a year after the flood, and during the 1920s, he was a truck farmer, the term used for a local farmer who sells directly to consumers and restaurants. On March 17, 1932, he passed away quietly, hopefully with his wife Tracy and their three sons and daughter at his side.

1921

The dams were meant to save communities, but one community was something of a casualty of Morgan's vision. In February of this year, the town of Osborn was moved to a new site. The land was purchased as part of the conservancy reservoir, with the idea being that it would store up flood water and pass it down to Dayton in reasonable amounts. The state was going to wreck Osborn's buildings but decided to sell them to be moved to the new site and gave the old owners the first chance to buy them. A company was formed to manage the moving, and bids were requested.

It was a major undertaking, as described in a December 1925 issue of *Popular Mechanics* that told the story of E. W. LaPlant, who had made moving large buildings his specialty. One of his finest moments was when he engineered the transport of a 4,800-ton department store in Montreal, Canada.

But with the town of Osborn, LaPlant designed a move that required 552 buildings to be hauled out of a valley to a hilltop a mile and a half away. The town is still on that hill, at least in part. Never able to regain its former self-sufficiency, Osborn and the neighboring town of Fairfield merged to become Fairborn in 1950.

1922

The year that Arthur E. Morgan wrapped up his work on saving Dayton from any future flooding, it was almost as if fate decided that John

H. Patterson would be called for duty in the next world. He died a little over nine years after the flood, passing away on May 7, 1922. He was seventy-seven and busy to the end, dying two days after working on plans with General Billy Mitchell, a U.S. Army general who is considered the father of the Air Force. They intended to build an aviation research center in Dayton, Patterson's beloved city. He was as generous with his time and his money as he was during the flood until the end of his days.

1927

Christian Dane Hagerty, the intrepid Associated Press reporter, died far too young. His life ended in Chicago at the age of fifty-one. It was a sad end, an ill-fitting one considering all of the adventure he appears to have crammed into his life. The hard liquor and hard living caught up with him, and in his last few years in life, he was, as one paper described him, "an invalid."

It was a fate worse than death for such an active and curious man, and on July 26, 1927, he sent a last telegram to his brother, went to his hotel room, picked up a gun, aimed it near his heart, and became the depressing subject of at least one short article in the newspaper.

1928

Hagerty's one-time nemesis and friend Ben Hecht fared much better. This was the year his stage play *The Front Page*, a comedy, which he wrote with Charles MacArthur, another former Chicago journalist, made its Broadway debut.

Hecht left journalism to become one of America's most successful screenwriters as well as a director, producer, playwright, and novelist. He was the first writer to get an Oscar for a screenplay, for the 1927 silent crime film *Underworld,* and he either wrote or worked on numerous movies including *Scarface, Nothing Sacred, Gone with the Wind, Some Like It Hot,* and the original comedy spy film *Casino Royale*, which was released in 1967, three years after his death at the age of seventy.

But Hecht never quite forgot what it meant to be a newspaperman. His well-received stage play, about newspaper men covering the crime beat, was adapted by another screenwriter and became the 1934 film of the same name starring Adolphe Menjou and Pat O'Brien, and then later, Hecht rewrote the film *The Front Page* into a new adaptation, which became a much more famous and beloved film classic, *His Girl Friday* (1940), starring Cary Grant and Rosalind Russell.

After being presented with a gold medal by the Ohio governor, life went on for telephone operator and Dayton flood hero Arthur John Bell. He remained at his post in Dayton into World War I, briefly working at his company's branch in nearby Middletown, and then being sent to the center of the state in Chillicothe, where he was in charge of the electrical installation at Camp Sherman. From there, he was transferred to Norfolk, Virginia, where he oversaw a crew of a thousand men loading munitions for the war effort overseas.

After the war, Bell decided to leave the telephone industry and with his wife moved to Detroit, and he got involved with construction work. He was given the position of overseeing a crew working on the Cadillac Building, which was completed in 1920 and is now part of Wayne State University. A few years later, he started working for a sewer contractor. It was at that job that he came to a noble and yet such an ignoble end.

On August 6, 1928, Bell, now forty-six, was leading his men in installing a new road sewer in Detroit. Bell noticed that one of the workers was missing and, according to conflicting accounts, saw him fall down in the sewer and went down after him or couldn't find him and then descended the ladder into the sewer.

Once again, Bell was heralded as a hero, but there would be no happy ending followed by a medal and a meeting with the governor. Like his coworker, Bell was overcome by fumes and passed out. After spending nights and days doing everything he could to help his fellow citizens avoid drowning, Bell once again tried to save another fellow human being but would meet his end drowning in a sewer.

1933

Twenty years after the Great Flood of 1913, three flood survivors made their annual trek up to the attic where they had spent three days with six other people, with nothing but crackers to eat. Edward Wagner, a manufacturer, and Clark and Edwin Stoner, grocers and brothers, gathered in the attic of the Stoner home and dined on cheese and crackers. It was the last such reunion, however. Edwin, fifty-eight, was in poor health and low spirits. He would commit suicide in his store before the year was up.

That same year, Arthur E. Morgan was appointed by President Franklin D. Roosevelt—who selected him from 150 suggested names—to be the first chairman of the Tennessee Valley Authority, which involved construction that was twelve times the size of the Egyptian pyramids. Morgan, who, in the midst of overseeing the dam work in Dayton, became the president of Antioch College in Yellow Springs, a charming village in Greater Dayton, in 1920. When Roosevelt offered him the job to create a flood control system in the same vein as the successful work in the Ohio Valley for the neighboring Tennessee Valley, which includes parts of Alabama, Mississippi, Kentucky, Georgia, North Carolina, and Virginia as well as the state it's named for, Morgan, forty-eight, jumped at the chance.

Roosevelt received some criticism as the cost of the construction mounted, but he defended his selection of Morgan, saying simply, "He builds good dams."

Roosevelt was correct; and that same year, Dayton was reminded of what Morgan had done for them. After a tornado invaded the nearby city of Xenia and crushed a house, killing its sixty-year-old dweller, George Gibbs, rivers and creeks left their banks, sweeping poor William Voelpel, forty-five, to his death in a drainage tunnel, and an emergency dam north of Dayton broke, sending waters through the villages of Miami Villa and Eldorado.

But the main dams of the Miami Conservancy District? Those held fast. In fact, the Miami Conservancy District would be a model that was imitated across the country, including in Minnesota, Colorado, Michigan, and Florida. American engineers and international delegations still make pilgrimages to Dayton to probe for lessons on how they have resolved their own flooding problems.

1937

This was the year when Morgan's magic truly came to light, and Roosevelt's wisdom in hiring the man was borne out. A flood swamped the Ohio and Mississippi Valleys, affecting cities from Pittsburgh to New Orleans, and killing, most accounts say, 250 people. In Ohio, which got off relatively lucky with ten deaths, Kentucky, and Indiana, it was estimated that one of every eight people were left homeless. Almost one-fifth of Cincinnati, Ohio, which had managed to mitigate much of the damage in 1913, was now only accessible by boat. The city had no power, although fortunately they were able to bring in some emergency power—from Dayton.

The streets of downtown Dayton didn't have a drop of water on them.

1961

On January 11, the little baby that miraculously survived the ravaging current, Lois Adams, died suddenly at the age of forty-eight. She was, in a sense, the last victim of the 1913 flood.

It sounds far-fetched, but it was always the theory of her twin brother, and there may be some rationale behind it. Two days after Charles Adams and Grandpa Adams began cleaning their house, both Lois and Charles Jr. developed pneumonia. It wasn't due to being in their flood-ravaged house. Viola's brother, Nelson Hicks, had come down, posing as a doctor since the National Guard wasn't yet allowing visitors to Dayton. Hicks—who at least was a pharmacist, if not a physician—convinced Viola and Charles to bring the babies up to his house in Fostoria, Ohio. A few hours before boarding the train, Charles, Jr. became very sick, and they called in an actual physician.

The doctor did what he could and apparently cleared them for travel. In any case, the Adams family traveled north, but before they reached Fostoria, Lois was ill, too. Both babies had the aforementioned pneumonia, and once again, Charles and Viola feared for their children's lives. For several weeks, in Charles's words, the two parents "nursed them back to life," and during the moments that the babies seemed like they might live, Charles would think about their house back home and wonder how moldy and dilapidated it was becoming. But after three weeks, Charles finally felt comfortable enough to leave Fostoria and return to the task of rehabilitating their house. Not that there was all that much to do. Grandpa Adams, who always seems to have put his family first, had been cleaning it for the last three weeks, largely ignoring his own home in the process.

So the kids grew up, and became quite famous in Dayton, being known locally as "the flood twins." They married and had kids, and the flood twins' parents lived good long lives as well. Charles Adams died in 1950 at the age of sixty-three. Viola passed away in 1973. She was eighty-seven. Then in 1961, Lois, who evidently had been healthy throughout her life, simply passed away. Her heart just stopped. Charles, Jr. would always feel her heart and lungs were permanently weakened as a result of the exposure and pneumonia from their near-drowning experience and suffering through weeks of pneumonia. It's hard to argue that.

1963

Sam Bundy, the American Indian, who it's believed saved as many as 160 lives and possibly more, lived a long life, and deservedly so, although his later years weren't his finest. When he was in his middle-aged years, he was hit by a car crossing the street in Fort Wayne, and his injuries were severe. In his later years, he was walking with two canes. He needed a walker, but he wasn't able to afford one, nor, apparently, could his family, and he became house-bound. In 1963, when the *Plain Dealer*, the paper for Wabash, Indiana, did a story on the octogenarian, Bundy's grand-daughter's husband told the reporter: "He would appreciate hearing from any old friends. He's dying from loneliness."

Bundy passed away the following year.

1975

Arthur Ernest Morgan, the architect of the Miami Valley Conservancy, the man who built dams that protect much of Ohio as well as Tennessee, Alabama, Mississippi, Kentucky, Georgia, North Carolina, and Virginia, preventing an incalculable number of flood deaths in later years, appears to have been rewarded with his own life. He was around for a long time, writing books, consulting in Finland on postwar reconstruction and in India as a member of a national universities commission and on a hydroelectric concept in West Africa.

Morgan was active up until the end when he finally breathed his last. He was ninety-seven years old.

1983

In April of this year, Charles Adams, Jr., Dayton's iconic living symbol of the 1913 flood, asked Jim Rozelle, then the Chief Engineer of the

Miami Conservancy District, "How many times would water have been at Third and Main Streets in Dayton, if the five dams had not been built?"

Rozelle checked his records and concluded that without Morgan's dams, there would have been seven more floods, on some sort of par with the flood of 1913: 1924, 1929, 1933, 1937, 1952, 1959, and 1963. He added that if the dams hadn't existed, there would have been minor flood damage 1,200 times.

2005

On August 23, 2005, Hurricane Katrina lumbered ashore and made landfall in southeast Louisiana, becoming one of the deadliest storms in history, and the deadliest hurricane since 1928 when 4,078 people were killed. That hurricane had devastated the Leeward Islands, Puerto Rico, and the Bahamas, but it really put a stiletto into the heart of Florida, after a storm surge from Lake Okeechobee flooded the dike surrounding the lake. Just as a lake was created on April 28, 1913, in the Tensas and Concord parishes of Louisiana, Lake Okeechobee flooded an area covering hundreds of square miles. That incident alone was responsible for 2,500 of the 4,078 deaths.

Hurricane Katrina's death toll was fewer, but still brutal (at least 1,833), and at first glance it seemed as if Louisiana and Mississippi had come out of the destruction without too much difficulty. But 238 people in Mississippi were soon known to be dead, and 67 more people were never found and thus officially listed as missing, and vast amounts of property from buildings to bridges were destroyed. Louisiana was in similar straits, but it was the state's largest city, New Orleans, that memorably played out like a disaster movie turned real-life. The surge from the storm caused water to spill over the levees in fifty-three different places, ultimately putting eighty percent of the city underwater.

Just as in 1913, and countless other floods throughout time, families and individuals were fleeing for their second floors and roofs. Thousands of people who had taken refuge from Hurricane Katrina at the Louisiana Superdome, a sports and exhibition arena, found themselves stuck on what had become an island.

But what was particularly galling and surprising for the victims, the nation, and the world that watched the catastrophe unfold on cable news networks was how powerless city, state, and federal officials appeared during the rescue efforts. For instance, at the Superdome, which had been designated as a shelter, there were enough MREs (meals, ready to eat) to feed 15,000 people for three days—but 26,000 people had shown up. Nobody had thought to have any water purification equipment on hand, or antibiotics or doctors to prescribe them. The toilet situation was less than ideal. All of that said, the mayor of New Orleans had warned people that they should consider the Superdome as a shelter of last resort and that they should bring their own supplies.

Still, people expected better. Fair or not, it seemed unreal that in 2005, with all of modern technology at one's disposal and after everything everyone should have learned about dealing with disasters, that a hurricane and its resulting flooding could make the government appear so spavined, to borrow newsman Ben Hecht's phrasing.

Entire books have been written about Hurricane Katrina and the federal, state, and local mismanagement of the disaster, and so it's probably not worth rehashing at length here, but in a nutshell, the Federal Emergency Management Agency (FEMA) was verbally eviscerated for moving far too slowly in getting supplies to the flood victims. President George W. Bush was roundly criticized for his role in Hurricane Katrina, from remaining on his vacation after it was clear New Orleans was facing a dire and unusual threat to its existence to him standing in front of news cameras and telling FEMA's director, Michael Brown, "Brownie, you're doing a heck of a job."

Brown wasn't considered by many to be doing a heck of a job, and when it came out that he had almost no experience in emergency management, Bush, who had appointed him, received even more criticism.

In many ways, what the hurricane victims went through was similar to what happened in so many disasters before it, particularly with the Great Flood of 1913. For a long stretch of time, everyone was on his or her own. Three million people in New Orleans were without electricity, and like thousands and possibly millions of Americans in 1913, many of those people were without food or clean drinking water. Scores of people who had remained in New Orleans began looting, some of them because they wanted to steal TVs, jewelry, and whatnot, but many people simply wanted to avoid starving to death. As with the floods in 1913 and the floods of 2005, if you were poor and black, odds were, you were at a disadvantage. In 1913, you may have lived on some cheap property in a flood plain; in New Orleans, many of the flood victims were impoverished African-Americans, too. They ignored warnings to flee the city not because they wanted to stay but because they couldn't afford to go. It takes money to gas up the car or pay for bus fare and find a hotel. That help was slow to arrive brought charges of racism or at least a slam on a social class—people were quick to suggest that if it had been a city full of white rich people, aid would have been much faster to arrive. The flood victims in New Orleans suffered many indignities, although at least nobody was asked to spend some time being a human sandbag.

Then and now, misinformation abounded. While there were many instances of violence in the wake of Hurricane Katrina, many of the reports of carjackings, murder, thievery and rape turned out to be wild, completely untrue stories undoubtedly born of panic.

In 1913, President Woodrow Wilson considered traveling to Ohio to see the damage and destruction firsthand, but he ultimately didn't, and it's unlikely anyone thought less of him for not traveling from Washington, D.C. to Ohio. Air travel for the president was out of the question—Franklin Roosevelt would be the first president in office to fly, although Theodore Roosevelt had, after his term, flown in 1910—and train travel, even for a president, took some serious time. But by the time 2005 had rolled around, it would have been unthinkable for President Bush, or any president, not to visit the flood-besieged region. As technology, travel, and life have modernized, so have the public's expectations of what kind of help they should receive. That may be a reasonable assessment, but human nature, no matter what the year, doesn't change.

Looking at a flood through that prism, it doesn't really matter what age or era you live in. Unless mankind ever learns to harness and control nature, if you're stranded on your rooftop, staring down at water that truly looks as if it wants to come up and get you, you will never be in a good place.

2011

As the centennial of the 1913 flood approached, Charles Otterbein Adams, Jr., who was ultimately saved by someone shouting out a window that there was a baby in the river, almost lived to see it.

He was ninety-nine years old when he passed on. The retired electrical engineer died of what he believed killed his sister and almost killed him shortly after the flood: pneumonia. If at some point in his last remaining hours, he realized pneumonia was going to bring him down, he wasn't surprised. He had had trouble with his bronchial tubes his entire life.

Adams obviously remembered none of his adventures in 1913, but always had a keen interest in history and must have felt supreme gratitude toward his parents, neighbors, and strangers for keeping him and his sister alive. Throughout his years, especially after he retired, he frequently gave lectures about the flood, sharing his and his family's stories not because, he said, that it was all that important people knew about him, but because he felt it was important people remembered the flood and its place in history.

It is worth remembering. The Great Flood of 1913 was a devastating correction, a rap on society's collective knuckles that we underestimate and ignore mother nature at our own peril, possibly a useful lesson going forward for civilizations concerned about melting ice caps and global warming stirring up extreme storms such as those that have hit the East Coast in recent years, including Hurricane Irene in 2011 and what became known as Superstorm Sandy in 2012. But if the Great Flood of 1913 caused a lot of hopelessness, it also offers much hope, too. That tens of thousands of people didn't die in the floods is because families stuck together, neighbors helped neighbors, and strangers instinctively risked their own lives to help strangers. People looked out for each other when it mattered most. Human nature tends not to change over the years, which is why it's nice to think that if another flood comparable to 1913's occurred again, people would rally and rise to the occasion, even if it might be hard to imagine such camaraderie with our community when so many of us now hang out with friends and neighbors on Facebook instead of drinking lemonade with them on our front porches.

But Charles Adams, Jr., would probably tell anyone today that it doesn't matter how you stay connected with your community as long as you are connected, because for a guy who thought a lot about the past, the 99-year-old flood survivor embraced the future. When Charles Adams was admitted into the hospital for his final visit, he asked the nurses for a computer.

Notes and Research and Acknowledgments

I knew I was getting somewhere with my research when I found myself dreaming about nearly drowning.

In what goes down as the most unpleasant nightmare I've so far had, one night—or maybe it was early morning—I found myself behind the wheel of my car, skidding off a rain-splattered road and careering into a roaring creek. That's when I looked behind me and saw my youngest daughter, her seat belt still on and waist-deep in river water and screaming for my help. I woke up instantly, shaking and terrified and trying to figure out if I would have been able to rescue her or not.

It didn't occur to me until much later that it might be a good sign that I was making considerable progress in researching and writing my book.

At the end of other nonfiction narratives, I always read other "notes and research" sections with envy. I learn how authors and historians traveled to the ends of the earth, retracing every step and path that real-life characters in their books once traversed.

I'm not so fortunate. Even though I always am working, writing for news wire services like Reuters and random publications like the Huffington Post and CNNMoney.com, the cash flow of a freelance writer is often a bit unpredictable. Instead of sharing details of how I spared no expense in traveling to the ends of the earth to collect data for my book, I'm telling you about some weird dream I had.

Still, because so much of the Great Flood of 1913 occurred so close to where I live, and in Middletown, Ohio, the town I grew up in, I was able to visit quite a few communities in the area that were affected by the flood and stand in areas I knew had once been underwater, getting a sense of the power and reach of a flooded river. That idea really came across as I neared the end of writing this book, on one summer day in 2012, when I traveled out to Mentor, Kentucky with my parents and daughters to see a house that had been on the edge of the Ohio River's flooding during 1913. My great-grandmother, Lillian Williams, who passed away before I was born, took the photo of the house, or at least it found its way into her scrapbook. We were able to find the house, which is still standing, and then drive as far as we could toward the river, which appears to have been about a three-mile distance.

But mostly during my research, I combed through newspapers, many of them online at NewspaperArchive.com, and many of them not, still on microfilm, and so I spent many evenings and weekends at the Public Library of Cincinnati and Hamilton County, which has been a trusted research refuge for me during the writing of this book and earlier ones. I also trekked up to Columbus, Ohio, to its impressive Columbus Metropolitan Library, and found a treasure trove of information about the city's role in the flood. I, of course, on a number of occasions, went to the Dayton Metro Library in Dayton, Ohio, about an hour's drive from my house, and burrowed into their local history room and pored over microfilm of their city papers.

And, you know, before I forget, I should say thanks to Nancy Horlacher, a local history specialist at the Dayton Metro Library. She steered many of the photos in this book to me, and she was invaluable in helping me make the most of my research time at the Dayton library. She was terrific.

I also found some great material at the Clark County Public Library in Springfield, Ohio, and at my hometown at the MidPointe Library in Middletown, Ohio. I used to go to the MidPointe Library when it was just known as the Middletown Public Library, and I have many fond memories from studying there in middle and high school.

As for the newspapers I utilized for the book, and I'm sure I've left some out of the list you're about to read, but I focused on the dates of March 23–27, of course, although I frequently was looking ahead into April and May 1913 and beyond, and immersed myself in the *Dayton Daily News*, the *Dayton Journal*, the *Dayton Evening Herald*, the *Middletown Journal*, the *Middletown News-Signal*, the *Springfield News-Sun*, *Xenia Daily Gazette*, the *Fort Wayne News*, the *Fort Wayne Journal Gazette* and the *Fort Wayne Sentinel*, the *Indianapolis Star*, the *Indianapolis News*, the *Columbus Dispatch*, the *Columbus Citizen-Journal*, the *Ohio State Journal*, the *Galveston Daily News*, the *New Castle News* (New Castle, Pennsylvania), the *Gazette and Bulletin* (Williamsport, Pennsylvania), *Lebanon Daily News* (Lebanon, Pennsylvania), *Chester Times* (Chester, Pennsylvania), the *Evening Record* (Greenville, Pennsylvania), the *Pittsburgh Gazette Times*, the *Neosho Daily Democrat* (Neosho, Missouri), *Moberly Weekly Monitor* (Moberly, Missouri), the *Daily Democrat-Tribune* (Jefferson City, Missouri), *St. Louis Post-Dispatch*, *Alton Evening Telegraph* (Alton, Illinois), the *Daily Free Press* (Carbondale, Illinois), *Monmouth College Newspaper Oracle* (Monmouth, Illinois), the *New York Times*, the *Los Angeles Times*, the *Washington Post*, and the *Atlanta Journal-Constitution*. I went through as many newspapers as possible, repeatedly, because so often during the 1913 flood, when communication was difficult and confusion reigned, an account would be wrong or wouldn't quite tell the whole story, but when two, three, or ten papers started reporting an incident from varying angles, and you compare it with other facts you pick up at sites like Ancestry.com, you start to get a clearer picture.

I used other sources, however, beyond newspaper articles, magazine articles, Web sites, and books. I need to thank Gregory McDonald, a forensic pathologist at the Philadelphia College of Osteopathic Medicine, who has performed many autopsies on drowning victims over the years and gave me as close to first-hand information as possible on what happens when you drown and what it's like. Donna Randall and Sara Houk, relatives of Theresa Hammond, the Fort Wayne teacher who saved two orphans, were able to fill me in on what her aunt was like and filled me in about Teresa Hammond Dinnen's life, post-flood. Ms. Houk was especially helpful, as were Helen Steele Lehman and especially Elinor Kline, who both provided information about the

Saettel family. (George Saettel, as you may recall, was the shopkeeper who was caught up in an explosion but managed to survive in the flood for a little while.)

Felicia Korengel, Lyn Keating, and especially Elaine Korengel Durham were all able to provide a little more information about Ralph Korengel, the ten-year-old kid in Cincinnati who almost became a flood statistic when he was sucked through a sewer tunnel. Ralph lived a good long life, married, but never had kids. I was pretty horrified to learn that in 1980, when he was ill with cancer, he ended his life in his garage, turning on his car. That was bad enough, but he didn't realize the carbon monoxide would go anywhere beyond his deathtrap. It did, the poisonous gas drifting up to the room above the garage, and killed his wife, Ruth.

Other people I should mention who helped out with a little advice, or pointed me in the right direction, include Edward Roach, a historian at the Dayton Aviation Heritage National Historical Park; Megan Griffiths, conservation technician at the Gerald R. Ford Conservation Center at the Nebraska State Historical Society; Eric Mankin; Leslie Mark Kendall, the curator of the Petersen Automotive Museum; and Patricia R. Shannon, the director of education at the Thurber House.

One of the most invaluable was a recounting that I found at the Dayton library written by Charles Adams, the father of the twin babies who almost drowned in the flood. He wrote about a ten-page manuscript, detailing the day it flooded in Dayton and of how he and his wife and their babies almost died. His son, Charles Adams, Jr., also wrote extensively about his role in the flood, and I think their stories really added a lot to our understanding of the flood; but of course, there are probably so many stories written by people and waiting to be discovered in libraries and probably in numerous aging trunks and shoeboxes heaved to the side in attics and basements.

Trudy E. Bell is a science journalist who wrote *The Great Dayton Flood of 1913* (Arcadia Publishing, 2008). I didn't utilize her fine book all that much—anyone familiar with Arcadia knows that their books are filled with more photos than prose—there are 200 in Bell's 128-page book—but Bell has written extensively about the 1913 flood on the Internet. Somewhere in the last few months of writing this book, I came across her Web site, in which she says, "My ultimate goal is to write the definitive book on the Great Easter national calamity of 1913."

I felt a twinge of guilt when I read that, since I hope *my* book is the definitive book on the Great Flood of 1913, but I hope she still writes her own all-comprehensive account. In my opinion, and I'm sure Ms. Bell's, there could and should be bookshelves full of tomes about the 1913 flood. What happened to America during the spring of 1913 is, I think, just as tragic, compelling, and relevant as other prominent historical disasters, like the *Titanic* and the 1906 San Francisco and 1871 Chicago fires, are today. Not to make it a contest or anything, but the flood victims and heroes of the 1913 flood deserve to be remembered as much as anyone else.

So, anyway, Bell's research about the storm and weather that hit the Midwest, Northeast, and South was very helpful to my understanding of the tornadoes and flood that pounded the country, and I'm grateful for all the work she has done in helping to unearth information about the flood.

I also have to sing the praises of John R. Repass, who wrote a lengthy document for the West Indianapolis Historical Society about his mother's family's ordeal during the flood and a tale of his grandfather, Philander Gray. That account, which the society put online, added a lot to the Indianapolis portions of the book.

In general, historical societies and counties in the region have stories about the flood on their Web sites, including the Shelby County Historical Society, which has a nice recounting of the flood from 89-year-old resident Gene Rees. The Emmitsburg Area Historical Society, of Emmitsburg, Maryland, also stands out; it had a little snippet on their Web site about John Hoke, possibly Maryland's only flood casualty, which sent me searching the newspaper archives to learn more.

In 2002, local historian Jim Blount published a 68-page book entitled *Butler County's Greatest Weather Disaster: Flood, 1913*. I found some invaluable material, especially on Hamilton!, Ohio, in his book. 'Sigh. I should mention here that Hamilton—wonderful, scenic community with good people—renamed its city in 1986, Hamilton!, Ohio. That's right. To the chagrin of many Hamiltonians even, there's an exclamation point after the city, although almost nobody, including mapmakers, uses it. I didn't in the book, in large part because it was set in 1913, long before the exclamation point was added.'

And, of course, there are others I would like to thank for their help with writing *Washed Away*, front and center my affable agent Laurie Abkemeier, who I mentioned at the start of this book and can't say enough nice things about, frankly. When I was trying to come up with an idea for another book, she pushed me to write about something local until I suddenly remembered all of the scattered stories I had heard about some flood a long, long time ago, and I definitely need to thank Jessica Case, my editor, who was able to tighten the prose and offer a lot of useful input. She is also unfailingly cheerful, never making me feel bad when I turned in my drafts slightly past our deadlines. Any author would be lucky to work with her.

I also would like to thank some of the people who have been everpresent in my life: my parents, of course, Jim and Rita Williams, who are about as perfect a pair of parents as you'd ever want; my younger brother and confidant, Kevin; my kind and generous grandmother, Mary Wellinghoff (born in Middletown, Ohio, twelve years after the flood); and some close friends of mine, Brian Kieffer, Mike Johnson, Richard Welch, and Stu Rubinstein. I'd also like to thank my ex-wife, Susan Kailholz. Our marriage not unexpectedly came crumbling to an end a few weeks before Pegasus Books gave me the go-ahead to write this book, and while divorce is obviously pretty unpleasant, ours was thankfully amicable, and I feel like we've kept our friendship intact.

Most of all, though, I thank our daughters, Isabelle and Lorelei, eleven and nine, who both inspire me, keep me on my toes, and simply make life interesting, exciting, and fun. One night at dinner, I told them that I wanted to dedicate the book to them, and Isabelle, who isn't one for mush, rolled her eyes. Lorelei, who loves history maybe as much as I do, cheerfully suggested that I dedicate the book to the flood victims. Isabelle quickly seconded that. And how could I argue? Those who survived the flood and those who didn't spent several harrowing days, famished and thirsty, often putting their lives at risk in order to save their families, friends, neighbors, and complete strangers. The 1913 flood may be mostly forgotten, but its victims and survivors should long be remembered.

Index

INDEX

INDEX

INDEX